DICKENS AND ROMANTIC PSYCHOLOGY

DICKENS AND ROMANTIC PSYCHOLOGY

The Self in Time in Nineteenth-Century Literature

Dirk den Hartog

Palgrave Macmillan

ISBN 978-1-349-18578-8 ISBN 978-1-349-18576-4 (eBook)
DOI 10.1007/978-1-349-18576-4

© Dirk den Hartog, 1987
Softcover reprint of the hardcover 1st edition 1987

All rights reserved. For information, write:
Scholarly & Reference Division,
St. Martin's Press, Inc., 175 Fifth Avenue, New York, NY 10010

First published in the United States of America in 1987

ISBN 978-0-312-19989-0

Library of Congress Cataloguing-in-Publication Data
Den Hartog, Dirk, 1945–
Dickens and romantic psychology.
Bibliography: p.
Includes index.
1. Dickens, Charles, 1812–1870—Knowledge—
Psychology. 2. Psychology in literature. 3. Self
in literature. 4. Romanticism—England. I. Title.
PR4592.P74D46 1987   823'.8   86–13006
ISBN 978-0-312-19989-0

To the late Harry and Margaret den Hartog and the late Alan Hughes

Contents

Preface   ix

1 Introductory: Dickens, Romantic Psychology and 'the
   Experience of Modernity'   1

2 The Ideal of Victorian Manliness in *Dombey and Son*:
   Radicalising Wordsworthian Psychology.   34

3 Wordsworthian Psychology and *Little Dorrit*: The
   Unresolved Dialogue   80

4 *Great Expectations*: 'Working Things Through'   123

Notes and References   156

Index   172

Preface

In this book I have attempted in a variety of ways to strike a balance between a number of opposing emphases. First of all, I have focused on Dickens in particular, whilst also attempting to locate him as a representative figure of his age. I have pursued a specific interest in the shaping presence within the major novels of a preoccupying theme of Wordsworth's, and in the developing resistance to and dialectical engagement with this presence. But I have also tried to examine this complex relationship as paradigmatic of the contradictions within post-Romantic literature and culture as a whole, in line with the conception of those recently set out in Marshal Berman's *All that is Solid Melts into Air: the Experience of Modernity* (1981).

In doing this I have proceeded along a path that is to some extent in accord with the contemporary critical emphasis upon the 'de-centred' author, but whilst continuing to insist upon the significance of individual authorial creativity. Both the acquiescence to and the reaction from the Wordsworthian presence are seen as inexplicable without recourse to the conflicting ideologies and sundry anterior textual 'presences' by which Dickens and his artistic expression are in general terms constituted. Nevertheless, I have equally worked on the assumption that the transformation of these into the individual acts of imagination and insight which in sum make up Dickens's novels, derives from a positively active authorial centre that we can meaningfully persist in talking of as 'genius', without thereby reproducing the fallacy of the divinely transcendental artist.

Finally, and somewhat in line with the above, this book has hopefully taken the point of recent developments in Dickens criticism, whilst resisting the full-scale inversion of approach these have announced. A unifying thread links the three most stimulating books about Dickens to have appeared in the last decade: John Carey's *The Violent Effigy* (1973), Garett Stewart's *Dickens and the Trials of Imagination* (1974), and, most recently,

S. J. Newman's *Dickens at Play* (1981). These have all sought to overthrow that conception of the most interesting Dickens as a maturely insightful novelist, deeply and intelligently critical of Victorian civilisation and responsible to the task that this imposed upon him. With some notable exceptions this was the orthodox Dickens of the several decades before 1970, when it reached its apotheosis in that centenary year with the Leavis's *Dickens the Novelist*. It is perhaps as a reaction to this excellent though only partially adequate book that we should see the bent of Carey and others, with their celebration of the anarchic and irresponsible in Dickens's imagination, and their sense of comic play as itself the bearer of central meanings, rather than as the rhetorical adjunct of meaning, as it had unfortunately become in much previous commentary. The current drift towards France in English-speaking literary criticism has possibly been influential as well, in that the 'new wave' Dickens criticism, whilst lacking French conceptual rigor and elaboration, has markedly shared its canonisation of the playful and the subversive. In writing the present book I have hoped to combine an acknowledgement of the value of such a re-orientation with a thus modified continuation of the previous mode. A professional colleague has commented on my *Dombey* chapter (read in shortened, article form) that it represents a 'renovated left-Leavisism'. I am happy to lay claim to that label.

One aspect of all this is that I have concentrated on works within the New Critical/'Leavisite' canon of Dickens's novels: I have written on *Dombey and Son*, *Little Dorrit* and *Great Expectations*, in contrast to the current re-emphasis upon the early novels and denial of a significant line of development in terms of maturation. It would also have been very much within the terms of my argument to have said much more than I have about both *David Copperfield* and *Bleak House*. However, to have done so would have entailed an unnecessary restatement of accounts already quite adequately given by others, most notably Robin Gilmour on *Copperfield*,[1] and William Axton and Alex Zwerdling on *Bleak House*.[2] Anyone curious as to how these two novels might be said to fit into my general argument more than my brief references to them suggest, should find these essays very helpful, and the alignment of their particular readings to my overall framework not too difficult.

This book originated as a Ph.D. thesis undertaken at the

University of Leicester, and its gradual transformation into its present state has been marked by a number of articles appearing in the Australian literary journals, *The Critical Review* and *Meridian*. Foremost amongst those to whom I owe acknowledgement for help with it are thus the sponsors and administrators of the Commonwealth Scholarship Scheme, who made the study for the thesis possible, and my Leicester University supervisor, Professor P. A. W. Collins, who patiently did his best to induct me into the procedures of scholarship, besides commenting helpfully upon the intellectual content of work in progress. The greater part of the work involved in rewriting the thesis into a book was done whilst on leave from the Footscray Institute of Technology, and I am grateful to the Institute for giving me this opportunity. I would also like to take this opportunity to thank my former teachers within the English Department at Melbourne University for the rigorous and stimulating training in literary criticism they gave me; in particular Sam Goldberg and Jock Tomlinson, who in their postgraduate seminar on nineteenth-century Literature and Thought threw out a number of suggestions that led me to my particular subject. I am also grateful to Mr Goldberg in his capacity as editor of *The Critical Review*, as I am likewise to John Barnes as editor of *Meridian*. I also owe thanks to Mr Graham Burns, of La Trobe University English Department, who read some of the first draft at short notice and made valuable suggestions, and to my father, the late Harry den Hartog, who made detailed and helpful criticisms of the prose of that draft. Mrs Susan Letts and Mrs Rosemary Lovett were invaluable as typists of the original thesis, and made many sacrifices of their personal comfort in the process. Finally, I am deeply grateful to my wife for her cheering support, despite the innumerable pressures upon her which the completion of my work has involved.

I have used and quoted from the Penguin English Library editions of Dickens's works. John Forster's standard biography, *The Life of Charles Dickens* (1872–74) is cited in the Everyman edition. Wordsworth's *Prelude*, which I frequently refer to, is cited in the 1850 version.

DIRK DEN HARTOG

1 Introductory: Dickens, Romantic Psychology and 'the Experience of Modernity'

Consciousness of the self as a living continuity in time is obviously a major form of our contemporary awareness. Be we devotees of psychoanalysis or merely dilettantish psychic explorers with a taste for thoughtful reminiscence, we tend to share a typically modern interest in the interrelation of our early experience and our adult selves. We collectively cultivate it: it is part of our intellectual culture, or rather, the bourgeois intellectual culture of the West. In our more detached moments we think of ourselves as the 'products' of our formative years, on the analogy of 'the way the twig is bent'. More intimately, we sense the relation as more threateningly, or more vivifyingly, mobile, as a matter of the past living actively on into the present, either nourishing it or tyrannising over it, or perhaps both. The very idea of the adult self as autonomous we now know to be *hubristic*, courting retributive invasion from the more archaic depths of the psyche. We are more likely to conceive the self in the terms in which the transactional analysts have elegantly formulated it, as an arena in which 'child' and 'adult' selves act out a never-ending drama of warfare and alliance.

In some sense, of course, the greatest works of literature, being the master explorations of the human soul that they are, have always had this to tell us. Euripides' Pentheus is the classic instance of a character who is made to discover the delusion of his too narrowly adult conception of himself. Likewise Shakespeare's curiosity as to what makes a Coriolanus what he is, leads him into taking an interest in Roman child-rearing habits, just as we are invited to understand Ophelia's fatal passivity in the context of the structure of familial authority of which she is the product. Nevertheless, the detailed consideration of the manifold and subtle ways in which the psychic past can press upon the present, would seem to have had its origin as a cultural activity in the eighteenth century, in that broad pre-Romantic movement of sensibility that we know as Sentimentalism. This cultural ethos, with its emphasis upon the value of feeling and of individuality, can be seen to have naturally prompted and legitimised the kind of introspective attentiveness from which a reminiscent sense of the self's unity through time emerges. The first important sign of this is a non-literary one, the 'Associationist' development in philosophical psychology. Besides this the interest in Memory in poets like Gray and Cowper is slight, albeit significantly distinct when compared with its mere absence in earlier eighteenth-century poetry, as is also the case with the eighteenth-century novel. With Rousseau's *Confessions*, however, and soon after with Wordsworth's poetry, memory comes into its own, not just as a literary topic but as a desired mode of awareness; and the modern way of being aware of the self arguably has its roots in these seminal works – Freud is by no means the first intellectual giant in the 'tradition'.

The subject of this present book is the developing exploration of this mode of consciousness within nineteenth-century English literature. I will be paying a good deal of attention to Wordsworth, of course, whose early investigations in the mode naturally became established as paradigmatic models that later writers could not but turn to when thinking along similar lines. My chief focus, though, will be the novels of Dickens, for it is their varied, uncertain but persistent engagement with Wordsworthian beginnings, I want to argue, that most fully explores and reveals the ambiguities and dilemmas that this way of conceiving the self entails. Such a focus, I hope, will also reveal a good deal of interest about Dickens's works and their creator, both taken in themselves and as the products of their age. I also want to pay some attention, in passing, to those other nineteenth-century novels that witness a similar preoccupation, works such as *The Mill on the Floss*, *Jane Eyre* and *Wuthering Heights*. Indeed, a list such as this suggests the degree to which the concern with the self's continuity (a concern which is both thematic and a medium for the investigation of other themes) becomes in the nineteenth-century English novel one of the established narrative schemas, one of the available types of novelistic structure. An eighteenth-century novel like *Tom Jones* is also patterned by the history of the protagonist's self, of course. But whilst we see Tom's self as being to an important extent *shaped* by his experience, just as Austen's *Emma* begins with a heroine whose character is predicated upon the shaping fact of the absence of a proper paternal authority, it is only in the nineteenth-century, post-Romantic, post-Wordsworthian works that the shaping past is seen as being *alive* in the present, the 'child' as persistingly the doggedly unrelinquishing 'father of the man'.

This, then, in broad terms, is the path I want to trace. However, in order to grasp the significance of the particular forms taken by the mode of awareness I am discussing – its complications and permutations – we need to go at least a little way towards seeing it not just in the context of the works themselves, but also in the light of the century's broader social and cultural development, and the general relationship between the tensions and contradictions inherent in this, and the literature of the period. It is with this in mind that I have taken my chapter title from Marshal Berman's recent book, *All that is Solid Melts into Air: the Experience of Modernity.*[1] Berman offers an illuminating account of post-French Revolutionary culture wrought by the modernising bourgeois revolution and the massive unleashing of aspiration and energy involved in its interrelated forces of individualism, capitalism, urbanisation, secularisation and technological progress. This is a quite familiar historical drama: such changes are obviously central to any account one might give of European culture since the eighteenth century. Berman's distinctive achievement, though, is the way in which he relates these factors to a phenomenological effect in consciousness, an effect both complex and unified, and one which, whilst respecting the individuality of the figures he discusses, he persuasively suggests to be collective. This 'effect' (which can also of course come to function as a cause within the circumstances which produced it) he calls 'the experience of modernity', meaning by this both the recognisably modern condition of responding with both delight *and* fear, in equal intensity, to the possibility of freedom and expansion, embracing it as liberation whilst shrinking from its threat of *anomie*, and, importantly, all the time undergoing such contradictions more or less simultaneously, so that ambiguity itself becomes the hallmark of the experience. It is as moulded within the condition defined by this collective 'experience', I want to argue, that the forms of evolution taken by the awareness of self-continuity make most sense. The continuities and tensions between, say, *The Prelude* and *Great Expectations* in their different senses of the personal past, disclose themselves most meaningfully when seen in the context of the age's Faustian (or Promethean) dialectic as a whole.

The best way of pursuing this (leaving aside the details of the case Berman himself presents) is perhaps to digress a little on to one of the chief factors involved in 'the experience of modernity'. Wherever we look in the relevant literature of the century, the interest in the self's continuity is inevitably bound up with the question of authority, with the authorisation or inhibition of certain feelings and desires. Morality and psychology reveal themselves as closely related fields of enquiry. Hence I want to look generally for a few moments at several literary examinations of the subversion of traditional conceptions of authority that 'the experience of modernity' entailed, and at the emergence within these works of new conceptions, albeit still problematical ones. The 'modern' life-situation (in Berman's terms) has naturally given rise to a love–hate fascination with authority, which is why modern life, collectively and individually, has been strewn with the grotesque consequences of both compulsive authoritarianism and obsessive anti-authoritarianism. This instability has also engendered an astonishing cultural creativity, however, in response to the challenge it poses. Indeed, the central motivating theme of nineteenth-century literature can best be seen as a continuing negotiation between an heroically expansive sense of human potentiality, and an equally powerful awareness of the limits to fulfilling this, together with an anxiety as to where attempts at its realisation might lead.

Promethean challenges to the constraints of established authority have loomed titanically, as with Blake and Shelley and their legacies. But equally important and creative has been the contrary response of seeking out, or reluctantly discovering, new rationales of authority, and intellectual-imaginative legitimations of it persuasive enough to allay and contain Promethean challenge – one thinks here, among the English Romantic poets, of Wordsworth and *his* legacy. For me the most interesting literary figures are those whose works span both these contraries, living fully within the dialectic of their opposition.[2] Dickens and

George Eliot in England, Tolstoy and Dostoevsky in Russia – it is most of all in such novelists that one finds this completeness of engagement. It is in their novels (though Professor Berman has his own canon) that I think we can find 'the experience of modernity' most vitally enacted.

The Promethean/Faustian expansive impulse (the choice of myth reflecting the authorial point of view) is the one we most immediately associate with the literature and culture of the last two hundred years. This is the crucial factor that most clearly separates pre- from post-Romantic periods, wherever in relation to 1789 we see this division as lying. It is one obvious expression of the bourgeois revolution's energy, the *welcoming* response to the world of change in which, to use the metaphor from Marx on the same subject that Berman has taken as his title, 'all that is solid melts into air'. A fascination with Promethean possibility is as old as the myth itself, of course, but there is a specifically Romantic form of it. The Renaissance–Baroque emphasis on energy, power and splendour exemplified by, say, Marlowe and Milton, is very different from the Promethean accent of either Blake or Shelley, notwithstanding the links between Milton and both these very dissimilar poets. Between the two periods, of course, stand the Enlightenment and the French Revolution, and from this background derive such distinctively Romantic emphases as the frequent (though not uniform) identification of the passion for life with passionate love, and the recasting of the classical Promethean *agon* (princely or demi-godly rebel versus metaphysical authority) into a new mould of the heroically rebellious social victim versus an essentially secular authority, though one often allegorised as godly. Both emphases grow out of Enlightenment optimism about the innate goodness of humanity, and the concomitant claim that what people are is essentially a matter of what their culture and society have made them. The Romantic Promethean's struggle is just as likely to be with 'mind-forged manacles' as with external ones. Both Romantic poetry and the nineteenth-century novel are deeply involved with these themes, and the very form of the novel changes radically to accommodate them.

Yet, as Berman has most cogently argued, such an impulse cannot be separated out, in the dialectic of modernity, from its opposite, from that reaching back to preserve established structures even in the act of joying in their demolition. Hence the fact, as Berman points out, that the writers of the nineteenth century and beyond – the 'modern' period in his definition – have been so often at once revolutionary and conservative. At the least impressive level this doubleness has typically taken the form of lurching from a naive and frothy Prometheanism into the grip of a wilfully simplistic, and hence strident but brittle Reaction, a phenomenon that the decades since the 1960s have made us depressingly familiar with. It is partly the spectacle of such human helplessness that makes so impressive the refusal to simply react (in whatever direction) which has so often, if not always, distinguished the major novelists' negotiations with modernity. It is this that has prompted me in this study to lay emphasis on the dialectic of modernity not just as an explanatory schema, as a way of making sense of Dickens and the other writers I discuss, but as a stimulus to creative *achievement*. I am interested, that is, in the positive contribution to imaginative human understanding that is the finest consequence of the best writers' engagement with it. Hence, whilst attempting to pay appropriate attention to contextual factors and to thus avoid the fallacies of the Romantic myth of the artist heroically creating in a social vacuum, I do want to maintain a stress upon that element of literary value that cannot simply be 'de-constructed' into its constituent social and ideological determinants.

The fundamental if implicit premiss guiding the kind of creative exploration I am singling out is that both poles of the dialectic, the expansive Promethean and the conservative reactionary – the anti-Faustian, one might say – must be allowed their full force and claim, allowed to clash freely against each other. To engage with disruptive Romantic propositions is not in these instances to ritually exorcise them. It is this steady openness that distinguishes Tolstoy, Eliot and (surprisingly) Dickens at their best, and also, in his way, Flaubert, prone to premature foreclosure and simplification of their dialectical allegiances though they always are. The novelists' post-Romantic problematic is well summed up in the first paragraph of the Prelude to *Middlemarch*, in the fond reference to the young Saint Theresa and her brother quixotically leaving home 'with human hearts, already beating to a national idea . . . until domestic reality met them in the shape of uncles'. It is the peculiar genius and preoccupation of the best nineteenth-century novels both to confront Shelleyan beating hearts possessed by crypto-Hegelian ideas, with the constraints of the mundanely, empirically real, *and* to maintain a commitment to keeping those hearts beating at least in some form or another. The particular complexity and tension (and even to some extent the length) of a work like *Middlemarch*, stem from its adherence to this dialectic, which dictates that Dorothea, say, must be brought at last to a life at once domesticated *and* (to quote) 'full of emotion'. George Eliot is prone to gush about Dorothea, of course but I suspect that this tendency is inseparable from an engagement with human actuality and possibility quite superior to that of, say, Conrad's preternaturally gushless *The Secret Agent*. One might compare Eliot's not entirely quixotic commitment to Dorothea and the Shelleyan Ladislaw, with Conrad's relentless satire of Shelleyan idealism in the figure of the mental defective Stevie, which typifies *his* novel's outlook, and the degree to which its achievement is a matter of purely 'aesthetic' perfection, being in this a major example of the transition to one main line of twentieth-century development in the *genre*. One might also compare *Middlemarch* favourably on this score with Thackeray's unequivocal stance of no-nonsense anti-Romantic dryness, which only leads to resurgent gushiness on certain special topics. His is a case of defective emotional plumbing that also says much about the age's peculiar complications.

What I am drawing on in these comments on the *manner* in which these writers involve themselves in the conflict of Romantically legitimated freedom and traditionally authorised restraint is the concept of 'negative capability'; and it is in this way that the idea has come to play an increasingly significant role in literary–cultural critical theory, through Arnold to Leavis and his associates, from the time of Keats's coinage of it. Both Arnold and Leavis found their criticism on the idea of the possible spiritual authority of literature, a conviction that associates them with nineteenth-century poets and novelists and divides them from the axiomatic relativism of contemporary structuralist criticism and the literature that corresponds to it. But neither do they conceive of such authority as something to be expounded in the magisterial manner of Dr Johnson. For them it is just something to be, if possible, discovered, and primarily (if not quite self-consciously) in the inconclusive maze of the dialectic I am discussing. What place is there, can there be, for expansively yearning energy in the world? What *are* the limits of freedom, of possibility, when seen in terms of the inevitabilities of real living? What, indeed, does a word like 'inevitability' mean? All these, except the last, are perennial questions, but it is the concern of the dialectic's explorers to ask them in a particular way – a way exemplified by the instance from *Middlemarch* just cited, and which one might summarise by rephrasing Johnson's characteristic title, 'The Vanity of Human Wishes' into something like: Are human wishes vain? Which ones and to what extent? Now or forever?

This present study is mainly about what all this means with regard to the awareness of self-continuity. But by way of filling out a bit more the sense of context in which, I am arguing, *that* can only be fully appreciated, I want to spend some more time in this introductory chapter approaching my focal theme, and Dickens in relation to it, via a brief discussion of some other of the period's 'landmark' novels, and the various 'answers' to the above 'questions' about freedom these arrive at. One recurrent answer, of course, is simply irresolution, the conclusion that there is simply no reconciliation possible between the Promethean and the Stoic, the longed-for possible and the realistically perceived actual. This is most pre-eminently so with that virtual genre that Tony Tanner and Judith Armstrong have both recently written about as 'the novel of adultery'.[3] Adultery is so frequently the central plot-situation in the nineteenth-century novel, Tanner argues, because it paradigmatically focuses the strain between the novelists' overt and abiding commitment to bourgeois morality and its institutional structures, and their deep attraction to expansive yearnings which neither that morality nor those structures can accommodate. The adulterous situation (actual in most of the works Tanner discusses, but one could also add many instances of narrowly averted adultery or spiritually adulterous marriage) is thus the representative arena for the working out of what Tanner calls 'the fate of awakened energy ... unsuited to time and place', a fate that is significant for social and cultural life as a whole. The origin of this strain in the legacy of Romanticism is obvious, as is implied in Tanner's phrase '*awakened* energy' – energy, that is, which has been culturally named, acknowledged, legitimised, and which therefore cannot be simply repressed. Hence the kind of resolution which such different novels as *Madame Bovary* and *Anna Karenina* enact – a resolution that characteristically balances a vindication of societal sanctions, through the tragic course of the plot, against a sympathetic evocation of illicit desires and relations, so that acknowledgement of the value of the subversive goes hand in hand with its cathartic exorcism. There is obvious point in Flaubert's famous 'Emma Bovary, c'est moi', whilst it is hard to imagine the pre-Romantic Jane Austen having anything similar to say for her heroine of the same name if the plots of *Emma* and *Mansfield Park* were somehow conflated and she had run off with Frank Churchill. Jane Austen is perhaps the last figure for whom the discrimination between morally sanctioned and thus good feeling, and immoral and thus bad feeling, can be regarded as unproblematic; and even in her the curtness with which she dismisses 'the high spirit and strong passions' of Maria Bertram sounds reactionary. We might also compare Pope's opening gambit in his second Moral Essay, 'Most women have no character at all', with Flaubert's fascination (brilliantly demonstrated by Tanner) with Emma Bovary's indefiniteness, with the way she persistently eludes the definitions, the characterisations, that men, and the social structures they dominate, seek to impose upon her. Of course one might wonder what sort of bourgeois allegiance Flaubert could be said to be demonstrating, given the un-English acidity with which he depicts the bourgeois males in Emma's world. A clearer distinction has to be made than Tanner allows, between a positive commitment to bourgeois morality and a pessimism about any more Romantic alternative. Though this suggestion perhaps also shows how the conventions of novelistic realism themselves pre-determine certain answers to certain novelistic questions. 'In adultery she found all the banality of marriage': one might adapt Dennis de Rougemont's case about Romance to argue that there is no better genre than the nineteenth-century novel, with all the mimetic specificity of its aspirations, in which to arrive at that insight.

However, to speak like this is to concede Flaubert's tale an inevitability it cannot really persuade one of. Or rather, whilst the Manichean dualism of desire and reality that determines Emma's fate does satisfy as an account of her as an individual, it surely represents a too dogmatically narrow sense of human possibility to compel us to accord her a universal significance. What it feels like to be Emma Bovary (or Flaubert), the sense of life as locked into that inexorable rhythmn of soaring release and claustrophobic reversion, is evoked with incomparable power and art in such scenes as Emma's visit to the opera, or the series of sexual encounters with Leon in the hotel room at Rouen. But we are left too aware of further avenues of negotiation between dreaming and living beyond the novel's scope, for the work to have, at least from a humanistic standpoint, quite the highest stature. Which is not to say, though, that the novel does not fully give itself to the contradictions of its problematic within its powers to envisage them.

Another way of putting this is to say that Flaubert has nothing very compelling to say to us about the grounds of moral constraint, about its possible authority. His Manichean pessimism offers a no more persuasive grasp of the wisdom of inhibiting sanctions than the ideologically-loaded 'common-sense' assumptions that determine the narrative of more conventional and more overtly moralistic and socially-committed stories of adultery: that adultery can never work because the seducer will prove faithless, etc. *Anna Karenina*, by contrast, does precisely this, as has been variously if not universally attested by the novel's readers and commentators. Even Judith Armstrong, who begins her discussion with a feminist version of Lawrence's well-known charge of Tolstoy's predetermined investment in Anna's failure, finally claims for her story a truthfulness that transcends ideological considerations.[4] Neither she, however, nor Michael Black in his admirable *The Literature of Fidelity*,[5] nor, for that matter, F. R. Leavis in his essay,[6] have quite managed to adequately specify in what this truthfulness consists. I want to take a little bit of time to try to do this myself, since the way in which this work challenges and tempers moral authority, in its profound interrelation of the moral and the psychological, nicely points to how my focal theme of the self in time grows out of the Promethean *agon* I have been digressing upon.

The reasons for Anna's failure are of course many and various, which is symptomatic of that liberating open-endedness in the sense of life in the nineteenth-century novel (*pace* qualifications of the above Flaubertian kind), that Lukàcs has canonised as its 'historical' nature. Tragedy here implies no *assumption* of an eternally unchangeable human nature, such as underlies the tragic vision of classical Greek drama, or Johnson's 'Vanity of Human Wishes'. Thus, where the protagonists of Johnson's poem, say, fall in order to demonstrate an inevitable futility which we are sternly enjoined to acknowledge, Anna's downfall can partly be analysed in terms of a cluster of contingent factors: the state of divorce laws, social attitudes towards sexual 'deviance', etc. One factor proffers itself as absolute, however, I suggest, and this is the crucial role played by psychological insecurity in destroying, in the vicious cycle of possessiveness and jealousy it engenders, the initially so vital and promising relationship with Vronsky, and thus destroying Anna herself. Anna and Vronsky's love does not 'inevitably' dwindle, after the pattern of Flaubertian pessimism or conventional moralism. Rather, it suffers a slow, agonising death, strangled by the cancerous growths of bad feeling that insecurity produces, though still – with the unique poignancy of this particular story – persisting valiantly to the last in despite of this. The insecurity is exacerbated by contingent factors, obviously, but I do think that it is Tolstoy's essential point to show us that it is the inevitable consequence of the adulterous situation *per se*. Critics may stress the importance of Vronsky's officerly limitations, for instance (if only Anna had fallen for someone with their own powers of empathy!); but what strikes me most of all about him in the closing stages of the relationship is the degree to which his love enables him to transcend these, desperately persisting with Anna until he is driven off in sheer emotional exhaustion.

What we have here, in fact, is a striking instance of the kind of deepening of moral understanding I have been talking about, in its relocation of the grounds of constraint away from the absolutes of social law and their traditional justifications in metaphysical dogma and prudential 'common sense'. Anna does not die because she offends against God's will (which ceases to exist when ceased to be believed in), or against historically specific social conventions and attitudes, however much these contribute to her suffering. Primarily she dies because she offends a deep-rooted need in her own psyche, a need presented as absolute and independent of social conditioning. The final grounds of morality, Tolstoy is suggesting, are in the nature of the human psyche itself, present there in equal force to that other psychic imperative which compels Anna to revolt against constraint.

In fact, one of the novel's most important meanings is the paradox it suggests of an underlying identity in these overtly opposing drives, which emerge as the positive and negative manifestations of the one life-force, alternately empowering and disrupting the self. This is why Anna's insecurity in the second half of the novel is not just a factor in her breakdown, as it is usually spoken of, but an almost *daimonic* presence. The paradoxical oneness of this vitality, at once impelling her into adultery and destroying her happiness in it, is, I think, what gives the depiction of Anna's decline its harrowing power. We can sense this clearly in the episode where she insists upon going to the opera, which begins with Vronsky's awareness that 'something unusual [is] taking place within her':

> her eyes glittered with strained attention when they rested on him for a moment, and there was that nervous rapidity and grace in her speech and movements which had so fascinated him in the early days of their intimacy, but which now disturbed and alarmed him.[7]

That continuing but now revalued 'nervous rapidity and grace' makes the point: the animation that was once the sign of an irresistible passion for sexual fulfillment, now speaks of an equally inexorable impulse to clutch and claw at Vronsky in jealousy and possessiveness, a desperate, counter-productive but, in her, totally uncontrollable attempt of the psyche to assuage the insecurity her situation besets her with. The connection succinctly exposes the contradiction at the heart of the kind of sexual ideology that counsels permissiveness in the name of freedom from repression, whilst at the same time holding up a repressive notion of aloofness from jealousy as a standard of enlightened maturity. Tolstoy elsewhere attacks such emotion-denying urbanity in Levin's comically undignified but essentially right expulsion of the amiable Vasenka Veslovsky (or *aimable*, as Mr Knightley might say, making the point more stiffly): such a suggestion is at the heart of the novel's whole case against the Westernising Petersburg and French-oriented influence. It is this awareness that accounts for the marvelous empathy that informs his portrait of the irrational, ridiculous, unbearable yet profoundly *true* behaviour that characterises Anna in her downfall; as in her meeting with Vronsky immediately after her return from the opera:

> Anna was already there. When Vronsky entered, she was still in the same dress as she had worn at the theatre. She was

sitting in the first arm-chair against the wall, staring straight before her. She glanced up at him, and immediately resumed her former position.

'Anna,' he said.

'It's all your fault, all your fault!' she cried, tears of despair and anger in her voice, and rose.

'But I begged, I implored you not to go. I knew it would be unpleasant . . .'

'Unpleasant!' she cried. 'It was awful! As long as I live I shall never forget it. She said it was a disgrace to sit beside me.'

'A silly woman's chatter,' he said. 'But why risk it, why provoke . . .?'

'I hate that self-possession of yours. You ought not to have brought me to this. If you had loved me . . .'

'Anna! What has my love to do with it?'

'Yes, if you loved me, as I love you, if you were tortured as I am! . . .' she said, looking at him with an expression of terror.

He was sorry for her, but angry all the same. He assured her of his love because he saw that this was the only means of soothing her, and he did not reproach her in words, but in his heart he reproached her.

And those assurances of his love, which seemed to him so hackneyed and commonplace that he was ashamed to utter them, she drank in eagerly, and gradually became calmer. The next day, fully at peace with one another, they left for the country.[8]

If Anna strikes one as a heroine more morally passive in the face of destructive emotion than, say, Eliot's Dorothea, it is largely because Tolstoy has, at this point of comparison, a more clear-sighted sense of certain truths of feeling and their tragically inevitable nature. Such 'neurotic' outbursts as this are manifestations of the psyche's god-like power of retribution, and Anna is Tolstoy's heroine precisely because of the depth to which she is possessed by it, in a fashion which Eliot would never have permitted her heroines. Such is the tragic cost of her vitality and spontaneity: the force that at first Romantically ennobles her in sweeping her into adultery, is now her own form of secular, psychologistic martyrdom. Of all the morally assertive resolutions in the nineteenth-century novel, it is perhaps the one that can still most persuade us of its authoritativeness, can still undermine our ethically liberal, relativistic dispositions. For one is almost tempted to see in Anna's *daimon* the revelation of a kind of psychological equivalent to the metaphysical deity who has lost his sway in the society of the novel, as in ours. Karenin may lecture Anna on marriage as a 'sacred duty', but this is a novel written very consciously about a modern world where only pedants and pseudo-mystics can invoke such traditional absolutes with confidence. Tolstoy's Russia is a world in which liberalism and a leisurely quasi-bohemian officer class (whose *joie de vivre* Tolstoy is still, at this point in his life, half in love with) have produced an ethos in which, as Betsey gaily informs Anna, the best people have all adopted 'the new fashion' and 'kicked over the traces'.[9] Tolstoy's deeply-explored response to this historical situation might arguably be said to have discovered a new kind of authority, perhaps the only kind which can have abiding relevance in a world (our world?) in which the old justifications have lost their power. In being this, Anna's story is one of the finest consequences of a general line of enquiry arising from the conservative impulses within the post-Romantic Promethean dialectic as I have outlined it. Tolstoy here stands linked with writers like Wordsworth, George Eliot, and, in our own century, Lawrence, in a common search to discover a moral authority in psychological law.

The tragic impasse of Emma's and Anna's stories is nevertheless not the nineteenth-century's definitive mode of resolution. The age's bourgeois optimism finally shows through in an equally strong reluctance to arrive at tragic conclusions. Hence perhaps the habit of multiple plotting which complements Anna and Vronsky with Kitty and Levin, Catherine and Heathcliff with the young Catherine and Earnshaw, Lydgate with Dorothea. And it is with these more achievement-oriented couples that we find attempts to imagine Romanticism and morality in a more harmonious relation to each other. These efforts to resolve the opposition of individual passion and social obligation issue in characters or character-types whose goodness is inspired by Romantically-acceptable energy. There is, for instance, the mixture of Romanticism and Puritanism, this-worldliness and otherworldliness, that informs the ideal of ardent selflessness espoused (pre-eminently) by Carlyle and George Eliot – somewhat grotesquely in the former case, much more interestingly in the latter. An outstanding example of this is Dorothea Brooke. As the opening chapters of *Middlemarch* show it, the energy of her heroine's social idealism proceeds from – is a *natural* sublimation of – a strongly alive sexual nature; and this is why the novel has to see her through to the attainment of the kind of marriage that offers her a fulfillment of that. For all its imperfections, the Dorothea story does seem to me to represent the most impressive attempt in the English novel of the period to imagine some productive social usefulness to which Romantic idealism and energy might be turned, a way that Romantic Prometheanism might possibly be harmonised with moral constraints.

The portrait also implies, however, a Romantic optimism about the availability of such feeling, a trust that there is more than simple commitment to principle in people that can guide and motivate the moral will. George Eliot has a good deal of such trust, but she is also naturally preoccupied with the problems that flow from it: which is why she leads Dorothea, in her first marriage, into a situation that epitomises the difficulty of being spontaneously good. Constancy, stability, fidelity, all these most testing aspects of the moral life pose special problems to any morality based on feelings, as the Regency anti-Jacobin satire 'The New Morality' had pointed out in deprecating 'feelings fine, that *float* about the heart'.[10] George Eliot tackles this problem in a number of ways. In *Middlemarch* her stress falls upon the potential for empathy and consequent compassion to energise the moral will against the temptations of seemingly justifiable (and in fact self-protective) egoism. The power of restraint simply maintains a clear space to allow into play a protective tenderness that is a more socially solidifying form of the energy of feeling that threatens disruption: thus that fine aspect of heroines such as Dorothea and Maggie, which is that their passionate natures express themselves equally as assertive individualism and as ardent sympathy. Rather differently in *The Mill on the Floss*, however, and by way of explaining Gwendolen's lack of moral will in *Daniel Deronda*, she looks to the most interesting development in moral understanding that Romantic poetry made available to the novelists of the century: Wordsworth's very original examination of the psychology of moral feeling, as observable in the development and continuity of the self in time. This view of the self locates the sources of moral feeling or the lack of it in the nature of the psyche, making the availability of that feeling seem less arbitrary and mysterious.

Equally, it offers a rationale for moral integrity by regarding it as an abiding by a more deeply inward principle than traditional ones of 'honour' and 'character', regarding it rather as an honouring of the most primary sources of the self, which is thus a way reassuring to post-Romantic assumptions.

This may well seem a misguided approach to Wordsworth the poet. Yet for Wordsworth himself, it is clear, being a poet goes hand in hand with being a psychologist. The same intimate examination of his experience that informs his poetry also informs his interest in ideas about the human psyche, ideas that are not 'metaphors for poetry' in the Yeatsian sense, but seriously intended propositions. *The Prelude* is nor more just a versified psychological treatise than it is a versified autobiography or diary of the times; nevertheless, to appreciate its achievement we do need to give full weight to the statement of theoretical intent that introduces the justly famous passage in Book Two about the 'infant babe': 'For with my best conjecture I would trace Our Being's earthly progress'. This conjecturing is an essay in what De Quincey, writing on Wordsworth in 1845, called that 'good psychology', as yet unestablished, which is the prerequisite of 'absolute and philosophic criticism'.[11] The passage itself is at the heart of Wordsworthian psychology:

> Blest the infant Babe,
> (For with my best conjecture I would trace
> Our Being's earthly progress,) blest the Babe,
> Nursed in his Mother's arms, who sinks to sleep
> Rocked on his Mother's breast; who with his soul
> Drinks in the feelings of his Mother's eye!
> For him, in one dear Presence, there exists
> A virtue which irradiates and exalts
> Objects through widest intercourse of sense;
> No outcast he, bewildered and depressed:
> Along his infant veins are interfused
> The gravitation and the filial bond
> Of nature that connects him with the world.
> Is there a flower, to which he points with hand
> Too weak to gather it, already love
> Drawn from love's purest earthly fount for him
> Hath beautified that flower; already shades
> Of pity cast from inward tenderness

Do fall around him upon aught that bears
Unsightly marks of violence or harm.
Emphatically such a Being lives,
Frail creature as he is, helpless as frail,
An inmate of this active universe:[12]

I think we can see a key to Wordsworth's psychological vision in the optimism these lines declare about the possibility of softening the developmental tragedy of maternal loss. They look to a process of psychological growth in which the mother's presence is both internalised and then sustained by being progressively replaced by things that are vestigially continuous with her: a process of metaphoric displacement, as Freud and Lacan would have it, but seen more hopefully. In this way the child's growth into the world is envisaged as a journey not from symbiosis to apartness, but into sublimated forms of the original rich relationship – the main one being that sense of instinctive harmony with Nature celebrated so often in Wordsworth (not, of course, that peace and harmony are the only ways in which Wordsworth experiences Nature).

A great deal in Wordsworth derives from this idea. In essence, it posits the development in early childhood of a healthy core of selfhood, a core manifesting itself primarily in a strong disposition to relate to the world in certain ways rather than others: 'No outcast he, bewildered and depressed', but a being that lives *emphatically*. The theoretical psychological understanding Wordsworth elicits from his life-history as *The Prelude* unfolds could be roughly summed up in two corollaries to this initial idea. First of all, sustained psychic (and thus spiritual) health depends upon living in such a way as to keep in touch with this core self. The self-in-time is repeatedly conceived in terms of a metaphor of organic plant-growth ('Fair seed-time had my soul'). For Wordsworth, this gives an especial importance to memory as the medium in which such organic continuity is sustained. Not only is the child seen to be the father of the man in a causal sense, but there is an emphasis upon an almost religious duty in maintaining fidelity to the personal past, of positively embracing it: 'And I could wish my days to be/ Bound each to each by natural piety.'[13] The second corollary, and a closely related one, is the manner in which Wordsworth sees the abiding influence of the personal past and its 'hiding places . . . of power' as a source of moral stability. As Christopher Salveson has pointed out in his *The Landscape of Memory* (1965), whilst writers of a 'sentimentalist' persuasion were increasingly interested in memory through the eighteenth century – interested, that is, in the continuity of childhood and adult selves – it is only with Wordsworth that memory comes to be thought of as having an important *moral* function. Hence the conception of Nature, or rather the conception of the memory of the experience of it, as:

> The *anchor* of my purest thoughts, the *nurse*,
> The *guide*, the *guardian* of my heart, and soul
> Of all my moral being. [my italics] (Tintern Abbey)[14]

Nothing more different from the restless turmoil of, say, Shelley's Nature could be imagined; and the serenity to which Wordsworth's poetry so often and so surely gravitates bears witness to the unity of the conscious idea and the poetic reality. It is an idea of inwardly-inspired rather than self-imposed quietness under constraint, supporting and steadying the self under the demands of normal social life – the eighteenth-century code of social obligation, as it were, with a distinctively Romantic inwardness. This is the point of the allusion in 'Tintern Abbey' to those feelings:

> As have no slight or trivial influence
> On that best portion of a good man's life,
> His little, nameless, unremembered, acts
> Of kindness and of love.[15]

All these notions are highly problematical, but we need to recognise their positive value. They form a poetic and intellectual account of a morality of feeling; poetic, in the so often assured and radiant calm of the verse's evocations; intellectual, in the very interesting attempt to ground vague sentimentalist optimism about natural goodness in precise psychological explanations, and thus offer an answer to the objections about inspirational instability I mentioned above. Coleridge, who shared these concerns (as did Thomas de Quincey), caught the drift of this enterprise when he glossed Wordsworth's 'The Rainbow' with the comment that 'continuity of . . . self-consciousness' is a *'law'* of man's *animal* life' (*The Friend*, 10 Aug. 1809).[16] In all of this, it seems to me, Wordsworth offers a subtly intimate articulation of just what it is in the self that expansive self-assertion violates when it over-reaches itself. The historical period of his own formative adulthood was (not unlike our own times) one when the ideological battleground tended to be divided between over-simple ideas about freedom, and hollow and outdated appeals to traditional restraints. In *The Prelude* especially, his recreation of his own moral life and his explanation of its psychological sources, provided just the kind of departure in moral understanding that the best novelists of later generations could look to for inspiration. It articulated, for instance, a defence against the anomic perils of 'self-fulfillment', a defence that was itself a form of self-realisation couched in acceptably Romantic terms. In being thus conservative *and* Romantic it was a psychology with an especial appeal to its age.

Nevertheless, such a psychological conservatism entails its own simplifications. Of course, like Tolstoy on Anna's insecurity, it arises from the reactive side of the post-Romantic dialectic, and thus in both the Tolstoy of *Anna Karenina* and the Wordsworth of the early 'adventure' episodes in *The Prelude* (and the one recounted separately in 'Nutting'), the elicited sense of sanctities is only one side of a tragic paradox that equally insists upon the inevitability of violation.[17] In the poetry where Wordsworth more consciously articulates a social ethic, however, the point of such a complexity is generally not taken up, so that in consequence the principle of self-continuity becomes the psychological grounding for a general philosophy of quiescence. Hence we have the political conservatism resolved upon in *The Prelude*, through the logic by which the poem moves from an affirmation of fidelity to the personal past, to a general advocacy of contentment with the given, a general renouncing of what it calls, in its post-Godwinian calm, 'impatient or fallacious hopes' of 'throwing off incumbrances'.[18] That logic has some cogency, admittedly: it *is* illuminating to see how the notion of maternally-derived creative perception suggested in the 'infant babe' passage – the 'virtue ... which irradiates and exalts' – does give a special force to an ideal of seeking 'for present good in life's familiar face'.[19] But this is hardly a universal and absolute truth, as Wordsworth implies it is. 'Life's familiar face' was understandably amenable enough in Wordsworth's particular experience of it; but he does want us to take his own spiritual recovery as exemplary for everyone else.

There is also a similar absolutist tendency in the ideal of femininity he enshrines in the portrait of his sister in the closing books of *The Prelude*, or in poems like 'She Was a Phantom of Delight' – the woman who, in 'the happy stillness of her mind', 'welcomed what was given, and craved no more'.[20] This ideal may be perennially appealing to restless male hearts; certainly with Wordsworth and, to a much more extreme extent with Dickens, as I shall argue later, it represents a consoling still point in fascinating contrast to the turning world of their own personal tensions. But its limited adequacy as a model for women in general is obvious.

Both the strengths and limitations of this Wordsworthian Romantic psychology can be seen in George Eliot, who stands out amongst the novelists as the one most visibly affected. One can see the general connection in the debt apparent in the depiction of Gwendolen Harleth's underlying insecurity, to Wordsworth's vertiginously excited evocations of 'troubled pleasure': one might compare something like the boating incident, say, in Book I, with the similar sudden collapsing of exultant self-assertion into dread in the tableau scene in Chapter 6 of *Deronda*. And both in *Deronda* and in *The Mill on the Floss* we can see something of the mixed benefit of a susceptibility to the conservatism of the Wordsworthian psychological 'model'. Hence, whilst it is intelligent enough of Eliot to conceive Maggie Tulliver's life and moral being in a modified version of Wordsworth's terms, this also leads Eliot, I think, to simplify or evade her own dilemmas as much as to resolve them. One can see the difficulty in a passage like the one at the end of Book 2, Chapter I, in which Tom's relief at returning home from boarding out is interpreted in terms of a gloss on one of Wordsworth's corollaries on his leading idea, the deeper appeal of places and things that are invested with early memories:

> There is no sense of ease like the ease we felt in those scenes where we were born, where objects became dear to us before we had known the labour of choice [cf. *Prelude*, XII, 188 . . . 'I felt, observed, and pondered; did not judge'], and where the outer world seemed only an extension of our own personality: we accepted it and loved it as we accepted our own sense of existence and our own limbs. Very commonplace, even ugly, that furniture of our early home might look if it were put up for

auction; an improved taste in upholstery scorns it; and is not the striving after something better and better in our surroundings, the grand characteristic that distinguishes man from the brute – or, to satisfy a scrupulous accuracy of definition, that distinguishes the British man from the foreign brute? But heaven knows where that striving might lead us, if our affections had not a trick of twining around those old inferior things – if the loves and sanctities of our life had no deep immovable roots in memory.[21]

The poised irony towards contemporary liberal optimism brings to mind Arnold, but it is the Wordsworthianly hallowed personal past rather than Culture that is offered as the bastion against anarchy. Eliot shares this defensiveness with Wordsworth – both, in their different ways, develop their positive ideals in the context of an anxiously sensed potential *anomie* in the prospect of freedom. And to some extent this is justifiable, and part of their achievement. But in doing so they both run the risk of simply saying 'no' to expansive energy *per se*, which is to withdraw too soon from the kind of dialectical endeavour I have outlined. The Eliot passage itself, given its particular context, does not encourage us to be fully aware of this implication: the warm mood of Tom's Christmas home-coming invites acquiescence, and there is a rhetorical advantage (and a blurring of the issue) in speaking of 'the striving after something better and better in our surroundings' as if it were simply materialistic in aim. It is not, and although (as Lukacs has said) the nineteenth-century novel typically reveals the reification of generalised Promethean yearnings into materialistic or equally mundane manifestations, it is the achievement of the novels themselves to keep alive at least the dream of fuller and finer possibility.

This is what Eliot herself sets out to do in *The Mill on the Floss*: there is the continuity between Mr Tulliver's educational hopes for Tom and the yearnings for self-fulfillment in Maggie which find their object in Stephen. But Maggie's final rejection of Stephen is understood and validated in largely Wordsworthian terms: a decision required not just by an external (albeit internalised) social code, but also, more broadly, by fidelity to her childhood. And what is surely unsatisfactory in the novel is Eliot's resolute assertion that this is a really viable decision, one that does not offend against life as much as the alternative would. Hence there seems something evasive in the rather cursory treatment of Maggie's ensuing inner state in the concluding chapters of the novel, marvellously telling though such things as the sarcasm against 'the world's wife' and the 'man of maxims' are. The love–death reunion with Tom in the concluding flood-scene climactically dramatises the Wordsworthian continuity with her past on which Maggie's integrity is founded. But it also reprieves Eliot from having to spell out fully the attenuating consequences in her of her noble resolve 'to be true to [her] calmer affections, and live without the joy of love'. Perhaps something of the same thing might also be said of Eliot's equivocations with Gwendolen Harleth – along the lines, for example, of S. L. Goldberg's comments (in his article in *The Critical Review* for 1980) about the motives behind her marrying Grandcourt and the novel's interpretation of these.[22]

Eliot then, one might say, characteristically resolves the strain between the integrity of the self and its proper expansion – between its roots and its full flowering – too narrowly in favour of the former. Or, to put it in the terms of Donald H. Stone's recent discussion of contending Romantic influences upon her, Wordsworth is allowed to win out too easily over Rousseau.[23] But what of other contemporary English novelists? Both Charlotte and Emily Brontë would seem to think within the kind of framework I am outlining, since the dilemmas of passion and control, and of the growth and continuity of the self in time, are also at the heart of their concerns. However, both seem to me to draw the lines of their various spiritual and psychological battles in a way that does not quite engage with the particular problem I have in mind. The peculiarities of Cathy Earnshaw's circumstances, for example, mean that in her case integrity to childhood and self-realising passion lie on the same side, so to speak, rather than in dialectical opposition. The melting of socially-acquired identity during her climactic trauma of passion and sickness (which compares with what Tony Tanner notes in Emma Bovary), goes with a regression to childhood that the novel presents (at least in part) as spiritually uplifting. Perhaps this might account for the special respectability amongst Anglo-Saxon readers that *Wuthering Heights* has traditionally had – might explain, that is, the willingness to interpret the bond of Cathy and Heathcliff in rather mystical terms. (If you must be immoral, at least be so with a childhood friend.) Something of the same goes for *Jane Eyre*, too, where the heroine herself is the orphan figure. This novel is arguably one of the two most powerful and intelligent expressions in nineteenth-century fiction of the urge to push out from the *constrictions* of the childhood self, constrictions seen both as external circumstance and as internalised psychic disablement. In this it represents a view of the relations between early and later life that is the direct antithesis of Wordsworth's. But persuasive as it is here, it addresses itself to the universal dilemmas of psychic development only within the self-imposed limitations implied by Jane's status within the Reed family. For as the Reeds are not her actual family, either by lineage or by early experience, her self-assertive drive away from them and from their influence on her can be a relatively clean-cut affair. It is, of course, interestingly complicated to some extent by internalised self-doubt; but since this is not entangled with any of the bonds of affection that would have entered the case had Jane's family been a natural and just normally oppressive one, there remains something rather melodramatically two-dimensional about her psychic struggles to assert herself against her childhood-derived self-deprecation.

It is in Dickens, I want to argue, that we can find the fullest dialectical engagement with the Wordsworthian psychological position. This may seem an odd claim, and it is certainly not *consistently* supported by his work. Of all the writers I have mentioned so far, for instance, his treatment of adultery (always only potential in his case) is by far the feeblest – compare Maggie's story, say, to Little Emily's or Louisa Harthouse's. Indeed only a dialectical relationship could significantly link two such opposed figures as the rarely comic poet of rural serenity and the manic comic genius of city life: only the dialectical thread of attraction within antagonism, and *vice versa*, could bind together such polar opposites. George Eliot seems a much more natural choice of a novelist in whom to trace the working out of Wordsworthian concerns. Yet it is in this very unlikeliness, the seeming paradoxicalness of such a conjunction, that my point lies, and it is in this way that the developing preoccupation with the self's continuity can be related to the broader paradoxes of Berman's schema that I have been discussing. One key to the unlikely relation perhaps lies in Forster's comment, writing of Dickens's restlessness in the 1850s, that 'there was for him no "city of the mind" against outward ills, for inner consolation and shelter'.[24] His very lack of this essentially Wordsworthian strength arguably explains that mixture of relative overt indifference and persistent underlying fascination, that stamps Dickens's involvement with Wordsworth. And such an ambivalence makes sense if we accept that the nuclear pattern informing both Dickens's life and art is, as is now more fully realised, neither that of the sentimental Victorian public persona nor the demonic inversion of this first offered by the late Edmund Wilson[25] (and restated more recently by John Carey[26]), but the complex whole which expressed itself with equal spontaneity in both of these extremes, and which found its spring of life in a creative see-sawing between them. This dividedness can also be seen to exemplify the paradoxical opposites I have been discussing as a general phenomenon. The aggressive dynamism of nineteenth-century bourgeois capitalism and the nostalgia for the sanctities this violated, express themselves in specifically Dickensian contradictions: the Dickens of energetic and extroverted comedy as against the introverted Dickens who sensitively explores the costs of childhood emotional disturbance in such *covertly* 'Dickensian' characters (vehicles of oblique self-examination) as Paul Dombey, Esther Summerson and Amy Dorrit; Dickens the hard-nosed businessman as against the national celebrant of Christmas and domesticity; the genial humorist, and author of *David Copperfield*, 'the perfection of English mirth', as Forster called it,[27] as against the humorist of the macabre.

Influence, of course, can take a number of forms. It can be something consciously alluded to or something unconsciously present within a work; something communicated directly through reading alone, or indirectly as dissolved into an author's formative cultural ethos. Or all of these things together, in various relations of reinforcement and selectivity. Certainly this latter blend best describes the Dickens-Wordsworth connection. On the one hand the Wordsworthian presence I will be showing Dickens to be engaging with is a matter of ideas and sentiments that we can think of as having passed into the general currency of Victorian educated culture. Yet there is also useful supportive evidence of the straightforward kind traditionally gleaned by 'influence study'. Dickens did read Wordsworth; Wordsworth's poems were in Dickens' library.[28] *Household words* published an obituary article upon Wordsworth's death, which was respectful albeit critical of the poet's conservatism;[29] the *Household Narrative* reviewed *The Prelude* upon its posthumous publication;[30] and popular Wordsworthian tags appear from time to time throughout Dickens's writings[31] Forster, of course, remarks in the *Life* that his friend 'had little time' for the poet.[32] However the painter Wilkie, in a letter of 1839 to a Mrs Ricketts, cites Dickens' praise of Wordsworth in a personal conversation. Dickens, Wilkie reports, had 'a very great admiration for Wordsworth's genius, of which he thought the little poem "We are Seven" was one of the most striking examples.' What he 'seemed to like in this was divesting death of its horror, by treating it as a separation and not an extinction. He deprecated what in families occurred of never alluding to a near relation deceased; said he lately met with a severe loss, but took every pains to recall the person deceased to his family about him'.[33] This is a significant piece of evidence, I think, as it shows Wordsworth touching Dickens deeply, the poetry becoming associated with what was to remain one of *his* most potent 'hiding-places of . . . power' – the 'severe loss' alluded to was, of course, the death of Mary Hogarth in 1837. Interestingly, too, the terms of Dickens's appreciation touch on what was one of Wordsworth's major achievements: the poetic definition of an ideal of stoic composure in suffering and loss which did not involve a simple overmastering of the potentially disabling feelings. This was a variation on the continuity idea. Dickens's regard for Wordsworth was further expressed when he recommended that poet and Crabbe to his philanthropist friend, Miss Burdett-Coutts, for inclusion in the library of Urania Cottage, her home for 'fallen women'.[34]

Perhaps more important than such pointers to a direct connection, however, is, as Philip Collins has suggested, the oblique influence of at least Wordsworthian ideas and sentiments that Dickens would have undoubtedly been subject to in his extensive reading of the Romantic essayists, Lamb, Hunt and De Quincey. All three can be seen as a source of Dickensian treatments of Romantic themes, and in later chapters I deal specifically with the role of the latter two in mediating the Wordsworthian stress on memory and the early self.

Nevertheless, we can find in the early Dickens novels various direct signs of an un-dialectically assimilated, quite un-problematised Wordsworthian influence, though with a sweetening and banalising effect. Philip Collins, for instance, has commented on the sad resurrection of 'The Idiot Boy' into the character of Barnaby Rudge,[35] where what is genuinely extraordinary in Wordsworth becomes simply ludicrous in Dickens. Similarly, as Angus Wilson has noted,[36] 'We are Seven' is the likely prototype of such things as Smike's grave tableau ending in Nickleby, or the scene in *The Old Curiosity Shop* where the child shows Nell his brother's grave. Again influence means dilution: Dickens 'works up' the child's feelings into an unreal lushness, whereas Wordsworth had presented them with a matter-of-factness that leaves them properly remote. More specifically relevant to our theme, too, are early instances where we can see the young Dickens' explicit interest in the Wordsworthian theme of the moral force of memory. In the Christmas story interpolated into *Pickwick*, for example, the Scrooge-like Gabriel Grub comes to see:

> those who had been delicately nurtured, and tenderly brought up, cheerful under privations, and superior to suffering, that would have crushed many of a rougher grain, because they bore within their own bosoms the materials of happiness, contentment, and peace.[37]

Likewise, the inset-tale 'The Five Sisters of York' in *Nickleby* is a parable in demonstration of the claim that 'memory, however sad, is the best and purest link between this world and a better'. At the beginning of the tale the sisters are seen working together upon embroidery. When challenged to justify this use of their time by a misanthropic friar, one of them answers that one reason they do so is that if:

> in later times, we went forth into the world, and mingled with its cares and trials – if, allured by its temptations and dazzled by its glitter, we ever forgot that love and duty which should bind, in holy ties, the children of one loved parent – a glance at the old work of our common girlhood would awaken good thoughts of by-gone-days, and soften our hearts to affection and love.[38]

The friar scoffs at this, and denies the moral value of such childish fancies, enjoining upon the sisters a stoical resignation to the inevitability of suffering. But the sister's prediction is of course borne out, for the embroidery does in fact awaken memories that give them strength and unity in suffering: *temps perdu* are recovered according to plan. Wordsworth's case against the stoical rejection of memory reappears as a keepsake trifle.

Such unmemorable examples hardly portend a substantial literary debt, but it would be wrong to conclude that the interest they express, even at this stage of Dickens's life, is merely a politely conventional one. A similar instance from *Oliver Twist* perhaps more clearly shows Dickens to be looking to Wordsworth as a way of articulating and understanding that obscure pulse of vulnerability and hurt that the buoyantly aggressive comedy of the early novels tempts us to ignore. A description of Oliver asleep, after his rescue by the Maylies, gives rise to this empathetic (and self-probing) reflection:

> The boy stirred, and smiled in his sleep, as though these marks of pity and compassion had awakened some pleasant dream of a love and affection he had never known; as a strain of gentle music, or the odour of a flower, or even the mention of a familiar word, will sometimes call up sudden dim remembrances of scenes that never were, in this life; which vanish like a breath; and which some brief memory of a happier existence, long gone by, would seem to have awakened, for no voluntary exertion of the mind can ever recall them.[39]

Unlike the first-quoted passages this has an authentic plangency: it bespeaks an appropriation of the Wordsworthian idea to express Dickens's own distinctive note of longing, a longing extreme and unassuageable, and therefore one which must inevitably be put by and again repressed as soon as awakened. And whereas the Wordsworthian allusions in *Nickleby* and *Pickwick* are decoratively peripheral to the novels as wholes, such longing is at the heart of *Oliver Twist*; Oliver's vulnerability, and the personal vulnerability that the author (London's literary darling but late of Blacking's warehouse) is now beginning to probe, are its governing problematic. But such melancholia, perhaps because it *is* irresolvable, can only exist in the novel as counterpoised by its psychic opposite, the manic energy which, by its criminality, denies human dependency and the longing it stirs, and thus seems to solve the irresolvable by evading it. A similar pattern is present in *The Old Curiosity Shop*, in the even clearer dual imaginative obsession Dickens reveals with Little

Nell's virtuous passivity on the one hand and Quilp's comically grotesque but demonic energy on the other. Donald H. Stone has recently written of this doubleness in Dickens as an alternation between his own versions of Wordsworthian passiveness and Byronic will-to-power. We might tentatively hazard an explanation of such ambiguity, in the light of the Oliver passage and our general sense of Nell's lyrical morbidity, by suggesting that since the Wordsworthian for Dickens came to represent unresolvable longing, or resolvable only in the fantasy of death (or the living death of an idealised quiescence), it was only logical that the manic denial of such longing, the Byronic will-to-power, should come to stand for him, with a peculiarly personal intensity, for life. This at least would seem to enable us to connect the paradoxical fictional pattern I have been outlining with what Edgar Johnson rightly emphasised, I think, as the crucially shaping psychological factor of Dickens's creative career, the fierce determination with which he mastered the trauma of the Blackings episode.[40] This determination imposed a personally distinctive repression, on which we can see the aggressive zest, the expansive (bourgeois capitalist?) dynamism of the life and work to be premissed. Conversely to this, as a complicating counter-melody, we then have, beginning with Oliver, a series of fictionally objectified explorations *of* the repressed material, of fictionally controlled returns of the repressed. These all involve characters who, *in* their quiescent passivity, function as concealed *alter-egos* of their publicly and predominantly dynamic author, each one portending the finally unstable foundations on which that dynamic ego was based, and each in turn embodying a fuller depth of characterisation as that ego approached its crisis in middle-life. Hence the strange contradiction that for all his male chauvinism and his mid-Victorian taste in female stereotypes, Dickens's finest moments of psychological understanding are so often achieved with figures like Esther Summerson and Amy Dorrit, or that weirdly un-boyish boy, Paul Dombey, with whom he has such an unlikely but revealing affinity.

In the early novels these contrasting impulses simply express themselves. Imagination flows and rips, here drooling over Nell's asexual but sexual innocence, there, starting manically into life with a vision of Quilp's grotesque concupiscence. What such Jekyll and Hyde-like behaviour *means*, for Dickens the individual or the age and culture in which he lives, is a question not asked, let alone answered: this writing is the apotheosis of that Dickens anarchically 'at play' who has recently been so persuasively celebrated by critics like John Carey, Garett Stewart and S. J. Newman.[41] Yet however winning such revivals of a 'spontaneous', unself-conscious Dickens are, and however timely the re-emphasis upon the early novels, it still seems important to maintain the importance of a 'mature' Dickens in whom imaginative play and concentrated thought co-exist, and who, from the time of *Dombey and Son* onwards, does come up with some very interesting answers to it.

In each case this questioning proceeds hand in hand with what we can see to be a critical exploration – a 'problematising' – of the Wordsworthian normative model of the self as it at once answers to and fails to answer to Dickens's own needs and his own sense of life. The involvement is an extremely varied one, the angle of attack shifting from work to work. In *Dombey and Son*, for example, we find a remarkable objectification of personal tensions into a fictional model of the socially typical, an extrapolation from self to society by way of obliquely seeing self as social product. There is a splitting apart of the mutually supportive relationship Wordsworth assumes between psychic fidelity and moral stability, so that the psychic ideal becomes the basis for a radically subversive social critique which penetrates beyond social institutions to the morality and the character-ideals that support them. Where Wordsworth presents the world, including the social world of duty and constraint, as one in which a child ought to be able to grow up without severe psychic discontinuity, the Dombey world is one in which to grow up is simply to renounce; and the pith of Dickens's critique of the Dombeyist character-ideal is his diagnosis of how that world works by heroically ennobling such alienation into an ideal of manliness. In this world psychic integrity of the Wordsworthian kind can exist only in the form embodied in the child Paul Dombey – i,e., as socially superfluous and hence regressive. Dickens's insight into the complications of sickness and health, naturalness and unnaturalness, is both illuminating and poised; and I think we need to recognise the extraordinary unconventionality of his leading intuitions, dependent though they are, of course, upon the kind of emerging Wordsworthian-Romantic tradition I have been trying to suggest. Nevertheless, one cannot deny all those things in Dickens's life and social circumstances that made it impossible for him to be as single-mindedly clear-cut and confident in his more subversive perceptions as, say, Blake. And it is predictable enough that his next (and openly more autobiographical) novel, *David Copperfield*, should attempt to heal the split between psychic and socially-moral allegiances through the artificially smooth development of the young hero into Mr David Copperfield the novelist and budding sage. The ending of *Dombey* had already begun to air such a possibility in the idea of Walter Gay as Dombey's successor, although the formally comic mode in which the ending is cast signals the author's awareness that such a resolution belongs to art rather than life.

Nevertheless, for all this, *Dombey* is still in a sense 'simply' Wordsworthian in that the denial of the personal past, seen as the Dombeyan 'taboo on tenderness', is depicted simply as repression and self-violation. Hence Mr Dombey, a petrified extreme form of that determination that Dickens himself forged by his own more partial and ambiguous personal repression, and which produced in *him*, as Forster acutely discerned, that curious co-existence of hardness and 'feminine' susceptibility.[42] It is one of the consequences *of* the novel's subversiveness that it nowhere acknowledges the positive element of the dynamism that required repression to fulfill itself; rather, through the identification of bourgeois capitalist revolutionary dynamism with the Frankensteinian monster of its worst consequences, Dickens denies the complexity of his own involvement with his age by trying to opt out of modernity's dialectic altogether. This is what is entailed by his championing in the Wooden Midshipman a warm-hearted maritime ethos which is seen to combine the *gemeinschaft* of primitive small-scale capitalism (seen through the rosy lens of Victorian domesticity) with that flavour of Romantic chivalry with which mid-Victorian ideology adopted the national past. Such radical-conservative nostalgia is of course very much in line with a good deal of nineteenth-century opposition to industrial capitalism, just as the idealisation of domesticity and the private realm was an (itself problematic) compensatory reaction to the alienation these forces produced.

But from this point, however, the novels begin to move, gradually and with great uncertainty, towards a deeper self-acceptance that entails an increasing engagement with the conflict that Wordsworth, George Eliot and the Brontës never really came to grips with: that between allegiance *to* the personal past and its positive sources, and an equally *positive* drive *away* from that allegiance – and a drive clearly acknowledged as such. That drive is magnificently expressed in Blake's 'Infant Sorrow' (a poem which contrasts interestingly with Wordsworth);[43] it is one that, whatever it may lead to in the entanglements of living, cannot simply be reduced to egotism in the negative sense, or resisted out of the fear of *anomie*. To use the language of developmental psychology, one might speak of it as the drive for *individuation*, as contrasted to the Wordsworthian preoccupation with *symbiosis*. It is a drive that from the early works on we can generally sense in Dickens's own voice within his narratives, in the anger, in the energetic comic zest. But because of its implicit conflict with Wordsworthian pieties and implication in their violation, it is never associated with the overtly 'good' characters, who remain pallid and drained of life by lacking it, but is always displaced into the demonic grotesques, being in this way at once expressed and disowned. *Dombey*, by its movement from moral melodrama to an attempted realism of analysis, confronts its author with the inadequacy of this procedure, coming to a head with the tricky question that looms towards the end of the novel of what is to happen to Dombey and Son the firm after Mr Dombey's therapeutic demise. Unprepared to see his radicalism through to having it simply collapse, Dickens the bourgeois and journalistic entrepreneur nevertheless balks the choice of a person possessed of something of that energy that Dickensian heroes so conspicuously lack. Unable to decide upon this, and embark upon the conflict with Wordsworthian loyalties that this would entail, Dickens plumps for the fictively neat but realistically quite implausible choice of Walter Gay, whose appeal throughout the novel has been closely associated with his romantic incapacity for business. It is a consciously contrived happy ending, superseding an earlier authorial intention of having Walter doomed by his social marginality. It is acceptable *as* the indulgently imagined whimsy of comic artifice, but the charm of this barely conceals the gap between the contradictory cluster of values and allegiances that Dickens himself lived out in his person and manifested in his work, and those he is prepared to explicitly accept as good or valuable. A similar sentimental blurring marks the resolution of *The Haunted Man*, the Christmas tale that followed upon the conclusion of Dombey's serialisation. The protagonist Redlaw's wish to be freed from the 'haunting' of memory, which sets the narrative going, expresses an unWordsworthian sense of memory as problematic. But the lesson he learns through his experiment in forgetting is the thoroughly Wordsworthian one that freedom at such a cost can only mean sterility, and the concluding prayer – 'Lord, Keep my memory green' – simply suppresses the tale's earlier, more double-edged awareness.

The novel after *Dombey*, *David Copperfield*, goes no further towards closing this gap. Ostensibly a record of its author's own success story within bourgeois society, it evades following through the split it discloses between psychic and socially-moral allegiances through the artificially smooth development of the immature hero into the mature Mr David Copperfield, a novelist and budding sage. Indeed, David's graceful, boyish charm depends upon his having been very carefully denied by his creator the kind of self-assertive energy that would have made his tender nostalgia for the past more problematic. '*Into* the dangerous world I *leapt*' – the kind of thrust upon life that this line from 'Infant Sorrow' celebrates, which we know to have been so much a part of Dickens himself, is totally lacking in David. It is also lacking, curiously enough, in the narrative voice which Dickens shares with David; indeed this novel bespeaks an especially charmed interlude in the author's middle life in which, under the thrall of a beguiling albeit simplifying nostalgic recall, Dickens seems to have been able to imaginatively indulge in the illusion that he was in fact someone of David's comparative inner serenity. Of course the novel does develop a deeply-probing critical analysis of its own fictional narrator, as has been excellently demonstrated in recent commentaries.[44] But the tone and spirit of its narrative voice is consistently David's, containing all of Dickens's characteristic wit and fancifulness, but purged of that humour's typically aggressive edge. In a way it is Dickens's most successfully Wordsworthian novel: its charming, if problematically wistful serenity witnesses a psychic continuity with childhood along Wordsworthian lines, a fact that the narrative itself self-consciously directs us to. Likewise the distinctive flavour of its humour, the note singled out by Forster as 'perfect English mirth',[45] is very close to that of the Romantic essayist Leigh Hunt, whose nostalgic pieces constitute an interesting link between Wordsworth and the Copperfieldian Dickens in their adaptation of the continuity idea to the purpose of the humorous exploration of memory.[46]

Nevertheless, the discrepancy between this tone, which presents David's boyishness as charming, and the novel's implied critical view of David as overly-boyish and fixatedly Dora-bound, suggests that Dickens's ventriloquil identification with David – with the David in himself – is a holiday respite, to use Edmund Wilson's phrase, from the toils of personal (and socially representative) self-division. As with the ending of *Dombey*, irresolution here would seem to point Dickens towards a more open acceptance of modernity's dialectic and its message that both the assertive, rebellious will and its submission to authority, both the anti-Wordsworthian and the Wordsworthian, represent equally persuasive truths about the self. This could explain the odd fact that in the ensuing two novels, and most clearly in *Little Dorrit*, a resurgent authorial ferocity is matched by a fascination with passive heroines who, especially the clearly Wordsworthian Amy, are even more acquiescent than David. The urge to escape the dialectic's demands by a surrender of the will is obviously very present to the energetic but inwardly wearying Dickens of the mid-1850s. Yet it is a temptation which it is the triumphant achievement of a novel such as *Little Dorrit* to resist, both in the reassuringly un-Amy-like presence of Dickens's voice and in the book's thought-out case about Amy and her opposite, the rebellious Tattycoram, which entertains perceptive doubts as to whether Wordsworthian lack of self-assertive will and fidelity to childhood bonds are necessarily good things. These themselves, though, are clouded in ambiguity and reticence, and it is only in the later *Great Expectations* where we find anything like clarity and confidence. Here the same crucial conflict is explored again, though this time, at last, in terms of a hero who embodies, in *himself*, the full range of Dickens's and the age's contradictions. In terms of the continuing engagement with Wordsworthian psychological theory it involves a working through of the recognition of the paradoxical necessity of at once honouring one's psychic origins whilst growing beyond them. In this sense at least it is Dickens's most mature work, and certainly one of the finest fictional evocations we have of 'the experience of modernity'. Yet even here there is a degree of confused equivocation as the novel works to at once acknowledge and disavow such an insight: the ideology of Romantic psychology is present at the very moment when Dickens seems to have transcended it.

2 The Ideal of Victorian Manliness in *Dombey and Son*: Radicalising Wordsworthian Psychology

> 'You are not so tolerant as perhaps you might be of the wayward and unsettled feeling which is part [I suppose] of the tenure on which one holds an imaginative life, and which I have, as you ought to know well, often only kept down by riding over it like a dragoon – but let that go by.'[1]

The complexities of Dickens's spirit are seldom so concisely revealed as in this well-known letter to Forster. The oft-quoted phrase about 'the wayward and unsettled feeling' is not so significant in itself as it is in combination with the stern-faced, Carlylean relish with which the simile of the dragoon is seized upon. What we thus get is simultaneously a positive valuing of the subversive and anarchic and an ennoblement of repression as the necessary cost of survival in the struggle of life. This duality of allegiance tells us much about Dickens as an individual and as someone participating in and shaped by the kinds of sociocultural contradictions dwelt upon in my introductory chapter. The imaging of self-control in military-heroic terms is of course a typical mid-Victorian note: the sustained manic energy of Dickens's life was, no less than Dombey's icy will, one of the ambiguous Smilesian triumphs of the Protestant work ethic. Yet that Dickens could be as aware as the letter shows him to be of the limitations of such heroic resolve was also due, perhaps, to another important fact about his contemporary ethos, one that sets it apart from other Puritanic cultures. By this I mean that continuance of something of the legacy of Romanticism within the alien framework of mainstream Victorian values, a persistence which functioned as an adversary sub-culture within the parent body, preserving the human values denied by the alienating dominant culture, albeit in a problematic (because marginalised) form, and offering an ideological perspective from which the destructive costs of the governing ethic could be diagnosed and articulated. Victorian literature is in consequence variously imbued with a sense of the havoc that could be wreaked upon life by the dragoon of Victorian will-power, though it often simultaneously hallows that same martial super-ego as a hero of the collective psyche (Charlotte Brontë's ambivalence is, of course, the classical case here.).

Such oppositional expressions vary greatly in their focus. Much Victorian poetry of the Tennysonian dream-world kind can be seen, as Terry Eagleton has recently put it,[2] as a marginalised repository of socially denied impulses which, being expressed in poetry typically as impossible or perilous longings, represent a safety-valve rather than a challenge (eg. 'The Lotus Eaters'). It is more in the novel that we see the adversary values used as a vantage-point from which to mount a serious critique of the mainstream ideology and the society it served and shaped. In general this sort of point has been made about the Victorian novel since Raymond Williams's *Culture and Society*. The peculiarity of *Dombey and Son*, however, is in the way in which it is at once a profound example of this overall novelistic pattern, while also containing an expression *and* diagnostic evaluation of the domesticated subversiveness of the characteristic poetic response. I want to trace how this comes about in *Dombey and Son*, and to do this, as I have foreshadowed, in terms of the novel's creative and subversive adaptation of the Wordsworthian Romantic psychology of the self in Time.

* * *

My offering to proceed thus at this stage of Dickens criticism, however, may well put a reader on guard. 'Surely there's enough of that sort of thing', one might say; 'surely John Carey's *The Violent Effigy*[3] was right in castigating the endless search for significance in the novels, which is so alien to their real spirit?' Well, Carey's book has its own kind of reductiveness about Dickens, of which one manifestation is the failure to discriminate between helpful and redundant interpretation, and the consequent gross parody of such practitioners of the former as the Leavises. Nevertheless, even their book does often leave one wishing for a more substantial treatment of how the novels, as it were, *perform* themselves. Subsequently, in venturing into *Dombey and Son* along a basically interpretative path, I still wish to keep steadily in view the easy balance the novel sustains between criticism of life and self-delighting artifice, between reference beyond itself and freedom of play within itself. The prose is uniquely Dickensian for-instance, in its willingness to take off from an objective perception into self-enjoying verbal inventiveness, pursuing a witty conceit across a field of designated scenic particulars, say, with the zest and stamina of a seventeenth-century poem.

Much to their shame, however, most interpretative critics have ignored this plain fact. Thus even otherwise lively critical minds have laboured to enumerate the imagistic analogues of Dombey's coldness dispersed throughout the novel, failing to indicate, in their lengthy barometric probings, that the repetitions for the most part do not extend the original perception, but are rather the kind of playful amplification one expects from a certain kind of poem, transposed into the novel's own narrative and descriptive procedures:

> Now, the spacious dining-room, with the company seated round the glittering table, busy with the glittering spoons, and knives and forks, and plates, might have been taken for a grown-up exposition of Tom Tiddler's ground, where children pick up gold and silver. Mr. Dombey, as Tiddler, looked his character to admiration, and the long plateau of precious metal frosted separated him from Mrs. Dombey, whereon frosted Cupids offering scentless flowers to each of them, was allegorical to see. (p. 596)

This Hogarthian scenic diagram hardly tells us anything we do not know about the Dombeys' marriage, though the detail about the scentless flowers does perhaps sharpen as well as illustrate more than the other particulars, or any of the similar ones that fill out the parallel scene of Paul's christening. The main point, though, is that quietly exhilarating sense of a difficulty overcome by the play of mind, of the significance (sterility) being plausibly yoked to the circumstantial detail (tableware) in the characteristic manner of witty elaboration. Consider, too, the even closer approximation to the extended conceit of the poem of wit – and the feeling of exuberance that accompanies such a performance – in the paragraph about Sir Barnet Skettles's 'voyage of discovery through the social system' (p. 418), or the startling telescoping of opposites in the joke about Cornelia Blimber as the 'fair bride, around whose lambent spectacles two gauzy little bridesmaids fluttered like moths' (p. 947). Such things are not entirely absent in, say, George Eliot, though in her the wit is always fairly tethered to a firmly referential text and an over-archingly sober tone. Dickens's more ludic and levitational prose used to be rather despised as a mark of his second-rateness, his exaggeration. What today seems more apparent, however, is the easy compatibility of such flights with a firm grasp of the socially real. Similar to this is the co-existence of 'rounded' developing characters such as Dombey with humorous, 'flat' ones such as Toots and Cuttle, in whom the fixed persona persists into situation after situation with the same triumphant sense of difficulty inventively overcome as we get at the level of the local prose in the amplifications of wit. Equally in harmony, for the most part, are thematic depth and seriousness with the presence of many of the formal patterns and devices of stage comedy:[4] complaints about the forced coincidence of Walter's return from the sea and Florence's flight from home seem to apply mimetic criteria at a too superficial level, for in the deepest sense the novel is mimetic, about life and offering a wisdom about it, albeit with a stylisation that it takes no trouble to conceal. The novel consists, one might say, of a rich core of significant perception that is its *vision*, plus a penumbra of amplificatory play that, in its genial exuberance, expresses the novel's *spirit*, in the same way that a style of architecture or of interior decoration can be said to express a certain spirit.

One way of illustrating the kind of mimetic refraction I am talking about, and which will serve to bring me back to my opening propositions, is to note briefly the way in which the novel can be said to be representing early Victorian society. For I do not think that it offers the sort of empirical directness that we get in, say, *North and South* or even *Hard Times* and *Little Dorrit*, stylised as these later novels themselves are. This is because there are problems in relating things in the novel to their likely social references. Dombey Senior, for instance, looks very much like a creature of the Protestant work ethic; yet the novel is totally uninterested in the psychological significance of his work. Similarly, whilst the forcing-house atmosphere of Blimber's school seems to point to the more drastic psychic costs imposed by the harsher aggressiveness and achievement-orientation of emerging Victorian society, with its increasingly bourgeois tone, the school's clientele and curriculum point rather to the past, and in fact much of Dickens's humour at its expense comes in the voice of railway-age radicalism. Against this looseness of surface reference, though, we have a very interesting attempt to grasp and render the interrelatedness of highly disparate elements of the social-cultural whole. Weaning, education, adult relations between the sexes, the economic system – the novel feels its way towards the constellation of all these, towards a picture of the underlying dynamics of a fictional world which stands as a helpful model against which to interpret its historically real context rather than as a would-be photographic replica of it. There is a certain incompleteness about the analysis at points: Dombey's 'Will' always seems to be about to be connected to his economic role – as a sort of psychic equivalent of the Railway – in a way which would compare with Thornton in *North and South*, or, more sophisticatedly, with Gerald in *Women in Love*. But it never is: it remains a too simply glacial thing to represent a socially representative dynamism; and we are thus left wondering just what the social significance of Dombey's psychic structure is.

Nevertheless, it is a failure to acknowledge the novel's *concern* for this kind of interrelation that mars what I think is the most interesting recent interpretation of *Dombey*, Nina Auerbach's account of it as Dickens's vision of 'the schism between masculinity and femininity as his age defined them', 'the story of male and female principles who can neither evade nor understand each other, whose tragedy and whose force come from their mutual exclusiveness'.[5] This emphasis is surely the correct one, and Auerbach shows convincingly how this thematic pattern pervades the novel, both on the levels of character, major and subsidiary, and of symbolism. Her mistake, though, is to take all this as a picture of the unchanging essence of things, beyond conventional sexual ideology rather than conditioned by it, and thus trapped within that ideology's mystifying sense of itself as being founded in Nature. Thus she misinterprets, for instance, the initial mock-heroic jibe at Dombeyan self-absorption ('The earth was made for Dombey and Son to trade in,' as a kind of truth, and therefore claims that 'Dombey and Son is defined in terms that are sexual and metaphysical rather than social'.[6] In contrast to this I would suggest that Dickens is much more aware of the gulf as a neurotic product of a particular culture, if not exactly the neurotic source of that culture's over-reaching dynamism.

One might begin to develop this claim by querying exactly what is meant by Dombey's masculinity, his 'inveterate phallicism', as Auerbach puts it. For what kind of masculinity is it, one wonders, that finds such a natural issue in the sexual (as well as moral) sterility that his marriage is clearly meant to be, given that Edith interests him more as testimony to his power than as sensual object? He does in fact fit rather neatly into Wilhelm Reich's category of the 'phallic-narcissistic' type of pseudo-masculinity[7], which designates the aggressive, often impressive and successful, but cold man, who has a 'high erective potency' but is in fact 'orgastically impotent', and who, whilst seeming very masculine and being therefore often sought after by women, is in fact contemptuous of them and often sadistic, since he unconsciously thinks of the phallus not as a source of love but as an instrument of revenge against an initially disappointing mother. As Shakespeare had insisted centuries before in *Antony and Cleopatra*, genuine phallicism requires the ability to relax from rigidity into deliquescence. The 'melting' that Dombey resists in Florence is of course the denial of tenderness rather than anything narrowly sexual, but the latter meaning is implied as well as a more general characteristic, as is hinted in the image of Dombey's embarrassed entrance into Edith's bedroom: 'Solemn and strange among this wealth of colour and voluptuous glitter' (p. 651).

All this Dickens knows, in his way, and one of his primary concerns in this novel seems to be to show how the oddly perverse kind of maleness that Dombey represents could come into being and come to have the status it had in Dickens's world. The novel, that is, despite the imprecision of social reference just mentioned, is still trying to capture and assess, with Dombey, a prevailing cultural ideal of manliness, this being that heroism of emotional self-discipline that so many of the Faustian, modernising forces at large in early-Victorian society – this-worldly

Puritanism, industrialism, social mobility – conspired to make appealing to the age.[8] Dickens himself, as my epigraph shows, was one of that ideal's exponents and victims, and his accession to the role of its critic as well is an act of self-knowledge as well as social analysis. We can sense this very well from an aside in a speech Dickens gave in 1851, two weeks after his father's death and just before learning of the death of his daughter Dora: 'how often it is with all of us that in our several spheres we have to do violence to our feelings and hide our hearts in carrying on this fight for life'.[9] Here again is that note of resolved sternness struck in the earlier-cited letter, though this time, in the echo of that determination to ride down the difficulties of his childhood that Forster rightly saw as the key to Dickens's character, it is the destructiveness rather than the heroism of emotional repression that is emphasised. Stern self-suppression is also the key to Dombey: the character is, one might say, at once socially representative in the broad sense and the magnification of something that Dickens was coming to be more and more critically aware of in himself as the Frankensteinian legacy of his own and the age's bourgeois dynamism. Mrs Chick's Dombeyan ideology of 'effort' is a telling parody of that gift.

If *Dombey and Son*, then, is a diagnostic study of the sexual ideal of a culture, Dombey himself, in his own world, is a culture-hero, 'a pecuniary Duke of York', as Miss Tox says.[10] Thus the sexual schism the book portrays is not founded in Nature, but arises, at least in the intense form it is shown in, from the repression that just such an ideal ennobles. For if it is unmanly not to be able to 'do violence' to one's feelings, what could be more natural than to see such vulnerability as feminine and essentially alien to oneself, and to be contemptuous or at least patronising to women as a way of sustaining this rejection of the 'feminine element' in oneself. Such, anyway, seems to be the essence of Dickens's case about Dombey, which is something he can manage to say because he himself was both Dombey and more than that, espousing and embodying the ideal in his conduct of life, yet remaining persistently aware, in his creative consciousness, of the psychic cost of this. Forster masterfully touches on this duality when he speaks of how he came to see in Dickens 'at chance intervals, a stern and even cold isolation of self-reliance side by side with a susceptibility almost feminine and the most eager craving for sympathy'.[11]

Dombey and Son: *Radicalising Wordsworthian Psychology* 41

However, as I said at the outset, Dickens's ability to articulate such an ambivalence surely owes something to the subversive legacy of Romanticism, an ideology which, significantly for my argument, has recently been characterised by Michael Cooke in terms of its 'incorporation of the feminine'.[12] To see the influence that may well have been of most use in helping Dickens come to his understanding of Dombeyism, though, we need to set aside the terms 'masculine' and 'feminine' for the moment, and turn to the connected Romantic, or especially Wordsworthian preoccupation with the relationship between childhood and adulthood, with the ways in which 'the Child is Father to the Man', as outlined in my first chapter. Dickens's relations with this conception were problematic, as we have seen, as also were those of Thomas de Quincey, who read *The Prelude* in manuscript before its publication, and whose individual reworking of Wordsworth's ideas about the self's organic continuity can perhaps be seen as the main specific Wordsworthian influence behind *Dombey* (see the appendix at end of this chapter) – there is of course no reason to think that Dickens had himself read *The Prelude* at the time of writing *Dombey*.[13] Dickens accepted from the Romantics, in contrast to modern psychoanalytic determinism, that for the adult to keep vitally in touch with the childhood self was both a psychological desideratum and a moral value: the childhood past is not just a determining force in the psyche to be acknowledged and negotiated with, but a crucial source of vitality and moral feeling. The self in Time is hence conceived in terms of a metaphor of organic plant-growth ('Fair seed-time had my soul'), with the implication that to lose touch with one's personal past, the repository of the emotional nourishment of primary relationships, is to invite spiritual malnutrition. Several years before his embarking upon *Dombey*, in 1843, *A Christmas Carol* had presented its mass readership with an ingenious popularisation of this doctrine in terms of straightforwardly accepting it – the very meaning and mood of the season must have cried out for such an adaptation. Yet five years later *The Haunted Man* saw Dickens introducing, as I mentioned in the foreword, even within the seemingly impervious sentimentality of the Christmas-story genre, a sense of the ambivalence of memory's gift, of its capacity to destroy the self as well as to nurture it. Problematic ambiguity similarly pervades *Dombey and Son*, though in different terms (those of *The Haunted Man* foreshadow, of all the novels,

Great Expectations). Interestingly, these terms closely match those of De Quincey's adaptation. All this bears significantly on the sexual schism portrayed in *Dombey*, for there the roots of that repression which I have characterised so far as a 'denial of the feminine' are examined as a socially-enforced rupture of that 'continuity . . . of self-consciousness' (to quote Coleridge's phrase from his gloss upon Wordsworth's 'My Heart Leaps Up'), an alienation of the adult from the childhood self, *the* cardinal sin, that is, against the Wordsworthian injunction. The details of the analysis are Dickens's own, and derive from the particular circumstances to which he addresses himself. Yet the novel's thought along these lines would seem to be dependent upon Wordsworthian formulations in the same way as any specific application is upon the theory in which it is grounded.

The case begins with the novel's first focal interest: the account of Paul's upbringing within the Dombey system. The operating principle here is the 'taboo on tenderness', the concept first coined over forty years ago by the late British psychotherapist Ian Suttie,[14] and now quite widely in use. The phrase refers to a culturally-enforced antipathy to the 'soft emotions' that are of primary importance in early childhood (the analyst Harry Guntrip has since substituted the 'taboo on weakness' for Suttie's phrase, in order to stress the relevance of the fear of seeming weak or foolish as well as that of showing tenderness or being sentimental[15]). This involves, in cultures where the taboo operates, the rigid exclusion of such feelings from what is felt to be acceptably adult behaviour, and consequently the drawing of a strict barrier between the adult and the child, marked by abrupt weaning. The taboo has traditionally been enforced more severely on male than on female, and has clearly been a major source of mutually exclusive polarity between the sexes, tenderness and vulnerability being often disowned (or even praised) by males in the name of their being girlish or feminine, as in Forster's comment on Dickens's 'feminine' eagerness for sympathy. The Dombey world is certainly a culture governed by the taboo, for in Paul's precipitate weaning and rapid force march towards male adulthood we see the childhood–adulthood rupture erected into a cultural ideal.

The novel's sense of how this is so is richly various, ranging from Dombey's obtuseness about Polly and the nature of the child–mother bond, to his impatient deprecation of childhood in general. Perhaps the most poignant incident we are shown, however, is Paul's first meeting with Dr Blimber:

> 'Ha!' said the Doctor, leaning back in his chair with his hand in his breast. 'Now I see my little friend. How do you do, my little friend?'
> The clock in the hall wouldn't subscribe to this alteration in the form of words, but continued to repeat 'how, is, my, lit, tle, friend? How, is, my, lit, tle, friend?'
> 'Very well, I thank you, sir,' returned Paul, answering the clock quite as much as the Doctor.
> 'Ha!' said Dr. Blimber, 'Shall we make a man of him?'
> 'Do you hear Paul?' added Mr. Dombey, Paul being silent.
> 'Shall we make a man of him?' repeated the Doctor.
> 'I had rather be a child,' replied Paul.
> 'Indeed!' said the Doctor. 'Why?'
> The child sat on the table looking at him with a curious expression of suppressed emotion in his face, and beating one hand proudly on his knee as if he had the rising tears beneath it, and crushed them. But his other hand strayed a little way the while, a little farther – farther from him yet – until it lighted on the neck of Florence. 'This is why,' it seemed to say, and then the steady look was broken up and gone; the working lip was loosened, and the tears came streaming forth.
> 'Mrs Pipchin,' said his father, in a querulous manner, 'I am really sorry to see this.' (p. 210)

Paul's gallant attempt at self-control here is a crucial step along the way to becoming the kind of man his father's world is intent upon making him. I say gallant because it *is* a brave effort: the novel is flexible enough in its responses to allow us to see it as that, as well as something else. Yet it *is* this other that we are really most aware of, for whilst Paul is rising manfully (!) to a major early battle in the fight for life, it is only by beginning to don his father's character armour that he can do so. The description of the act of self-control is phrased to bring out the underlying destructiveness of what, on the surface, could pass as simply admirable: 'beating one hand proudly on his knee as if he had the rising tears underneath, and crushed them' – 'proudly' strongly recalls those other moments of parental imitation that F. R. Leavis has drawn attention to as a sign of Dickens's sensitively realistic focus upon Paul[16] – the chip off the old block becoming the wooden man complete. Consequently, Paul's failure here is a triumphant weakness, an act of Nature delivering itself from the 'tenderness taboo' of Dombeyan civilisation. Thus, given the novel's basic pattern of fluid and solid imagery, the free and spontaneous vitality about the way in which the tears finally come *streaming* forth from the shattered facial defences, re-affirms, in Paul's turning back to Florence, that continuity with the rich warmth of the maternal bond that his world is intent to rupture, scorning, in the name of heroic manliness, any more gentle transition.

Such triumphant tearfulness strikes me as a domestic echo of the eruptive sacred river in *Kubla Khan*, though the association may well strike most readers as a purely whimsical one on my part. More significant, however, is the comparison one can make here with *The Prelude*'s account of psychological growth in childhood.[16] As I argued in Chapter 1, that poem conceives the self with an optimism about softening the developmental tragedy of maternal loss by a process of substitutive identification by which the mother is progressively replaced by things which are at once different from yet vestigially continuous with her. This process is poetically delineated in the 'Blest the Infant Babe' passage I quote in that chapter (pp. 16–17). In this passage, thus, the modestly sublime metaphor of the 'virtue which irradiates and exalts' suggests quite precisely a means by which the maternal presence suffuses things beyond the mother and child, so that the original filial bond becomes one that spontaneously connects the child 'with the world'. In this way such a child's growth into the world is not necessarily one from symbiosis to apartness, but into sublimated forms of the original rich relation, one of the main ones being that sense of instinctive harmony with Nature (terrifying as well as soothing though this may be), that is celebrated time and time again in *The Prelude* and in Wordsworth in general. Freud was later to call this, of course, 'the oceanic feeling', detecting in it, as the relevant passages of Wordsworth could have told him, echoes of the primal harmony. In this light the broader, less strictly psychoanalytic Wordsworthian stress on fidelity to the personal past appears as a kind of homeostatic strategy, a way in which the adult self can keep steady and whole by attending to that inner core of early experience in which that developmental continuum has been least disturbed.

By contrast with this the Dombey world is one in which to grow up is simply to renounce, one in which there is no consequent restoration of the lost object in an altered form. The Wordsworthian model, one might say, is exactly the model of health and normality by which the nature of the Dombeyan disease can be illuminated. For the strict exclusion of the feelings of childhood from adulthood is shown to alienate precisely in the terms suggested by the 'infant Babe' passage: the image of Paul that closes the chapter from which I have quoted shows him, bereft of Florence, very much Wordsworth's 'outcast ... bewildered and depressed':

> He sat, with folded hands, upon his pedestal, silently listening. But he might have answered 'weary, weary! very lonely, very sad!' And there, with an aching void in his young heart, and all outside so cold, and bare, and strange, Paul sat as if he had taken life unfurnished, and the upholsterers were never coming. (p. 215)

As well as leavening out pathos with whimsy the closing simile also, in its way, points seriously to that domestication of 'objects through widest intercourse of sense' in reflections of the original source of life and warmth, which the Dombeyan 'tenderness taboo' interdicts.

Before going any further with Paul I want to turn back to Dombey himself. I am not, however, thereby implying that the two cases are separable, for one of the novelistic functions of the young Paul would seem to be to offer us an oblique understanding of the buried life in his father that it is the nature of Dombey's own suppressed character to obscure for us – Dickens's own vaguely portentous signallings about 'secret clues' and 'darkened rooms' when dealing with the patriarch do actually catch something about the way he himself must experience his own inner life (as well as inciting us with an enigma to decipher – it is another good example of that co-existence of mimetic and formal modes that I spoke of earlier). Much interpretation of the novel has rested on the rather vague diagnosis of Dombey as being 'alienated from life': more precisely, in the interview with Blimber, Paul's attempt at self-control, in its very suggestiveness of his father, could well be taken as a re-evocation of his father's own childhood past. The same goes for those other instances where we see Paul growing up in imitation: in reflecting Dombey Sr in a diminishing mirror he seems to throw forth a reflection of his model's own beginnings.

The difference between them, obviously, is that whereas Paul somehow manages to elude the 'tenderness taboo', his father has clearly grown up to be its very paragon, the collective super-ego incarnate, or, as Dickens himself puts it in a catchy but acute formula that collapses fictive distance to claim Dombey as a specifically contemporary phenomenon: 'the beadle of private life; the beadle of our business and our bosoms' (p. 113). This explains the novel's introduction of Dombey in those settings which suggest that he is as much the victim of his social order as its mainstay and exponent:

> From the glimpses (Polly) caught of Mr. Dombey at these times, sitting in the dark distance, looking out towards the infant from among the dark, heavy furniture – the house had been inhabited for years by his father, and in many of its appointments was old-fashioned and grim – she began to entertain ideas of him in his solitary state, as if he were a lone prisoner in a cell, or a strange apparition that was not to be accosted or understood. (p. 76)
>
> He had risen, as his father had before him, in the course of life and death, from Son to Dombey (p. 50)

Dombey's salient characteristics – his name, and the physical setting which is so integrally a part of our sense of him – are shown more as the impersonal properties of family tradition than as marks of his individuality. His chair, one feels, is a kind of throne to which he has acceded after following a course not unlike that which he now expects his son to undertake. Dickens in fact seems to betray his own fine grasp of the case when, at Dombey's downfall, he allows him to moralise sermonistically upon his *personal* guilt in rejecting Florence:

> He knew, now, what he had done. He knew, now, that he had called down that upon his head . . . (p. 935)

One feels the need of some partially exonerating authorial ballast to the anaphoric surge here, though it is oddly left to Edith to remind us, thirty pages later, of 'the causes that had made him what he was' (p. 968) (Dickensian poise often composes itself over long distances and seldom finds its way into the author's explicit assessments).

What we are shown more directly in Dombey, however, are the consequences of the 'taboo', the distortions wrought upon the adult personality by its alienation from the child-like. These fall together in a manner which curiously resembles the syndrome of this kind of repressed person as outlined in Suttie's pioneer work – here, as elsewhere, Dickens shows something of the psychoanalytic thinker's grasp of the significant interrelatedness of symptomatic traits. Dombey is, for instance, markedly lacking in those qualities other than adult sexual love which Suttie argues to be the natural substitutes for the rich warmth of early bonds: sociability and cultural interests. He is a Philistine, not through lack of education but from a deeper numbness to the colourful and the lively. His attraction to Edith is really only a matter of enjoying power over what others find desirable and inaccessible: Reich's postulation of a disappointing mother as the origin of the 'phallic-narcissistic type' fits well here. Similarly, though too sure-willed to be ill-at-ease in society, he moves in it with an Olympian remoteness, enjoying it merely for the testimonials to his power that it offers him. It is this lack of any developed convivial sense that makes him prey to the flattery of the grotesque Major Bagstock, just as it is his blankness about people in general that opens him to the Major's insinuations about Miss Tox's designs, a telling instance of the characteristic Dickensian point that instinct as well as rationality is necessary to moral discrimination. Bagstock's charge, after all, does have a specious plausibility.

Bagstock is also the product of a 'taboo on tenderness', of course, enforced upon him by the aristocratic-military ethos: '[it] made us what we are', he brags, with unwitting self-irony. In his case the taboo has licensed sensuality whilst inhibiting tenderness, as we see both in his raffish gallantry and his eating; the oft-stressed monstrousness of his gourmandising makes one suspect that Dickens has perhaps intuited this as an unconscious substitute (albeit a desperately inadequate one) for the repressed emotional appetite. (One would be hard-pressed to 'prove' such a point against sceptical objections that the trait is simply a bit of comic padding; it is just that, as is often the case with literary interpretation, the unexplained collocation of this piece of behaviour with other things seems to interestingly bear out and enrich a pattern not explicitly declared.) Dombey's flat-footed inability to rise to the Major's attempted camaraderie about women is, in fact, a point in his favour:

> 'Edith Granger is Edith Granger still, but if tough old Joey B., sir, were a little younger and a little richer, the name of that immortal paragon should be Bagstock.'
> The Major heaved his shoulders, and his cheeks, and laughed more like an over-fed Mephistopheles than ever, as he said the words.
> 'Provided the lady made no objection, I suppose?' said Mr. Dombey coldly. (p. 365)

A similar authorial fair mindedness is implicit in Dombey's abstention from games, which equally calls for double-judgement when compared with Carker's facility at them; there is a discriminating intelligence in pairing Dombey against someone who embodies sensual lubricity bereft of tenderness, as it accords the former's austere presence an edge of sad dignity, without in any way denying its neuroticism. In this way the well-meaning blindness with which Dombey anxiously consigns Paul to Mrs Pipchin, ironically in deep concern for his health, is poignant as well as critical in its implication. The Blimbers, too, are treated in the same even-handed manner suited to the realistic novel, in contrast to Mrs Pipchin, who, in the humorous tradition, is simply a hypocrite. Whilst critics like Carey are right to stress the fallacy of talking of Dickens as if he were another George Eliot, it is also important not to neglect those moments in which he does have something of her liberalism, for all his more anarchic nature.

Dombey's presentation, then, is profound both in conception and in execution. It displays, in fact, that quality which many of the best novelists share with the best psychoanalysts in their readings of character: that beautifully dynamic concurrence of explanatory inner schema (often tacit in the novelists' case) and

Dombey and Son: *Radicalising Wordsworthian Psychology* 49

surface concrete detail, by which, as we reflect upon the details as we come to them, we find them neither opaque nor redundantly illustrative. At their best, that is, they give us the pleasure of seeing how they at once clarify the underlying schema that, if it is a novel we are reading, we are probably just beginning to perceive, and surprisingly reveal to us *inherencies* of the schema *within* particularities, conjunctions of surface and depth, that we may otherwise never have fathomed (the previously mentioned humoristic *amplification* is a separate matter).[17]

A few more illustrations of this are perhaps in order. There is, for instance, the superb third paragraph of the novel:

> Dombey exulting in the long-looked-for event, jingled and jingled the heavy gold watch-chain that depended from below his trim blue coat, whereof the buttons sparkled phosphorescently in the feeble rays of the distant fire. Son, with this little fists curled up and clenched, seemed, in his feeble way, to be squaring at existence for having come upon him so unexpectedly. (p. 49)

Here one cannot but admire the subtlety of metaphoric suggestion achieved through the Hogarthian manner of having details in the surrounding scene comment upon the human foreground. It is very appropriate, given what I have suggested to be the terms of the novel's understanding, that the portrait of Paul should begin with the separation-trauma of birth and the Dombey world's false way of coping with it: the comic-pathetic fancying of the infant babe in a precociously pugilistic posture foreshadows the novel's essential theme. Beyond this, the overt analogy between the 'feeble rays' of the distant fire and Paul's "feeble way" of "squaring at existence" is metaphorically enriched by having the buttons, the objects from which the rays reflect, seeming to drain the light from its natural source, imprisoning it in the unnatural intensity suggested by phosphorescence – the unnatural intensity, we infer later, of the Dombeyan will. The psychic condition of the Dombey world is revealed in a single but complex image, in a way that compares favourably with Lawrence's use of the imagery of fused heat and coldness to introduce Gerald in *Women in Love*. This does not preclude, however, the similarly poignant comic-pathetic touch in which

Dombey's residual humanity is insisted upon: that (for him) almost unguardedly boyish way in which, inspired by the occasion, he jingles his watch.

Again, one needs to also recognise in the rendering of Dombey those small surface inflections of behaviour which serve to briefly lay bare the deep tentacular roots of his sickness. Whilst a number of Dombey's particularities *are* so commonplace as to be almost conventional *signs*, in the semiological sense, of the kind of man he is (the humoristic amplificatory detail discussed earlier is of this kind), Dickens's symptomalogical talent, by virtue of which he is the master amongst novelists of the external rendering of character, typically affords him the surprising *indice* of inner life, as in Dombey's handshake: '[Mr. Chick] gave Mr. Dombey his hand as if he feared it might electrify him. Mr. Dombey took it as if it were a fish, or seaweed ...' (p. 110), a divination which is then conventionalised into the novel's own code of representation. Or his skin:

> Mr. Dombey, who was one of those close-shaved close-cut moneyed gentlemen who are glossy and crisp like new banknotes, and who seem to be artificially braced and tightened as by the stimulating action of golden shower-baths. (pp. 68–9)

– in which instance one can sense the figurative play straining the observation past the conventionality of sign towards the freshness of nakedly observed indice. Another particularly interesting example, one in which a seeming triviality of surface and richness of inner import are especially conjunct, is Dombey's way of reacting to Paul's tears in that passage I discussed earlier:

> 'Mrs Pipchin,' said his father, in a querelous manner, 'I am really very sorry to see this'. (p. 210)

'Querelous' strikes an engagingly odd note for someone of Dombey's marmoreal composure. It resists common-sense interpretation, but yields to the tenderness taboo schema, however, being in this a mark of the highly unconventional perceptiveness informing the portrait. Suttie argues that the person who, like Dombey, is fully insulated from feeling by the 'taboo', is not only inaccessible to appeals for sympathy from others, but is also positively resentful, in that the appeal tends to rearouse a longing that has been suppressed but not extinguished. This *would* seem to explain why Paul's failure to control his own longing in this scene has the effect it does. As often in Dickens, it is by pondering the unexplained and thus easily-missed nuance playing around the edge of the seemingly predictable in presented behaviour, that we can arrive at the real nature of the understanding that guides the characterisation.

Such a detail, of course, only gives us the external symptom. The inner processes of Suttie's pattern in this respect, however, are pursued through Dombey's relation with Florence, whose unfortunate fate is to be for her father the embodiment of pathetic appeal. Not only is her persistent love towards him akin to introducing a female nudist into a celibate's refuge (the tenderness-tabooed person's reaction to sentiment is akin, Suttie argues, to the prude's response to sexual suggestion, and for the same reason); her behaviour at her mother's death-bed has already given a doubly disconcerting resonance to the echoes she can not help sending down to her father's hidden depths:

> The last time he had seen his slighted child, there had been that in the sad embrace between her and her dying mother, which was at once a revelation and a reproach to him. Let him be absorbed as he would in the Son on whom he built such high hopes, he could not forget that closing scene. He could not forget that he had no part in it. That, at the bottom of its clear depths of tenderness and truth, lay those two figures clasped in each other's arms, while he stood on the bank above them, looking down a mere spectator – not a sharer with them – quite shut out. (p. 83)

It is this memory, we are told, that changes Dombey's 'previous feelings of indifference' towards Florence into 'an uneasiness of an extraordinary kind' (p. 83), one which soon resolves itself into a positive aversion. Here, I think, we can improve upon Julian Moynahan's helpful argument that this development stems from Dombey's fear of love, arising from an intuition that any yielding to Florence's sentiment must involve his dissolution, a drowning of his strong ego.[18] For while this accounts for Dombey's apprehension, it does not explain the accompanying longing which is so evident in this passage, why he cares so much about being shut out from a scene between two people to whom he is ostensibly pretty indifferent. Pertinent here, I think, is the fact that the image that haunts Dombey is not just one of love in general, but of love between mother and child. Thus it should not surprise one that the final words of the passage have an oddly emphatic tone that reminds one strangely of David Copperfield, for the implication is that the memory troubles Dombey because it reminds him that there once *was* a time, perhaps, in which *he* was something of a Copperfield, a time when even he felt the Dombeyan ethos with acute pain and not simply as the proper climate for the fulfillment of Dombeyan destinies. The image, that is, threatens to make him painfully conscious that he is, now, 'an outcast ... bewildered and depressed', insinuates itself beyond the heroically-styled defences on which his whole character has been based.

Given all this, I think we have a clue to something psychologically clairvoyant about the denouement of Dombey's story, to which criticism has so far not done proper justice. Moynahan for one has objections to this resolution, arguing that given that surrender to Florence involves a lapse into a passive and unmanning invalidism, Dombey's previous proud and lonely state could well be deemed preferable. One can see his point, given the way Florence is presented, though his argument draws heavily on his much too wide-eyed admiration for Dombey's dubious *machismo*: 'his career', he says, matches Stavrogin and Coriolanus in its 'superb desolation of pride and obstinacy'.[19] I do feel, in fact, that there is a profound realism in Dickens's insistence upon Dombey's necessary salvation on the extreme terms to which he has been reduced. His first words to Florence upon her return are 'Oh my God, forgive me, for I need it very much', and, as Arlene M. Jackson has convincingly shown[20] (following upon Kathleen Tillotson's earlier suggestion[21]), this conversion has been thoroughly prepared for during the course of the novel – the confession is in no way just an extemporised rationale for a magical change of heart. His collapse has, as my discussion of him would also imply, the 'inevitability' of any nervous breakdown, which is what it is, even though, as is Dickens's nineteenth century novelist's habit, the psychic condition is partially veiled by being spliced together with a physical illness (one thinks also of Esther Summerson and Pip here, and, in this novel, of Mrs Skewton). Ms. Jackson's own account rather misses the significance at work here, in that Dombey's debility coincides for her with the final admission of need mainly as an anti-sentimentalising ballast against a potentially too lofty conclusion. It *is* arguably that, but in the main it suggests itself to me as Dickens's striking recognition, given the time at which the novel was written, that the only cure to Dombey's psychological disease is his complete sloughing off of that strong egoistic identity that has functioned as a false solution to his childhood deprivation, sloughing off, as Carker has earlier put it, 'that triumphal car' to which he 'has been yoked' (p. 717). And this, Dickens sees, entails nothing less than living through the emotional state of childhood anew, this time securely and gratifyingly.

Unlike Pip's therapeutic breakdown towards the end of *Great Expectations*, we are not allowed to see this process from the inside. Dombey is an early attempt of Dickens's at depicting this phenomenon, and, after all, the flurry of formal novelistic business at this stage of the book – romantic resolutions and general tidyings-up – requires Dombey to be moved somewhat off the centre of the stage, rather like Captain Cuttle during Mrs Mac Stinger's spring-cleaning. Nevertheless, given his world's rigorous equation of maleness with patriarchal self-sufficiency (the 'stern . . . cold isolation of self-reliance' Forster detected in Dickens), Dombey's new 'docile submission' to Florence does seem to intimate an inner psychic reversion beneath the surface of morbid-seeming pathos. The suggestion is supported, too, by the way in which his new position towards his daughter now clearly echoes his son's previous relations with her, and in which his behaviour seems almost to re-enact scenes from his son's past. Musing upon his own past with a significantly new openness of reminiscence (given the novel's Wordsworthian affiliations), he seems almost to become the young Paul in pondering, 'as if it had never been proposed to him until that moment . . . that childish question, 'What is money?' (p. 957) His convalescent posture also seems designed to recall the focal image of his late son's withdrawn, contemplative decline:

> It was dimly pleasant to him now to lie there, with the window open, looking out at the summer sky and the trees: and, in the evening, at the sunset. To watch the shadows of the clouds and leaves, and seem to feel a sympathy with shadows. It was natural that he should. To him, life and the world were nothing else. (p. 958)

The iconography of breakdown is a bit sentimentalised, as, in contrast to the treatment of the young Paul, there is no hint here of the possessive aspect of regenerated feelings: the end-of-novel Madeira-broaching mood pervades, though Dombey's new capacity to clink glasses with the Captain nicely signals his release from one, consequence of the tenderness taboo – comic pattern and social vision again being nicely concurrent. The essential psychological significance *is* there, however, as well as the superficially conventional depiction. Much modern psychoanalytic thought has come to affirm the value of regression during therapy: the English object-relations theorist D. W. Winnicott was one of the first to argue for the need of some psychotic patients to 'regress . . . to re-enact the failed mother–child relationship . . . with the analyst filling the role of the adapative mother', thus giving the patient a chance to grow properly by discovering the seeds of a 'true self . . . hidden away in cold storage behind the false-self facade'[22] (a formulation one can accept without necessarily subscribing to the teleological implications of its true–false terminology). This could easily be a description of Dombey and his fate, just as in Florence we can recognise at least the idea of an 'adaptive mother', heading, with Walter and their children, the kind of supportive therapeutic community needful, as Winnicott and others argue, if the regression is to be properly managed. Though Dickens did not have modern psychoanalysis to help him, it is, after all, not so surprising, given his experience and his growing gift for appraising it, that he should have intuited some of the major insights of that body of thought and have found his own fictional way of articulating them, obscured though they might still be from an audience committed to purely moral or physiological modes of interpretation. Which brings us back again to the fact that Dickens did have, at least, a Wordsworthian developmental psychology at his disposal. For whilst necessary regression in the sense that we see it here is not a Wordsworthian notion, it does seem to me that one might well explain its exemplification in Dombey's case as a creative extension of the basic Wordsworthian principle of self-continuity into the kind of character – Dombey – who simply does not exist in Wordsworth's world. Is not Dombey's regression, in one sense, his redemption from the cardinal Wordsworthian 'sin', the rupture of continuity, upon which his life has been based?

Now one crucial aspect of this extension, if such it is, is that it involves a disjunction of the principle of self-continuity from one of the basic assumptions of traditional morality. As I outlined in Chapter 1, the continuity idea originates in Wordsworth as a deepening and renovation of moral convention, or rather that stoicism that was the predominant eighteenth-century moral form.[23] It represents one way of accommodating the subjective and emotional vitality of Romanticism with the stability provided by reliance upon a fixed and objective code – only in the exceptional case of the tale of Margaret do we find in Wordsworth any questioning of such an established assumption as that embodied in Dr Johnson's dictum, 'The business of life is to go forwards'.[24] In *Dombey and Son*, however, we are given a world in which the claims of continuity and those of conventional practical morality are irreconcilably at odds. In this world all the stoical, non-sentimental elements of traditional morality, things such as firmness of will, self-discipline and resistance to nostalgia, have become localised in a particular and obnoxious social order: subservient to it and without any independent validity, they can be accounted for as the masked ideological legitimations of the prevailing 'system'. Strength of will and purpose here survive only as the 'effort' beloved of Mrs Chick, and stoicism in adversity as Mrs Pipchin's suspect 'triumph' over the loss of her husband in the Peruvian mines. The novel draws on the Romantic critique of these values as being by themselves insufficient, to present a picture in which their operation as a social code is seen simply as a denial of life – Dombey's fit acquiescence in his breakdown, for instance, is predictably deplored by his sister as lack of effort (p. 930). The century's conservative anti-Faustianism is given on especially radical and widely subversive edge, perhaps because Dickens's own political liberalism rules out its being incorporated within a Disraeli-like neo-feudal framework (though the novel does of course have its own more whimsical nostalgia for a colourfully nautical early-capitalist past). It is interesting to note, too, that the satire against Mrs Chick here does have a specific social reference, whether by intention or not, in progressive mid-Victorian psychiatric theory about insanity, which was governed by a concept of 'moral management' which stressed the capacity to keep insanity at bay by the exertion of self-control over disruptive feelings. Such an outlook did and still does have much to be said for it, though divorced from diagnostic understanding it hardly represents anything more than Meagles's advice to

Tattycoram in *Little Dorrit*. The Smilesian zeal with which it was promoted at the time, however, makes it seem very much a phenomenon of the Dombey world (and the parallel between psychiatric 'moral management' and Smiles's economic morality is obvious).[25]

* * *

So much, then, for Dombey. In contrast to his father, Paul has attracted much less critical attention, perhaps because the aura of Victorian religiosity still clings around him. Nevertheless, Dickens's achievement with him is of equal standing, I think: it displays an intelligence of a similar nature. This has not gone quite unrecognised, of course, for we have had F. R. Leavis' very helpful essay, which has rightly commended the 'intense concern for the real' shown in rendering such things as the disconcerting strangeness engendered by the privations of Paul's upbringing.[26] Yet despite his overt praise for the Paul section of the novel as a whole, Leavis does steer clear of the latter, more religiose half of Paul's story. And this, I feel, is somewhat misleading. For the whole portrait, it seems to me, is marked by a careful balance struck between the rhetoric of pathos and diagnostic perceptiveness.

There is, for example, the conclusion of Paul's well-known enquiry about money:

'Why didn't money save me my Mama?' returned the child. 'It isn't cruel, is it?'
'Cruel!' said Mr. Dombey, settling his neckcloth, and seeming to resent the idea. 'No. A good thing can't be cruel.'
    'If it's a good thing, and can do anything', said the little fellow, thoughtfully, as he looked back at the fire, 'I wonder why it didn't save me my Mama?' (p. 153)

Here, against the image of Paul as the wise child, somewhat precociously in command of the novel's themes, we have the very deliberate repetition of that phrase 'save *me* my Mama' (my italics), which realistically stresses that Paul's feeling for his mother is a reflex of intense personal need. And soon after this, amidst what looks like a purely set-piece bit of pathos, with Paul

Dombey and Son: *Radicalising Wordsworthian Psychology*   57

languishing idyllically by the sea, Dickens complicates the mood by insisting upon the possessiveness of this need:

> 'Go away, if you please', he would say to any child who came to bear him company. 'Thank you, but I dont want you.'
> . . .
> Then he would turn his head, and watch the child away, and say to Florence, 'We don't want any others, do we? Kiss me, Floy.' (p. 170)

But surely, it might be argued, the appearance of the sea marks a turning-point, after which insight is drowned in sentiment. And one does have sympathy for those critics such as John Lucas and John Carey who still, for all the talk about the symbolism of land and sea, find themselves unimpressed by Paul's groping oracularities about the speech of waves.[27] Still, whilst Dickens is rather ill at ease in this solemnly poetic mode, there *is* more going on, I think, than meets the no-nonsense critical eye. Take, say, Paul's discussion with Toots about the sea, which Carey cites in support of his view that 'whether the sea represents death or love or eternity or God is neither clear nor of much moment':

> 'I say!' cried Toots, speaking the moment he entered the room, lest he should forget it, 'what do you think about?'
> 'Oh! I think about a great many things,' replied Paul.
> 'Do you though?' said Toots, appearing to consider that fact in itself surprising.
> 'If you had to die,' said Paul, looking up into his face—
> Mr. Toots started, and seemed much disturbed.
> '—Don't you think you would rather die on a moonlight night, when the sky was quite clear, and the wind blowing as it did last night?'
> Mr. Toots said, looking doubtfully at Paul, and shaking his head, that he didn't know about that.
> 'Not blowing, at least,' said Paul, 'but sounding in the air like the sea sounds in the shells. It was a beautiful night. When I had listened to the water for a long time, I got up and looked out. There was a boat over there, in the full light of the moon: a boat with a sail.'

> The child looked at him so steadfastly, and spoke so earnestly, that Mr. Toots, feeling himself called upon to say something about this boat, said, 'Smugglers.' But with an impartial remembrance of there being two sides to every question, he added, 'or Preventive.'
> 'A boat with a sail,' repeated Paul, 'in the full light of the moon. The sail like an arm, all silver. It went away into the distance, and what do you think it seemed to do as it moved with the waves?'
> 'Pitch,' said Mr. Toots.
> 'It seemed to beckon,' said the child, 'to beckon me to come! – There she is! There she is!' (p. 235)

Contrary to Dickens's elevating intentions, comments Carey, in his own rather too self-consciously down-to-earth way, it is Toots here who has all the sense. The comedy, that is, works for rather than against him, and Paul's persistent high-mindedness in the face of comic deflation reads as mere inanity.

This certainly is a persuasive point if the passage is taken in isolation. Yet it is still worth paying attention to the mode of Paul's speech here. It is, isn't it, that of Victorian poetry, in which an intimation of the sublime is achieved through associative reverie, and in which the particularity of denotation is clouded over by vaguely suggestive connotation – Toots's comments, on the other hand, are starkly denotative, though the context suggests in him an underlying sensitivity that he can not even begin to comprehend or articulate. Here too, as in much Victorian poetry, spirituality manifests itself as a flight from a pedestrian reality which is felt to be too oppressive – the 'higher realm' is a consoling refuge, and Paul's imagery of moonlight and water significantly anticipates Arnold's favourite poetic décor. It is for this reason that Victorian poetry can be seen to have had that function I mentioned at the outset, of being a 'marginalised' form of the age's 'ideological production', cathartically venting feelings hostile to the ideological mainstream (the Puritan, bourgeois world-view alluded to by Mrs Chick's adulation of 'effort'), though in a form that inhibits their issuance into action, prevents any return from the 'spiritual' to the practical.

None of this in itself refutes Carey's objection: to say that the would-be prose-poetry of Paul's decline is working within a certain mode is not to prove that it is in any way a distinguished instance of it as such – it is not that. Its value, I want to suggest, lies rather in the way that it both works within this mode and, to some extent, *places* it by laying bare its mystificatory function. The point might be summarised like this: Victorian poetry (both in the literary mainstream epitomised by the more naïeve side of Tennyson and Arnold and in other forms of 'the poetic' as evinced, say, in certain strains of evangelical religiosity) *expresses* the regressive longings produced by the aggressively 'manly' (Dombeyan) Victorian ethos, whilst at the same time masking the true nature of these feelings in a poetic, transcendental language – *Dombey and Son*, on the other hand (along with a handful of exceptional Victorian poems such as, to some extent, *The Princess*), at once does this and clearly fathoms the sources of such religiosity. The novel, thus, contains in Paul the character a kind of Victorian poet, spontaneously uttering Victorian poetry, albeit crudely; but the character is seen objectively, and a psychological logic is revealed beneath the surface of conventional poeticism:

> Presently he told her that the motion of the boat upon the stream was lulling him to rest. How green the banks were now, how bright the flowers growing on them, and how tall the rushes! Now the boat was out at sea, but gliding smoothly on. And now there was a shore before him. Who stood on the bank!—
> He put his hands together, as he had been used to do at his prayers. He did not remove his arms to do it; but they saw him fold them so, behind her neck.
> 'Mama is like you, Floy. I know her by the face! But tell them that the print upon the stairs at the school is not divine enough. The light upon the head is shining on me as I go!' (p. 297)

If one pauses to really look at this climactic passage one can not help noticing the distorting effect of the last-minute re-routing towards Christ of Paul's essentially psychic journey, the last-minute superimposition of the public symbolism upon the individual pattern. For it is of course his lost mother who has been the gradually revealed goal of his voyage to death, and if there is a perhaps too conscious specificity in Paul's early wondering 'why the sea should make [him] think of [his] Mama that's dead' (p. 217), the needful vagueness of his growing awareness is more satisfactorily conveyed in that earlier-quoted exchange with Toots in that detail of the 'sail like an arm, all silver', which beckons from the waves. In fact, if we look at it in the context of the whole of his story, Paul's speech throughout that exchange with Toots perhaps suggests itself as Dickens's rudimentary illustration of how the imagination can lead the way at the growing point of consciousness, in this case instinctively and unconciously working to restore the actual lost mother with a symbolised maternal presence (just as the momentary ambiguity of the cry 'There she is!', with which Paul ends, establishes Florence as the actual maternal surrogate). Paul's career is at once spiritual progress and psychological regression, which may be why his disease is one that he seems almost deliberately to embrace:

'Shall we make a man of him', repeated the Doctor.
'I had rather be a child', replied Paul. (p. 210)

The relationship between these two levels, however, the spiritual and the psychological, is not simply that of the former being undercut by the latter. Rather, the religious framework functions to enforce a paradoxically positive significance in the regression. For the novel's insight here is, I think, that given that Paul's world replaces an organically continuous transition from childhood to adulthood with a precipitate thrusting from one state to another, his refusal to be made a man, which in his constrained situation is eventually a refusal of life itself, is in fact a desperate attempt to preserve his psychic integrity. Only this, I feel, can explain why his lapsing into 'weariness' is presented not just as a willing passivity, but as an oddly active and searching state:

Yet, in spite of his early promise, all his vigilance and care could not make little Paul a thriving boy. Naturally delicate, perhaps, he pined and wasted after the dismissal of his nurse, and, for a long time, seemed but to wait his opportunity of gliding through their hands, and seeking his lost mother. (p. 149)

Dickens is not just being casually facetious here, for the almost conscious elusiveness this passage notes in Paul is one of his characteristic expressions, that look, 'half of melancholy, half of slyness', or the 'shy and quaint yet touching look' which accompanies his answers to his father's questions. Again, too, as with his father's therapeutic collapse, the radical questioning here achieved of clear-cut distinctions between health and sickness, maturity and immaturity, would seem to represent a creative extension of the Wordsworthian insistence upon the self's necessary self-continuity, an extension achieved by sensitively pursuing the implications of that basic doctrine when applied to vastly differing circumstances. By allowing the claims of continuity to clash *against* those of traditional morality, a striking and paradoxical awareness is won of how what looks from a moral point of view to be weakness (however understandable) is also a kind of strength, at least in comparison with the other ways in which the people of Paul's world have allowed their lives to be shaped. Dickens's formula in Chapter 47 about natural unnaturalness is explored further in this novel than the explicit context of its appearance, that of humanitarian social concern for working-class deprivation, would suggest.

Of course, one does run a danger here of falsely bestowing a radical psychological understanding upon something much more conventional. In this, too, we are not helped by the way in which certain key things about Paul seem to yield themselves to both such lines of interpretation. One is tempted to take the contemplative aspect of his withdrawnness, for example, his preoccupation with 'what the waves are saying', as a stylised rendering of an imagination working in a compensatory fashion to foster Wordsworth's 'gravitation and . . . filial bond/Of Nature', the difference being that in Paul's social situation the connections necessarily lead not *to* the world but progressively out of it. Thus my interpretation above of Paul's transformation of the sail into the 'silver arm'. Yet it would be hard to insist upon this line of argument against an alternative reading of such a passage, especially if taken in isolation, as being a relatively thoughtless revamping of, say, the imagery of Wordsworth's *Immortality Ode*, that poem in which psychological vision is dissolved into philosophical vagueness. Does the obliqueness with which the psychological import of the passage is communicated stem from Dickens's wish to be faithful to the necessarily indirect way in which such significances intimate themselves to the mind, or does it proceed from Dickens's own vagueness about what he is doing? Certainly recourse to Dickens's social situation can not by itself resolve anything. It might be useful to explain the tantalising ambiguity of the text in terms of the need to express individual and unconventional insight in the conventional language and concepts that the reading public would understand, a constraint that can then be seen to have led to a kind of kabbalistic concealment of psychological insight within the rhetoric of popular religiosity. This would seem to be a natural outcome of Dickens's dilemma as both a master explorer of human behaviour and popular mentor, and other instances of such a tactic can be confidently located elsewhere in his works. Yet such an account does depend upon a willingness to assume that Dickens does have such an unconventional awareness here – and what if this is denied?

Well, in answer to this I can only say that I do not think it is tenable to argue that this section of the novel is simply uplift. Not only does the generally social-psychological orientation of the novel predispose one to accept as deliberate meanings which fall naturally and interestingly into the pattern of the book's argument as a whole. Beyond this, too, certain key details have a merely superficial resemblance to conventionalities, which fades upon closer scrutiny. The image of Paul by the fireside, for example, with his 'old, old face peering into the red perspective with the rapt attention of a sage' (p. 151) may at first seem just a gloss on the 'seer blest' of Wordsworth's Ode, but it is really too disconcertingly *odd* in its suggestion of weird precocity to quite square with this: Paul's particular kind of inner absorption is really more like that common ground shared by one kind of creative artist and some schizophrenics. Paul never ceases to be a 'case', and his spirituality a symptom, a point which Dickens actually spells out in the analogy he has Mrs Wickham draw between Paul and a previous charge of hers, Betsey Jane, who also, in her 'old, old . . . look . . . made people's blood run cold' (p. 167). Though he is, of course, as Mrs Wickham's bewilderment implies, just that kind of case that baffles analysis in received terms – Cornelia Blimber's confident pretension to grasp the meaning of Paul's character by means of her scientifically exact 'analysis' is thus no advance upon Mrs Wickham's recourse to a kind of fairy-tale typology. Only Dickens himself is in touch with a typology that can adequately take Paul's measure, one which, as I have been arguing, he can arguably be seen as having derived from Wordsworth's Romantic psychology. Yet even he, of course, is in no position to write about this typology in an explicitly psychological language – no more than his readers does he have that available to him. The most he can do is what is, after all, the dramatically appropriate thing: to have Paul articulate his inmost feelings in that culturally-bound religiose language which, given that he *has* to express himself fully, it is socially suitable for him to use. It is then only by setting such speech within the larger dramatic whole of the novel – the total pattern of significance as I have been outlining it throughout this chapter – that Dickens can then hope to inflect the meaning of such speech in the directions I have been claiming that he has.

* * *

I have not space here to go much into those minor characters who round out the novel's exploration of the Dombeyan system. I want to mention Miss Tox briefly, however, as an acute humorous–pathetic portrait of the painfully odd form into which femininity is seen to be twisted by patriarchal pressures. Her infatuation with the 'pecuniary Duke of York' ('But his deportment, my dear Louisa . . . his presence! His dignity!' (p. 58) is thoroughly in accord with the sexual code of the Dombey ethos, as epitomised by Dombey's first marriage, in which, we are told, he 'had asserted his greatness . . . and she had meekly recognised it'. Miss Tox's sexual typicality in this scheme of things is further enforced by the way in which her 'faded air' associates her at the beginning of the novel with the first Mrs Dombey, so that she becomes that lady's living continuation. Consonant with Suttie's analysis, her comic debilitation images the depreciated subordinate role permitted to femininity in a world where the male ideal is founded on the heroic repression of the feminine element in men. Thus we have the telling perception that her idolatry of Dombey's particular kind of strength naturally goes with a lack of confidence in the contrasting femininity in herself that the Dombeyan self-enclosed hardness denies. For her feminine feeling for Dombey leads her to adopt his own standards in self-judgement, and hence we have that pathetically comic image of a gauchely hesitant sexual identity conjured up by those 'odd weedy little flowers' and those shyly exotic 'strange grasses' that adorn and define her, or by her painfully apologetic presentation to Dombey of her feminine fancywork:

> 'It is only a pincushion for the toilette table . . . one of those trifles which are insignificant to your sex in general, as it's

very natural they should be – we have no business to expect they should be otherwise – but to which we attach some interest.' (p. 57)

It is perceptively appropriate, furthermore, that for the first half of the novel she should be under the thumb of Mrs Chick, the ideologist of Dombeyism, who mystifies its harshness as firmness in the manner of the Murdstones, and its coldness as an admirable objectivity, as when she lauds Mrs Pipchin's 'judiciousness' and refers to her as having devoted herself 'to the study and treatment of infancy'. As this Mrs Chick derives power over her timid friend by appropriating the only role in the Dombey world in which a woman is granted prestige, that which Suttie calls the 'protégé', a subordinate replica of the male.

In Miss Tox, however, femininity is suppressed but not crushed: it keeps on slipping out inadvertently. In interesting corroboration of my main argument, one sign of her femininity, and something of a turning-point in the novel's growing sympathy for her, is her habit of nostalgically pondering her childhood. She too has her 'hiding-places' of what, even in her, is a kind of 'power', and her recollection of the 'chains of dandelion-stalks' she has made in sentimental moods of her youth (p. 488) adds extra resonance for us to those fanciful little ornaments that burgeon in her apartment after she joins the Dombey ménage. It is this persistence of a 'continuity . . . in self-consciousness' in her that prepares the way for her conversion to the anti-Dombey party late in the novel.

A brief word is also needed about Mr Chick, who is generally recognised as a felicitous presence in the novel, an amiable domestic rebel sporadically assaulting the Dombeyan chill with his cheering if ineffectual bursts of liveliness. For though a peripheral figure, he is still a bit more than a stock joke:

'Don't you over-exert yourself, Loo,' said Mr. Chick, 'or you'll be laid up with spasms, I see. Right ol loor rul! Bless my soul, I forgot! We're here one day and gone the next!' (p. 61)

There is just a hint of something really peculiar in the blitheness of his last words: without sacrificing the comedy the writing manages to glance at a real psychic dislocation, an inner world of

Dombey and Son: *Radicalising Wordsworthian Psychology* 65

private gaiety that in its defensiveness has become quite estranged from the normally human. Comic oddity of this kind is not just a humour, as is Captain Cuttle's dextrousness with his hook, but a way of disclosing the pressures of a social world upon the shape of the individual personality. Here as so often elsewhere in the middle and later novels, the imaginative taste for the bizarre and the systematically ordering diagnostic intelligence work as one. Like Miss Tox Mr Chick is an 'enforced distortion' (to quote again from one of the novel's generalising asides), a natural consequence of unnatural conditions. Though to say this is not to depreciate the more traditional comicality of Cuttle and Toots, whose humorous traits are not in any way socially engendered. These other figures have their own kind of relevance, in that the warmth and innocent spontaneity of feeling that their comedy genially celebrates in them is very much in keeping with the novel's thematic affirmations.

What, though, of that other seemingly enforced distortion: Florence Dombey, who is usually associated with the weak side of the novel? This judgement seems for the most part quite proper: we find little of the balance of feeling and intelligence in the novel's handling of her that we do with Paul, and one is tempted to agree with A. E. Dyson's claim that Dickens has passed up the opportunity to present her as a realistic study in emotional deprivation and its consequences in favour of simply indulging her in the allegorical role of Redeeming Love, interesting to us only as a catalyst in her father's conversion.[28] One reason for this, perhaps, lies in that dilemma that A. L. French has pointed to in his discussion of *Great Expectations*: the contradiction apparent in that novel's thought about character between an increasing awareness of psychological determinism and an equally strong wish to continue to believe in Free Will.[29] Similarly in *Dombey and Son* we can see this strain pretty close to the surface when Dickens is dealing with Florence, most notably in the following passage from Chapter 47:

> Thus living in a dream where the overflowing love of her young heart expended itself on airy forms, and in a real world where she had experienced little but the rolling back of that strong tide upon itself, Florence grew to be seventeen. Timid and retiring as her solitary life made her, it had not embittered her sweet temper, or her earnest nature ... (p.743)

As with Arthur Clennam in *Little Dorrit*, Dickens here simply takes over the character in order to make her an inspiring exemplar of the way in which the morally good person can soar above psychological conditioning.[30] Dickens's own susceptibility to the kind of feminine ideal he criticises in Miss Tox seems to come into play here. At the beginning of the novel he is prepared to see Florence's quietness as a somewhat disturbing symptom: describing her reaction to Mrs Brown he refers to her habit 'unusual to a child, but almost natural to Florence now, of being quiet, and repressing what she felt' (p. 129). But by Chapter 47, however, 'timid and retiring' are redolent of delicate female charm, and so the contradiction Dickens has to assert is considerably muted. Nevertheless, directly after the passage I have just quoted we see Dickens's confidence in Florence's immunity from her background almost creaking at the seams when he qualifies a lyrical tribute with the comment that:

> in her thrilling voice, in her calm eyes, sometimes in a strange ethereal light that seemed to rest upon her head, and always in a certain pensive air upon her beauty, there was an expression such as had been seen in the dead boy. (p. 743)

– but as the thinly-veiled reference to the halo suggests, it is a purified image of Paul that is summoned up to make the comparison. A similar hesitancy in acknowledging the appropriateness of an ironic view likewise mars what could have been one of the novel's most astute moments with Florence, in Chapter 24, 'The Study of a Loving Heart':

> Yes, she thought if she were dying, he would relent. She thought that if she lay, serene and not unwilling to depart, upon the bed that was curtained round with recollections of their darling boy, he would be touched home, and would say, 'Dear Florence, live for me, and we will love each other as we might have done, and be as happy as we might have been these many years!' She thought that if she heard such words from him, and had her arms clasped round him, she could answer with a smile, 'it is too late for anything but this; I never could be happier, dear Father!' and so leave him, with a blessing on her lips. (p. 426–7)

Florence here is fantasising herself as a kind of death-bed flirt, tempting her father on to an agonising surrender of his pride, and then flitting off into immortality, almost as if in ingenious revenge. This could be a moment of intentional comedy and real perceptiveness. But as there is absolutely nowhere else in the novel where we are allowed to look at Florence with the faintest whisper of *comic* irony, it seems more logical to conclude that Dickens here is just blank to the absurdity of what she is thinking.

Nevertheless, though, there are moments in which the novel does seem to show something of the same kind of perceptiveness about her as it does about her brother and father – though it is a perceptiveness that is not at all incompatible with the solemn pathos that governs our attitude towards her. Take, for instance, her initial reaction to her father's remoteness:

> But her own mother, she would think again, when she recalled this, had loved her well. Then, sometimes, when her thoughts reverted swiftly to the void between herself and her father, Florence would tremble, and the tears would start upon her face, as she pictured to herself her mother living on, and coming also to dislike her because of her wanting the unknown grace that should conciliate that father naturally, and had no truth in it, or base to rest upon; and yet she tried so hard to justify him, and to find the whole blame in herself, that she could not resist its passing, like a wild cloud, through the distance of her mind. (p. 420)

I disagree with Dyson at this point, for it strikes me that here emotional lushness by no means drowns out a quite remarkable and objective apprehension of the neurotic emotional logic of the child starved of affection – at moments like this we can sense a continuity between Florence and Dickens's more assured explorations in similar psychological territory in later novels, with Esther Summerson and Pip. Elsewhere, too, scenes which come across with the predominant effect of simple pathos seem to touch on a reality about Florence that is blurred by sentiment but never quite obscured:

> 'Oh, Walter,' exclaimed Florence, through her sobs and tears. 'Dear brother! Show me some way through the world –

some humble path that I may take alone, and labour in, and sometimes think of you as one who will protect and care for me as for a sister! Oh, help me Walter, for I need help so much!' (p. 788)

Though to have shown us how *much* help Florence really did need would have involved quite a different kind of treatment; as it is, the comfortable comedy in which Florence's fate is worked out excludes the actuality consequent upon her deprivation that her plea for help seems to indicate.

Again, something of this ambiguity even attends Florence's marriage, for with her, in any case, there is a certain rightness as well as sentimentality about the sexless brother–sister terms in which it is celebrated:

> Blessed twilight stealing on, and shading her so smoothly and gravely, as she falls asleep, like a hushed child, upon the bosom she has clung to. (p. 806)

There is a rightness about the image of Florence as a 'hushed child' at this moment that has less to do with early Victorian convention, perhaps, than with the individual pattern of her psychology. For just as with Dombey himself a regression to the emotional equivalent of a compensatory childhood is a necessary precondition for his renewal, so the logic of Florence's case would seem to imply that she too needs to live through a natural childhood – again in surrogate form – before she can properly become a woman.[31] Hence it is right that Walter, as brother-husband, offers her what her father has previously withheld: 'now, no more repulsed, no more forlorn, she wept indeed, upon the breast of her dear lover' (p. 806). Where Dickens goes wrong is not in *what* he presents but in his attitude towards it: as with Dombey he speaks of the therapeutic half-way house as fulfillment itself, and his valuable concern for continuity with childhood slides into a dangerous unconcern for continuation beyond it. His intuitions in these instances are perhaps too entangled in Victorian conventions to know themselves fully – it was not until he came back to Florence's situation with Esther Summerson in *Bleak House* that he was to get things straight on this score.

* * *

Walter Gay is scarcely one of the more interesting figures in the novel, and critical commentary might properly be expected to let him tactfully alone. He is a paragon of the Romantic ideal of childhood – a 'cheerful looking, merry boy, fresh with running home in the rain; fair-faced, bright-eyed, and curly-haired', a youth distinctly akin in type to the 'race of real children'[32] celebrated in *The Prelude* at the expense of the model child beloved of the kind of hyper-rationalistic didacticism the Romantics generally campaigned against in their writings.[33] Yet he is quite clearly such a paragon as to be a gross unreality himself. However, the novel displays some thoughtfulness in its initial conception of Walter – as an idea if not as a realised presence – and the resolution of his fate takes us directly to its vulnerability as a critique of early-Victorian society. So it is perhaps worth devoting the concluding portion of this chapter to him.

Dickens's stated initial intention to 'disappoint all the expectations' Walter's introduction 'seems to raise'[34] was perfectly in keeping with what he actually wrote. For beneath the play of high spirits his doom is contrived with an almost clockwork precision. His upbringing at the Wooden Midshipman, it goes without saying, is in pointed contrast to that which Paul undergoes, and the connection between his affectionate bonds with his uncle and Captain Cuttle, and his own freshness and cheerfulness, is clearly implied. Less obvious, perhaps, is the contrast between education as perpetrated at Blimber's and the informal but real education that Walter is shown to have undergone at the hands of his uncle. For Walter's enthralment with the marvellous and adventurous life of the sea (p. 43) is clearly in line (modestly and comically prettified, but, in its stylised way, not without point) with the positive idea of education the earlier Romantics had counterposed against their sense of a prevailing pedantry. It concurs, for instance, with Coleridge's insistence that the education of the young should awaken 'by the noblest models the fond and unmixed love and admiration which is the natural and graceful temper of early youth';[35] and with Wordsworth's celebratory recollection of his own youthful enthusiasm for Romance, in the fifth book of *The Prelude*. Even more specifically it matches J. S. Mill's own Romantically oriented objection to some forms of utilitarian education, which he voiced in 1838:

Not what a boy or girl can repeat by rote, but what they have learnt to love and admire, is what forms their character. The chivalrous spirit has almost disappeared from books of education, the popular novels of the day teach nothing but (what is already too soon learnt from actual life) lessons of worldliness, with at the most the huckstering virtues which conduce to getting on in the world; and for the first time perhaps in history, the young in both sexes of the educated classes are universally growing up unromantic.[36]

We are surely meant to see that Walter's informal education has had a hand in the formation of his character. His trouble is, though, that whilst he has all the chivalrousness in the world, he is perhaps *too* deficient in those huckstering qualities, at least for the world he lives in. Dickens hints at this, light-heartedly for the moment, in one of Walter's earliest exchanges with his uncle:

'Come along then, Uncle!' cried the boy. 'Hurrah for the Admiral!' 'Confound the admiral!' returned Solomon Gills. 'You mean the Lord Mayor.' (pp. 38–9)

Having himself infected his nephew with his own romanticism, Gills is now worriedly trying to bring him around to present realities, which demand the quite opposed qualities suggested by Gills's chilling advice to Walter on his new job at Dombey's: 'Be diligent, try to like it, my dear boy, work for a steady independence, and be happy!' (p. 42) The old world – a conflation of Victorian domesticity, patriotic nautical mythology and Dickens's own class-based preference for small-scale capitalism – has passed away, and the Sea is now a matter of fiction only. Such prudence goes against the grain, however, and before long Gills and Cuttle are themselves revelling with their nephew in a riot of nostalgic reminiscence, inciting him with wild fantasies to become a second Dick Whittington. We accept this genially enough, but Dickens has clearly intimated the danger inherent in an idea of education, however good in itself, which is too far out of step with realities. Walter, as we see him here, is clearly designed to be a misfit; likeable, but with little more chance of success or even acceptable survival in life as presented in the novel than the Wooden Midshipman itself. Later in the century England's surplus of Walter Gays were to find an outlet for their romanticism in the Empire – Walter's nautical imaginings anticipate Kingsley and Public School muscular Christian Romanticism, with its heavily anti-trade bias (an ethos which was to contribute to the relative decline of English industrial power remarkably prognosticated by Dickens in the Doyce-Barnacle sections of *Little Dorrit*). However, this new lease of life for anti-bourgeois ideals is not foreseen, understandably enough, in the scheme of history envisaged by *Dombey and Son*: Walter, it is strongly implied, is a youth fated to grow up into a world in which he can have at most a marginal place.

Yet, it so turns out, it is his destiny to rise rapidly into the commercial world, to be head of another House of Dombey and Son. This is manifestly unbelievable as realism, though we can accept it in a comic spirit as another fanciful improbability in the consciously fairy-tale atmosphere of the novel's conclusion – it has its appropriateness within the terms of a genre designed to indulge human hopefulness rather than to reflect life. Nevertheless, one can not but suspect that Dickens is resorting to this mode in order to smooth over awkward contradictions raised by the quite serious attempt to come to grips earlier on with the question of human value and social progress. It is not just that he is reluctant to show us Walter going to the dogs, as originally intended, though this is one reason for the falsification. It also relates to the fact that for all the dislike he shows here for the Dombeyan forces of the new railway age, if not for the railway itself, Dickens is firmly committed to living within its 'stern realities',[37] to cite that phrase of Carlylean, ebullient stoicism that recurs so often in Dickens. For someone with his finally bourgeois sense of the real, the radically alienated position that would be implied by simply having the House of Dombey collapse is simply not available. And besides, he does at least partially welcome the progress the railways exemplify: as his wholehearted approval of the new developments in Staggs Gardens makes quite clear, he is no *simple-minded* conservationist, and in fact parodies such neo-feudal sentimentality in the grotesque attitudinising of Mrs Skewton. Thus, prepared neither to disown Walter's Romanticism nor the newly predominant economic reality, the novel conjures away the contradiction between what they stand for that is at the heart of its serious social analysis. Someone is needed to run things in the world of Experience, and rather than falling into the hypocrisy of relying on someone he can not admire, Dickens will have us believe that

Innocence can assume the controls, divagating into comedy because he can not believe this himself either.

Did he have any other alternative? Other, that is, than the extremist ones of writing Walter's history as a tragedy (with the rejection of the bourgeois–capitalist success-oriented character ideal that this would imply), or utopianly envisaging the transformation of that capitalism on to a new order to which Walter's character would somehow seem appropriate? One possibility was the person who could perhaps manage to live in both worlds, who might endeavour to hold together in himself the Dombeyan toughness and bourgeois self-discipline, while at the same time preserving in himself a humanising core of anti-Dombeyan tenderness and fancy. A person who could at once, or alternately, violate and abide by the Wordsworthian psychic taboos, who could be, in the special Romantic sense of the words, at once adult and child (Walter Gay, of course, is not this, being permanently boyish). Dickens himself, as we have seen, embodied such contradictions, though, as I have argued, the difficulty of being like this and living with any wholeness or stability – living free, as it were, of the dialectic of modernity – can be seen as a key to both the explanation and the motivation of his work. This is why the projection into the work of a proper self-portrait, focused in a single character, is something he so conspicuously chooses not to do until late in his life – it is as if to do so would involve either gross falsification or a too disturbing admission of deep confusion. The apparent self-portrait in *Copperfield* is of course not one at all: whilst David is presented as public success as well as private sentimentalist, his particular charm consists, as I suggested in Chapter 1 (pp. 32–3) in his failure to convince us of this, in his lacking the self-assertive energy necessary for it. Hence it is not surprising that one of the chief interests of *Little Dorrit is* its confusion, its sustained, deeply pondered doubt as to whether such energy is the vital essence of life or simply demonic, and its acquiescent opposite a sacred or a foolish thing. Nor is it surprising that the heroine from whom the novel takes its name is the author's polar opposite and concealed *alter-ego*, her existence a sign of his self-division, just as *his* irresolution about her betokens the difficulty of his achieving any sort of wholeness.

APPENDIX A: DICKENS AND DE QUINCEY

In his modification of Wordsworth's Romantic psychology Dickens is perhaps highly indebted to the person through whom his sense of that doctrine had most probably been mediated at the time of writing *Dombey*: Thomas de Quincey.[38] We know that Dickens knew and liked De Quincey (his American friend James T. Fields cites De Quincey as one of Dickens's favourite authors[39]), and although the thirteen-volume collected edition that was in the Gads Hill library[40] did not begin to appear until 1853, we can be fairly sure that Dickens would have read a good while before then the well-known *Confessions of an English Opium-Eater*, and would quite probably have also read the series of essays entitled *Suspiria de Profundis*, which, announced as a sequel to the *Confessions*, appeared in *Blackwood's* during 1845 (*Dombey* was begun in 1846). This contained a chapter of autobiographical analysis, 'The Afflictions of Childhood,[41] which must surely have caught Dickens's eye (his familiarity with that magazine is attested by allusions to it in his letters and his recommendations to aspiring writers to submit to it[42]).

Assuming then, that Dickens was familiar with De Quincey's account of his own childhood, it is interesting, in the light of my present argument, to see how De Quincey himself used Wordsworth in order to interpret his own very different experience. This, in contrast to Wordsworth's own comparatively untroubled youth, was dominated by a certain parental inadequacy and the traumatic death of a favourite sister when he was six:

> About the close of my sixth year, suddenly the first chapter of my life came to a violent termination; that chapter which, ever within he gates of recovered Paradise, might merit a remembrance. '*Life is Finished!*' was the secret misgiving of my heart; for the heart of infancy is as apprehensive as that of maturest wisdom in relation to any capital wound inflicted on the happiness. '*Life is finished! Finished it is!*' was the hidden meaning that, half unconsciously to myself, lurked within my sighs; and, as bells from a distance on a summer evening seemed charged at times with an articulate form of words, some monitory message, that rolls round unceasingly, even so for me some noiseless and subterraneous voice seemed to chant continually a secret word, made audible only to my heart –

that 'now is the blossoming of life withered for ever' ... Yet in what sense could *that* be true? For an infant not more than six years old, was it possible that the promises of this life had been really blighted? ... Raptures there might be in arrear; but raptures are modes of *troubled* pleasure. The peace, the rest, the central security which belong to love that is past all understanding – these could return no more. Such a love, so unfathomable – such a peace, so unvexed by storms, or the fear of storms – had brooded over those four latter years of my infancy, which brought me into special relations to my eldest sister.[43]

The lofty plangency of this is De Quincey's own manner, but the thought of the passage obviously draws heavily on *The Prelude*, which De Quincey had read in pre-publication manuscript form.[44] One can best see his grasp of that 'great philosophic poem', as he called it,[45] in the way in which he has transposed the phrase 'troubled pleasure' from the boat-stealing passage in Book One ('it was an act of stealth/And troubled pleasure'). This enables him to understand his own underlying sense of unease by invoking the Wordsworthian distinction of vital interrelatedness and estrangement upon which the psychology of *The Prelude* is premised: De Quincey's phrase 'central security' seems conversely to be his approximation to the state of wholeness and harmony more subtly delineated in things like the 'infant Babe' passage. By looking to Wordsworth, one might say, De Quincey is able to transform an eloquent expression of intense feeling into an understanding of the meaning of that feeling, and its bearing upon the possible growth of the self. Wordsworth has enabled him to see that his early childhood loss had made him an 'outcast ... bewildered and depressed', the condition implicit in the above passage, and explicitly named later in the sketch, when he compares his state on leaving the room in which his dead sister is lying with that of the archetypal outcast, the wandering Jew.[46]

Wordsworth's own subsequent alienation in his period of Godwinian intellectual *hubris* is, of course, the focus of the later books of *The Prelude*. However, where *his* affliction was remediable, De Quincey presents his own state as an irreconcilable rupture. Because of this his judgements upon his later life are interestingly contradictory: whilst at times accepting in traditional terms the necessity of putting his past behind him,[47] his Wordsworthian commitment contrastingly vindicates an instinctive preoccupation with it, even though, given the impossibility of making it productively continuous with any future, this inevitably results in a very un-Wordsworthian destructive morbidity, a progressively enervating obsession with the lost 'Paradise' of that 'central security' beyond which present life was felt to be 'Finished' and thus only superficially engaging.

One certainly does not have to strain too hard to see how suggestive all this may have been to a Dickens struggling to comprehend and articulate his own divided feelings about his equally problematic childhood. In general, hence, the acknowledgement of the tension between the demands of continuity and those of practical morality that we have seen in *Dombey and Son* may well have been facilitated by De Quincey's own adaptation of Wordsworthian psychology in applying it to himself. Furthermore, any latent intuition on Dickens's part that the 'tenderness taboo' could do no more than *repress* the child-victim's emotional need, driving it underground, would have found helpful confirmation in the theoretical sketch amongst the autobiographic collection, 'The Palimpsest of the Human Brain', which argued that early experiences persist ineradicably:

> The romance has perished that the young man adored; the legend has gone that deluded the boy; but the deep, deep tragedies of infancy, as when the child's hands were unlinked for ever from his mother's neck, or his lips for ever from his mother's kisses, these remain lurking below all, and these lurk to the last.[48]

Similarly, the nature of Dombey's regressive collapse is foreshadowed:

> Yes, reader, countless are the mysterious handwritings of grief and joy which have inscribed themselves upon the palimpsest of your brain . . . But by the hour of death, but by fever, but by the searchings of opium, all these can revive in strength. They are not dead, but sleeping . . . . In some potent convulsion of the system, all wheels back into the earliest elementary stage.[49]

– where the construing of Wordsworth's sense of past-present relations into a convulsive 'return of the repressed' is very close indeed to the Dickensian pattern.

Perhaps the most striking anticipation of *Dombey and Son* in De Quincey, however, is the resemblance between Paul's 'old-fashionedness' and the life-long proneness to brooding introversion which De Quincey recalls as having begun as a reaction to his sister's death:

> Now began to unfold themselves the consolations of solitude, those consolations which only I was destined to taste; now, therefore, began to open upon me those fascinations of solitude which, when acting as a co-agency with unresisted grief, end in the paradoxical result of making out of grief itself a luxury, and a luxury such as finally becomes a snare, overhanging life itself, and the energies of life, with growing menaces .... At this time, and under this impulse of rapacious grief, that grasped at what it could not obtain, the faculty of shaping images in the distance out of slight elements, and grouping them after the yearnings of the heart, grew upon me in morbid excess. And I recall at the present moment one instance of that sort, which may show how merely shadows, or a gleam of brightness, or nothing at all, could furnish a sufficient basis for this creative faculty ...[50]

Here we find clearly pre-figured that regressiveness which, as I have argued to be the case with Paul, is paradoxically a strategy to preserve, in the Wordsworthian sense, the integrity of the self. As with Paul's similar 'thoughtfulness and abstraction', too, De Quincey's inner absorption is marked by a peculiarly concentrated power of the imagination to sustain a highly private inner world at the cost of destructive isolation from the normal flow of life – De Quincey's written fantasies elsewhere amply confirm the hint here that the instinctive goal of such imaginings was the restoration of the lost idyllic relationship in surrogate form. In De Quincey no more than in Dickens is there an *explicit* acknowledgement of a positive logic in the morbid imbalance, open admission that in the circumstances the springs of life are in danger of drying up without such creative regression. But such is the strongly implicit burden of what both are saying.

APPENDIX B: THE TABOO ON TENDERNESS AND 'SOMEBODY'S LUGGAGE'

In a broad sense, an attack on the 'taboo on tenderness' is at the root of much of Dickens's social criticism: it is a natural complement to his characteristic positive values. It is certainly relevant, for instance, to his progressively deepening critique of the harsher traits of Nonconformity – David Copperfield, Esther Summerson, Arthur Clennam and Pip are all, in their varying ways and degrees, shaped, or rather mishaped ('enforced distortions') by a religiously inspired or sanctioned antipathy to what, from the Romantic viewpoint, is a natural childishness.[51] Even Dombey himself is a distinctively Protestant type, though of a secularised form. It is worth noting, however, than on at least one other occasion Dickens took up the idea of the taboo as operating on a diffused, not specifically religious level, making itself felt, that is, as a general feeling about what is and is not 'manly'. This was in the *All the Year Round* Christmas story for 1862: 'Somebody's Luggage'.[52]

The story concerns an Englishman, an officer and gentleman, who is on holiday in a French town in which a number of French soldiers are billeted. The soldiers are helping to pay for their lodgings by making themselves useful domestically, a state of affairs the Englishman finds ludicrously unbecoming to military dignity. He is especially offended by the daily sight of a soldier playing with a young child. He is, in fact, emotionally of a Dombeyan mould, with, as Dickens puts it, 'very little gentleness, confounding the quality with weakness'.[53] Visiting a nearby cemetery, he condemns as 'frippery' the tributes left at the grave of a recently deceased soldier by his friends. They are, he feels, 'offensively sentimental',[54] and very un-English. The deceased soldier is the very one he has disapproved of for playing with the child, but now, ironically, circumstances conspire to make the child the Englishman's responsibility. His reaction is predictably one of intense embarrassment; and he is shown 'creeping forth like a harmless assassin with Bebelle (the child) on his breast instead of a dagger'.[55]

Up to this point the story turns on the portrayal of the inhibition of tenderness as the characteristic of a social type, an emotional malady seen as peculiar to the English gentleman. Dickens was convinced that, compared with their continental neighbours (which for him meant mainly the French and the Italians), the English middle-classes were a stuffy lot, lacking, as a class, the spontaneity and vivacity he delightedly recorded as common to both the plebeian Cavalletto in *Little Dorrit*, and the 'rare old Italian Cavaliere' sketched in the *Household Words* essay 'New Year's Day'.[56] The latter, epitome of the Dickensian-Romantic social virtues ('Brown is his face, but green his young enthusiastic heart'), is reported to keep at his bedside 'the mechanical appliances of the whole circle of the arts . . . ready against inspiration in the night'.[57] One also thinks of the Moccolletti festival described in *Pictures from Italy*,[58] the *Uncommercial Traveller* essay 'In the French-Flemish Country',[59] or Dickens's angry attack on the falsity of many of the grounds of superiority on which the English were accustomed to plume themselves, in the *Household Words* essay 'Insularities'.[60] Dickens's outlook is essentially English in many ways (one thinks of his reference in a letter to Forster to 'what we often said of the canker at the root of all that Paris life'[61]). Yet Orwell's comment that it is free of 'vulgar nationalism' seems to me to be quite right – 'Insularities' even goes so far as to contend that the Frenchman is a 'more domestic man than the Englishman'.[62] Interestingly, the Victorian critic R. H. Hutton pronounced that Dickens's 'picture of the domestic affections' was 'not really English', tending 'to modify English family feeling in the direction of theatric tenderness and an impulsiveness wholly wanting in self-control'.[63]

This socially-diagnostic theme, nevertheless, is touched upon rather than explored in 'Somebody's luggage', and the story is of interest to us here more as evidence of Dickens's preoccupation and attitude than of his creative achievement. It is a likeable story, though, and there is no cause for critical rue in the fact that the unfolding plot slides away from the idea put forward at the outset, confusing the issue by making the protagonist's emotional defensiveness the product of a particular family quarrel, the upshot of which is unrelated to him in his representatively social and national aspects. It is of interest, however, that Dickens uses the account of his reconciliation with his estranged daughter and her family, and his accompanying recovery of his powers of tenderness, as an illustration of the abiding and restorative power of Memory; though it is not, in this case, his suppressed memory of his own childhood that is in question, but of his memory of his daughter when young:

Dombey and Son: *Radicalising Wordsworthian Psychology* 79

the windows of the house of Memory, and the windows of the house of Mercy, are not so easily closed as the windows of glass and wood. They fly open unexpectedly; they rattle in the night; they must be nailed up. Mr. the Englishman had tried nailing them, but had not driven the nails quite home.[64]

though one can not help feeling that the generalisation here is glancing at other kinds of memory, especially the kind we have been dealing with.

3 Wordsworthian Psychology and *Little Dorrit*: the Unresolved Dialogue

Nobody reading *Little Dorrit* would be surprised to learn that it was written during a period of personal crisis for its author.[1] Of all Dickens's novels it is the one where his violent contradictoriness is most dramatically foregrounded. Rebellious anger and the longing for rest, a vivid and derisive satiric imagination and an *authentic* sensitivity – unmatched in his work – for the beauty of the serenely demure: these contraries come to a head with a unique force, and their clash gives the novel its distinctive vibration. Equally distinctive, too, is the novel's inability, or refusal, to resolve the conflicts it explores; unlike *Great Expectations*, which to some extent therapeutically 'works through' its material, the play of modernity's dialectic in this work is at every point locked in the impasse of insoluble ambiguity. Its virtues are partially liberal ones, its achievement as a work of imaginative thought the negatively capable one of an intelligently sustained uncertainty, though of the genuinely disinterested kind that maintains itself against the pressure of a powerfully felt wish for certainty. Its scepticism is an affliction rather than a pleasurable convenience. An engagement with the Wordsworthian Romantic psychology of the self in Time is, too, a crucial focus of this non-progressing dialectic. Where *Dombey and Son* used this psychology to its own subversive ends, *Little Dorrit* enters more openly into dialogue with it, held inconclusively between a fascination that its conservatism might offer the answer to life's problems after all, and a persistent distrust of such an appeal, in part fidelity to the troublesome expansive impulses that are irreconcilable with self-continuity in its Wordsworthian definition.

This dialogue can be traced, primarily, in the complexities, confusions and ambiguities that attend the novel's treatment of

Amy Dorrit and Tattycoram and their respective situations, complications of which criticism has so far failed, oddly enough, to take adequate account. Yet these aspects need initially to be set in the context of the social depiction and agonised debate out of which they proceed. This is a work most obviously and systematically written out of the drive to throw off the 'incumbrances... of social life', to again cite the conservative Wordsworth of *The Prelude*, book thirteen.[2] In this it pulses with those 'impatient... hopes' and that 'heat of passion' that Wordsworth dreaded in Jacobinism and his own early self, hopes that run the whole paradoxical gamut of the bourgeois revolutionary impulse, from the middle-class radical challenge (itself forced somewhat on the defensive by the 1850s) to the rule of aristocratic gentility, to sympathy for that universal challenge to inequality as such which issues in Tattycoram's revolt against her bourgeois employer. Constantly, though, this dynamic radicalism finds itself checked by the unavoidable recognition of ways in which this 'zeal' might indeed be, as Wordsworth had said, 'fallacious' and 'excessive'. It is out of this spiritual state of tensed, energetic *arrest* that the novel's persistently ambivalent interest in Amy Dorrit and Tattycoram emerges.

One might start detailed discussion, then, with the marvellous study – centred upon William Dorrit and radiating outwards to the Gowans and Barnacles – of the operations of genteel hegemony. A decade after the appearance of *Dorrit* the principle of deference to gentility was to get its definitive celebration at the hands of Walter Bagehot, ideologue for the Barnacles and firmly critical of Dickens, in his famous political treatise, *The English Constitution*.[3] Dickens the opponent of 'the English gentilities and subserviences'[4] paints a contrasting portrait of this system as the social creation of unreality. It is perhaps the first thing one might point to to show how the mature Dickens had moved away from the eighteenth-century tradition of static and self-contained characters, towards seeing both main protagonists *and* whole social worlds in terms of processes, from the stable equilibriums of which identities are shaped into merely provisional and contingent solidity. Where earlier Dickensian comic characters had performed themselves as a spontaneous emanation of their being, the maturer intelligence moves from this fictional convention to a sophisticated psychological realism in its perception of performance as a crucial element in the self's continuation. This is certainly the case with Dorrit's chosen identity of lordly gentleman, which requires the continual assumption of the patronising role, the theatrical artificiality of which is masked, as the novel acutely implies, by the available social legitimation of the act as 'keeping up a position' and the 'strength of character' to 'preserve . . . self-respect'.[5] Here too, as in life, the performance requires the active compliance of others, a willingness in them to assume a complementary role, to take appropriate parts in the 'drama' the main character is initiating. Flora Finching and her 'legacy' are survivals of the earlier kind of character, and in this context their imperviousness to the response of others, which is simply a normal trait of the earlier type, is an especial mark of their comic eccentricity. One of the finest touches of Dorrit's portrait, by contrast, is his increasingly desperate insistence, as he himself declines, upon his brother's debility, against which he has always measured his own well-being.

Like the earlier works, however, much of the liveliness of *Little Dorrit* stems from Dickens's delighted parody of the language of performance. Yet where linguistic extravagance had formerly been registered as an expression of vitality, for all its ludicrousness (even Pecksniff joys in the verbal coruscations of his hypocrisy), the pleasure we are invited to take in picking our way through the evasions of Dorrit's pompously evasive circumlocutions is largely that of penetrating a maze to arrive at its empty centre. In contrast to the gusto of his predecessors' rhetoric his is voluble but stiff, a linguistic counterpart of the ceremonious formality into which his manners have hardened. This is a sign of the other most interesting trait of his performances, which is their brittleness. For along with Pip, and to some extent David Copperfield, Dorrit is a major study in that kind of insecurity we might call social vertigo, meaning a sensed fragility of the assumed identity. (The insight shown here, in fact, as with the two *Bildungsroman* protagonists, could be argued to represent Dickens's negative version of the Wordsworthian continuity idea, in its sense of the liability of the past to implode destructively upon the present.) This nervousness is seen to derive from the tenuousness of the whole system of interlocking roles, of which Dorrit is the jittery centre. As he is so dependent upon the confirmation of his performed self by others, it requires only a slight slip in their complementary enactments – Amy's obliviousness of the properly hierarchical way of being kind to Nandy, or the elder Chivery's momentary lack of deference – for his sense of himself to be annihilated. Thus his later barely-suppressed dread of servants, whose deference he correctly intuits to be simply role-playing. This is especially so with the Merdles' Chief Butler, whose look proclaims the fact: with a splendid *aperçu* we are shown Dorrit grasping at Burkean hauteur ('there was no reverence in the man, no sentiment'[6]) in a vain attempt to allay the anxiety the (sharply observed) 'glazed fixedness' of the Butler's eye creates in him.

Dorrit's psychology touches, perhaps, on something in all of us, whilst taking the heightened form it does in him from the particularities of his circumstances. One can also sense, though, his specific social typicality: he represents, partly by analogy, Dickens's deepening interpretation of the psychic condition of the socially mobile person, a condition which he seems to have been the first to treat compassionately from the inside, as we can see by comparing him on Dorrit with the traditional view as expressed in Pope's Sir Baalaam. It was also, of course, Dickens's own state, and his problematic relationship to memory has its socially representative aspect as well. The novel's dividedness shows itself both in the fact that such a trait can only be shown to belong to an unsympathetic character like Dorrit, and also in the paradox that his fictional exposure and demolition proceeds from Dickens's self-assertive anger whilst at the same time throwing into exemplary contrast the Wordsworthian Amy, who, as a heroine of fidelity, has a contrastingly solid and permanent identity which derives inevitably from this. Since the cause of Dorrit's insecurity is largely his denial of his past, his case points to a consideration of the Wordsworthian prerequisites for psychic stability, yet automatically exposes Dickens's problematic relationship to these.

The second of the social explorations in the novel to which Amy is relevant is its running argument with itself about what one might call the moral status of discontent – which is another way of posing the terms of Berman's concept of the dilemma of modernity. A number of commentators have seen this as one of *Little Dorrit's* main concerns, taking Amy as one 'answer' in the contest between the appeals of passionate rebellion and Christian resignation. Lionel Trilling's pioneer modern essay in *The Opposing Self* is still especially useful.[7] Grasping the importance of the allusions to the Bastille and the 'Marseillaise,' it locates the novel in the context of a post-French Revolutionary debate about the possibilities of liberation (Berman's 'modern condition'), and demonstrates the novel's complexity of moral attitude, its awareness of imprisonment both as a remediable social ill and as an inevitable human condition (an argument that interestingly refutes Bagehot's Victorian-neo-classic censure of Dickens's supposed *naïveté* about 'irremediable evils'[8]). Trilling's is a convincing case and it also makes sense of much in the novel that his discussion does not mention. Thus, for all the novel's outrage at how the deferential gullibility of the Plornishes and the Meagleses sustains 'the system', it nevertheless feels bound to acknowledge *something* of value in John Chivery's capacity to revere the genteel, which equally makes him a lover of Amy and an awe-struck admirer of her father. Cavalletto similarly challenges the novel's radicalism in his oddly cheerful submissiveness. Likewise, whilst Arthur Clennam is introduced with brilliant and characteristic volleys of anti-Nonconformist satire, he soon changes from a man who has good qualities despite his upbringing to one in whom they are paradoxically inseparable from it. Dickens has Amy perceive, of course, that though Arthur's earnestness brings his mother to mind, his is the earnestness of gentleness rather than of asperity. However it is not just gentleness that is shown to drive Clennam on in the tenacity of conscience with which he pursues his suspicions, but a sternness that seems rather the unqualified consequence of his mother's code:

> It was in vain that he tried to control his attention by directing it to any business occupation or train of thought; it rode at anchor by the haunting topic, and would hold to no other idea. As though a criminal should be chained in a stationary boat on a deep clear river, condemned, whatever countless leagues of water flowed past him, always to see the body of the fellow-creature he had drowned lying at the bottom, immovable and unchangeable, except as the eddies made it broad or long, now expanding, now contracting its terrible lineaments; so Arthur, below the shifting current of transparent thoughts and fancies which were gone and succeeded by others as soon as come, saw, steady and dark, and not to be stirred from its place, the one subject that he endeavoured with all his might to rid himself of, and that he could not fly from.[9]

'Criminal', 'condemned': the sensibility here directly recalls that nonconformity which in opening chapters was merely the object of satire, and the sermonic eloquence of the narrative syntax is at ease in evoking the awesomeness of the inflexible moral imperative. Dickens shows a range of sympathies here not usually accorded to him, reaching beyond his habitual assumptions in the location of something undeniably impressive here in Clennam's quite 'un-Dickensian' dour toughness. Later, in a kind of subsidiary echo of this that seems to have been overlooked by the novel's critics, Mrs Clennam herself is allowed to break free from our normally comic-diagnostic image of her to achieve a telling dignity in her final confrontation with Blandois. The dramatic pairing is aptly managed, for against his empty melodramatics her Puritan discipline, perverse though it is, shows well:

'You are a bold woman.'
'I am a resolved woman.'[10]

Her ready rejection of the banally Romantic linguistic mask he offers can not but compel our respect.

In all these cases (except, perhaps, Mrs Clennam), Dickens is recognising various ways in which the good and the bad are inextricably linked. Taken together their cumulative effect is to deeply question the novel's powerful wish to believe in and proclaim the possibilities of liberation. For Arthur to win complete freedom from his repressive background would be to become, so Dickens sees, so much the lesser man; and to simply dismiss Chivery as a *petit-bourgeois* dupe would be to opt for moral stupidity in the interests of political convenience. Hence the fact that the pervasive social anger of the novel finds fictional gratification only in the minor and comic uprisings of Affery and Pancks, while the central thrust of the plot *might* seem to affirm the quietist resignation of Amy, in whom the conservative implications I noted at the outset in the Wordsworthian ideal are strongly marked.

Little Dorrit, then, is a restlessly exploratory novel, which at once reveals its passion for change and liberation and radically ponders the validity of such hopes. In this it exemplifies the awareness of difficulty and complexity which is the hallmark of the specifically liberal intelligence (Trilling has written finely on this point in *The Liberal Imagination*[11]). Such values are of course very much under attack today by the literary-critical *avant-garde*, who argue that post- Arnoldian criticism has used them as ideology under the guise of a proclaimed disinterestedness. Terence Hawkes, for instance, is fairly typical in claiming that the pre-eminence accorded to complexity has legitimised the evasion of political commitment.[12] In this context *Little Dorrit* is of great use in the making of the crucial discrimination as to where such a charge is true and where it is not. For far from ministering to an underlying complacency, the kind of recognition of complexity and difficulty we get here strikes me as something won very much *against* the work's emotional temper, which boils fervently for simplicity and action. For this reason it seems to me that the novel's liberalism is genuinely disinterested, as the play of intelligence that yields the inclusiveness of vision is visibly free of determining pressures. Actually, much of what has traditionally struck some critics as Dickens's ungentlemanly rawness is arguably a matter of what in this light can be seen as an oddly admirable dissonance of feeling and perception; by contrast the smooth poise of, say, Bagehot's attack on Dickens reveals no sign of anything in *him* that resists his counsel of acquiescence to man's 'inevitable condition', and thus what he offers as philosophical urbanity comes across with a blandness that *does* seem to justify Hawkes's point – and Bagehot certainly has his present-day counterparts.

* * *

I come, then, to a detailed consideration of Amy, who, in keeping with this complexity, signifies, I think, neither a 'solution' to the dilemmas of discontent, nor an evasion of them. She is, as I have already said in anticipation, a character conceived very much in terms of the self-continuity doctrine. In this, though, she is placed, almost experimentally, in a situation radically altered from the Wordsworthian norm. And here, true to the flexibility I have been pointing to, the continuity ideal is both considered as an 'answer' to this situation and is in turn tested by it.

One can make a beginning with the detailed Wordsworthian echoes in Amy by considering her family's charge that she is a 'complete prison-child'[13] for her inability to join in their pretensions. They *are* in a sense right, though in this they are mainly paying her an unwitting compliment. What they do incomprehendingly register, in fact, is the quality of spirit that links her closely to Wordsworth's feminine ideal. For her spontaneous, unwilled contentment with the restriction of her life is close to the philosophy of the Wordsworth who, 'moderated and composed', regained health and sanity at Grasmere under the influence of a sister who:

> Welcomed what was given, and craved no more:
> Whate'er the scene presented to her view
> That was the best, to that she was attuned
> By her benign simplicity of life.[14]

This ideal reconciles active domestic responsibility with the essentially Wordsworthian value of the mind's self-possessed repose. The major locale for and physical analogue of such repose in the poetry is the scene of contained space, felt not as constriction but as refuge: phrases such as 'a fixed centre of a troubled world' are paradigmatic. A minor sonnet, undistinguished but representative in outlook, indicates the transition to Amy:

> Nuns fret not at their convent's narrow room;
> And hermits are contented with their cells;
> And students with their pensive citadels;
> Maids at the wheel, the weaver at his loom,
> Sit blithe and happy; bees that soar for bloom,
> High as the highest Peak of Furness-fells,
> Will murmur by the hour in fox-glove bells:
> *In truth, the prison, into which we doom*
> *Ourselves, no prison is* . . .[15] [italics mine]

The vacuous collocation here ('Nuns . . . weavers . . . bees') already expresses a smugly High Tory vision of social harmony as a pastoral idyll (the poem appeared in 1807). Amy Dorrit, on the other hand, might be said to represent Dickens's inquiry into the validity of such an ideal, under the complicating pressures of life as typified by the Marshalsea rather than Grasmere. For her 'the prison . . . which . . . no prison is' is a prison indeed, although she apparently bears it without sign of struggle.

It could of course be argued that such parallels reveal merely a common allegiance to post-Romantic assumptions in general about the nature of goodness. Yet I think there is a more direct reverberation at work, registering as a shared inflection in the interpretation of an idea. Most specifically this reveals itself in Amy's affectionate relationship with the Marshalsea itself:

> To speak of home, and to go and look at it, it being so near, was a natural sequence. They went to the closed gate, and peeped through into the court yard. 'I hope he is sound asleep', said Little Dorrit, kissing one of the bars, 'and does not miss me.'
> The gate was so familiar, and so like a companion, that they put down Maggy's basket in a corner to serve for a seat . . .[16]
>
> With a pitiful and plaintive look for her wayward sister; for her idle brother; for the high blank walls; for the faded crowd they shut in; for the games of the prison-children as they whooped and ran, and played at hide-and-seek, and made the iron bars of the inner gateway 'Home'.[17]

Her 'still surviving attachment to the miserable yard and block of houses as her birthplace and home'[18] seems very much to be Dickens's variant upon Wordsworth's insistence that the spiritually healthy self be necessarily rooted in a particular place, or places, hallowed by memory – a proposition that naturally follows from the premisses about continuity. The above passages anticipate the kind of adaptation I earlier cited George Eliot to have made of Wordsworth in *The Mill on the Floss*, and later elsewhere.[19] As in Eliot, too, there is a toning down of the Wordsworthian sublimity:

> Was it for this
> That one, the fairest of all rivers, loved
> To blend his murmurs with my nurse's song,
> And, from his alder shades and rocky falls,
> And from his fords and shallows, sent a voice
> That flowed along my dreams. For this, didst thou,
> O Derwent! winding among grassy holms
> Where I was looking on, a babe in arms,
> Make ceaseless music that composed my thoughts

To more than human softness, giving me
Amid the fretful dwellings of mankind
A foretaste, a dim earnest, of the calm
That nature breathes among the hills and groves.[20]

The life of the river here derives from its association with the nurse's presence, yet in contrast to the past things and places cherished in Dickens and Eliot, it is not simply a neutral medium in which the human memory is invested, but has its own life and voice, into which the nurse's presence has been dissolved and idealised in recall. In a manner typical to Wordsworth, the imaginative resonance of the memory is at once rooted in the immediacies of time and place, and yet opens out, through these, towards recognition of the 'beyondness' of the immanent Spirit – a delicate continuity is preserved here, for instance, between the actual mothering figure and Nature conceived as a maternal presence. No such reciprocal process is at work in the Dickens and Eliot examples.

Their secularisation, however, opens up possibilities as well as closing them off, for it enables both novelists to see the relevance of the organic continuity of the self to people whose past experience has been more commonplace. It provides Dickens, for instance, with an interesting and plausible psychological explanation of how Amy's extraordinariness arises realistically, 'out of the situation and the routine of daily life that produced her', as F. R. Leavis has put it.[21] Likewise it also enables both novelists to bring the conservative implications of the continuity idea within the range of common life: in a way alien to Wordsworth's world those 'old inferior things', around which Eliot (in *The Mill on the Floss*) claims our affections have 'a trick of twining', really *are* inferior – Wordsworth's imagination cherishes subdued and temperate beauty, but 'commonplace ... even ugly furniture', in its un-ennobled bareness, is not a generally obtruding presence in his sense of things. This gives a note of dourness to her conservative piety, as when she concludes a description of the Tullivers' environs with the rhetorical question, 'What novelty is worth the sweet monotony where everything is known, and *loved* because it is known'.[22] 'Sweet monotony' could also well describe Amy Dorrit's experience of *her* home, though in Dickens's application of the Wordsworthian doctrine to an urban setting the paradox is enforced more severely. Resignation here is an even grimmer business than in Eliot, and this relates directly to the ambivalences in Dickens I have already touched upon. (Dickens would also have almost certainly have read Charles Lamb's adaptation of the notion of the memory-hallowed place to his own London-based experience, in his letters and his essay, 'The Londoner'.[23])

The key to Amy's spontaneous goodness, then, is thus the Wordsworthian one of her unresisting fidelity to her childhood affections, either as invested in place, or situated directly in people. Wordsworth's point, of course, is that the two are inseparable, so that Amy's self-definitive gesture of kissing the prison bars, and her feeling the gate to be a companion, are acts of filial piety. It is in keeping with the intelligent psychological realism of her portrait that she *does* have something to be faithful to: her upbringing in the unwholesome Dorrit family *has* made available a kind of affection and given her a subsequent sense of security. Unlike Clennam, whose loveless childhood has left him very much, in Wordsworth's phrase, 'an outcast ... bewildered and depressed', the primary bonds of feeling have been freely implanted in her innermost being, and her relationship with the immediate world which is interfused with these bonds is consequently one of affectionate belonging, by virtue of which the sordid and dreary nature of this world is redeemed, 'irradiated', if not 'exalted'.[24] In one sense she has even been the favourite of the family, 'by far the best loved of the three',[25] as her father puts it, with a kind of honesty. Wryly enough, his very lethargic conceit and hidden infantile dependence (perceptively allowed to surface only in his break-down)[26] are shown to contribute to her emotional stability, for as he has never rejected her ministering attention in prison she has consequently never felt unwanted. The novel is never simple-minded about the play of feeling within the family, and never just rewrites Cinderella for us. Fanny's embrace, for instance, we are told at one point, is 'a really fond one'.[27]

The crucial deviation of her case from the Wordsworthian norm, though, is that with 'love' she has drunken in massive doses of exploitation and condescension. This again brings up the ambiguity in Dickens's own feelings towards his past, and to Amy as one way of dealing with this. It also raises again my related suggestion that this is matched by something unresolved in the depiction of Amy, something uncertain about how we are meant to see her. Certainly several critics in the last few years have moved towards this viewpoint: the earlier debate about Amy's reality as a heroine has given way to a questioning of whether she really is given to us as a heroine at all. Instead of 'The Paraclete in human form' (Trilling's unfortunate phrase) or 'miraculously intervening goodness' (Raymond Williams[28]), we are offered Amy as a conscious or semiconscious study in neurotic self-denial – the decades of feminism and self-assertion therapy have left their mark, though a number of persuasive earlier reinterpretations of Esther Summerson along similar lines have also prepared the ground. Both of the critics that I have in mind, Kathleen Woodward and P. J. M. Scott',[29] do in fact notice a lot of things previous discussions have missed, and do, I think, make the traditional view untenable. The trouble with both their accounts, however, would seem to be that they assume too readily (perhaps hindered as well as helped by the current cultural climate) that what they register as inadequacies in Amy are in fact recognised as such by the author; consequently they offer no satisfactory explanation of why Amy is proclaimed so explicitly *as* a heroine pure and simple (something which in fact is never done with Esther). Neither makes real sense of the novel's disunity, and though Woodward does *acknowledge* the fact of division she is rather too pat in explaining this in terms of a surface commitment to a conventional Victorian ideal of feminine selflessness masking an underlying scepticism. I myself do not think this kind of interpretation will quite do, whether we see the contradiction as an imperfectly conscious one, as Woodward implies, or whether we adopt Mrs Leavis's suggestion that the mature Dickens solved the dilemma of feeling bound to protect in his readers pieties which he himself could not fully share, by deliberately offering an equivocal text, which could be understood according to the reader's varying level of sophistication.[30] Both these variants illuminate a good deal in a number of the novels. With Amy, though, Dickens seems at different points deeply and personnaly committed to *both* of the conflicting evaluations of her. This may be a case of him at once being and not being a typical middle-class Victorian, as William Myers has persuasively shown about the novel in general. A better key in her particular case, though, can be found in the work's curiously unsteady attitude to her serenely untroubled relationship with her past.

We can make a start on the detailed evidence by looking at the handling of the first focal issue in the presentation of Amy: her burdensome role as the mainstay of a family of spongers. The way she is introduced to us suggests that the 'Paraclete in human form' may well be what Dickens has in mind:

> how much, or how little of the wretched truth it pleased God to make visible to her; lies hidden with many mysteries. It is enough that she was inspired to be something which was not what the rest were, and to be that something, different and laborious, for the sake of the rest. Inspired? Yes.[31]

We can sense a hovering between realistic and allegorical-moralistic modes here, an inclination towards 'miraculously intervening goodness'. The mood continues as the résumé of her early years proceeds into her childhood:

> No matter through what mistakes and encouragements . . . She took the place of the eldest of the three, in all things but precedence; was the head of the fallen family; and bore, in her own heart, its anxieties and shames.[32]

The first passage concedes, in its high-toned way, that Amy as a young child may well have been happily ignorant of much of her family's moral squalor. The second would seem to be saying that later years brought full knowledge, as is distinctly implied by her '(bearing) . . . in her own heart, its anxieties and shames'. This is not an unbelievable claim, and it is very consonant with the lofty conception of her Dickens seems to be unfolding. Nevertheless the next chapter, when she first meets Clennam, hints at a quiet modulation to a somewhat lower plane:

> Her look at her father, half admiring him and proud of him, half ashamed for him, all devoted and loving, went to his inmost heart.[33]

There is nothing critical of Amy here, but one does not wonder why, if she's bearing the family shame in quite the way the first passage suggests, she could be shown as even *half* admiring her father. One understands how she *needs* to do this, and the next dozen or so chapters go on to develop a poignant and well-observed picture of her struggle to believe in her father's illusions. In a painful first interview with Clennam she rationalises Dorrit's behaviour by explaining it as the consequence of his being in prison,[34] and as a just exaction of the tribute due to his gentlemanly superiority;[35] and then hopefully tries to convince Clennam that it is simply her father's 'anxiety' about his children that makes her hide the fact that she and Fanny go out to work. Later she even develops a theory that it is not really his 'true' self that Clennam is seeing – she's a great believer in his illusion of a nobler past self (which is quietly placed in anticipation by our own first image of him in Chapter Six). I do not think, either, that all this can be seen as a mere keeping up of appearances, as Scott claims when, rather on the hunt for Amy, he charges her with deceit in pretending not to see through her father: her 'innocent', 'boastful' 'pride' in speaking of her father's manners hardly suggests this. Rather, her protestations to Clennam have the ring of sustaining a faith by declaring it, one clue to this nuance being her remark to Clennam after talking to him of her father: 'I did not mean to say so much ... But it seems to set it more right than it was last night'. Her faith is fragile enough, understandably, and her 'boasting' is soon followed by the discomfiting admission that 'People might not think so well of him outside as they do in prison'.[36]

Despite its discrepancy with the initial heroic image, Dickens's commentary still attempts a purely ennobling interpretation of her persistent belief in her father, seeing it as just generosity. Her 'innocent' boastfulness about her father's manners is capped by an authorial standing ovation (if Dickens's characters give performances, he himself as narrator often acts the part of live audience):

> What affection in her words ... what a great soul of fidelity within her, how true the light that shed false brightness round him![37]

But the metaphor here surely glosses over the fact that her faith also makes things a bit easier for her. Against the overtly idealised figure, in fact, a somewhat different image begins to emerge; not of a moral or psychological cripple, as Woodward's and Scott's interpretations of similar things in her rather imply, but of a human being with a human propensity towards self-protective illusion, and who has not yet achieved the difficult maturity of laying this aside. And this doubleness has perhaps some relation, I feel, to Dickens's own double attitude to his past. If he overtly indulges her tendency to evade those perceptions which would most challenge her fidelity, this obviously goes with an impulse to celebrate her in the Wordsworthian terms in the way I have been discussing. On the other hand, his own incapacity for Amy's kind of single-minded acceptance, much as he would like to have it (the ambiguity we can see revealed in the *Autobiographical Fragment* – see next chapter, pp. 128–9), is surely behind his capacity to show Amy's heroic devotion as dependent in her on what we must finally call as weakness, albeit tolerantly so. The same also could be said about her attachment to the Marshalsea in general, if one considers the sentimentality on which her nostalgic gratitude to its prisoners is based.[38] If weakness sounds too moralistic, it is certainly an absence in her of a clear-sightedness that could hardly be deemed immoral, but which certainly makes Christian resignation more difficult for those people who possess it, like Tattycoram (to some extent), or Dickens himself (though his temporarily harmonious reconciliation with his past in *Copperfield* might be said to represent a conscious version of Amy's evasiveness, his sense of his father as Micawber, for instance, being a safe cordoning off of his positive memories within the restraints of the genially comic mode). It is we, of course, who are doing the calling; but the presentation of the facts seems to deliberately invite us to do so: where the overt sanctification of Amy is Dickens's apology for his inability not to resent, the implicit qualification of this might seem to reverse the judgement into something of a self-vindication.

A similar interpretation is suggested by the Dorrit family's treatment of Amy. Exploitation and injustice certainly figure prominently here, and her situation within the family is one of the main domestic foci of the novel's general engagement with these things as the prevailing conditions of its world, and of its inquiry into how people ought to live in such circumstances. This latter question is raised explicitly in Meagles's comic-serious disagreement with Miss Wade in the second chapter about whether or not a prisoner forgives his prison.[39] Despite the balanced sympathies invited by this exchange, where we see equally Miss Wade's relentlessness and Meagles's complacency, Amy's ostensible moral heroism would seem to bring the novel down firmly on one side, for her achievement is precisely that of forgiving her (very real) prison. Nevertheless, one cannot but wonder what exactly she has to forgive, as she never seems to quite face the fact that she is being treated unjustly. One major cause of this is a (somewhat convenient) failure to discriminate between genuine kindness in others and the odiously patronising benevolence that her father goes in for. Thus, when attacked by him and Fanny for walking arm-in-arm with Nandy, she protests that if she had not known of his kindness to the old man, she would not have done it.[40] She might perhaps be fibbing here, adroitly turning a family fiction to her own advantage; but this would imply a wittier and more agile woman than she ever really is, someone, in fact, rather more like her sister. One must take her as speaking in all innocence, and take this as a clue towards understanding how much of the truth about her family's behaviour towards her she does comprehend (her obliviousness to Mrs General's designs on her father is another[41]). It is interesting, too, that one *does* need clues on this score, for Dickens is curiously reserved about exactly how she does see things at times: where his earlier reticence about probing the mysteries of a young child's consciousness is quite proper, one sometimes feels that with the elder Amy he is choosing rather deviously how much to know about her knowledge. The narrative neither reveals her thoughts immediately after this scene, nor after a similar one later where she is charged with unfeelingly resurrecting the past; and in the one explicit comment upon her reaction to Fanny's condescension towards her the phrasing is teasingly ambiguous:

> One comfort that she had under the Ordeal by General was more sustaining to her, and made her more grateful than to a less devoted and affectionate spirit, not habituated to her struggles and sacrifices, might appear quite reasonable; and, indeed, it may often be observed in life, that spirits like Little Dorrit do not appear to reason half as carefully as the folks who get the better of them. The continued kindness of her sister was this comfort to Little Dorrit. It was nothing to her that the kindness took the form of tolerant patronage; she was used to that.[42]

'Used' hovers between 'habituated, and thus able to put up with', and 'inured, and not noticing' – it is almost as if Dickens himself is a bit embarrassed about the implications of admitting her to be so unseeing. For her to be this does not represent a telling perception into the kind of mystification of the innocent that a family such as hers could breed in someone like her. But it also threatens, or should be seen as threatening her status as moral heroine, for 'us' at least, by suggesting the relative ease of the moral life to her, when compared with that of those 'folks' given to 'reason'. The passage here does its best to champion her in this, for by a sleight-of-hand blurring of reasoning as thinking and as sordid calculation it sets up a false opposition between the base who think and the noble who feel too much to be able to, ignoring the alternative and more persuasive possibility that the fullness of feeling is *dependent* upon not thinking as well as the cause of it. This may be partially just a stock piece of Victorian anti-intellectualism; but it also savours more particularly of the author's own self-dislike: 'if only I could blind myself to the bad aspects of my memories', he seems to be saying through her, 'how virtuously free of resentment I would be'. There is a lot of Victorian manly chivalry in Dickens's championship of Amy, but there is also an element of *trahison des clercs*, of evading a fraught modernity of consciousness through a longing for simple solutions.

We seem to have a case here, then, of the novel's explicit judgement actively obscuring what the presented facts of the portrait imply, which is someone in whom the difficulty of the moral life is alleviated to the point where one can only accept her as a moral heroine in a special or qualified sense, as one does with, say, Miss Birdseye in James's *The Bostonians* (one of Fanny's names for her sister, of course, is Miss Bat[43]). Is Dickens simply unaware of the significance of the behaviour he reveals? This could perhaps hold for the first half of the novel; but as one begins to look closely at Amy during her travels with her family in Part Two, one cannot resist the impression that now at least we are being given an *analysis* of someone whose exemplary fidelity derives not from moral virture pure and simple but from a dominating need, sympathetically but dispassionately seen:

In this crowning unreality, where all the streets were paved with water, and where the death-like stillness of the days and nights was broken by no sound but the softened ringing of church-bells, the rippling of the current, and the cry of the gondoliers turning the corners of the flowing streets, Little Dorrit, quite lost by her task being done, sat down to muse. The family began a gay life, went here and there, and turned night into day; but she was timid of joining in their gaieties, and only asked to be left alone.[44]

The atmospheric details splendidly catch the meaning of the beautiful but disconcerting charm that Venice has for her. Bereft of the familiar things of her life, it is as if the very solidity of her identity – that which makes her a touchstone of value when set against the unreality of many of the others in her world – is in danger of dissolution. She is caught in an obscure, but significant inner state that the hallucinatory strangeness of Venice ('streets . . . paved with water', 'death-like stillness', 'softened ringing of the bells') arouses and expresses. Amy's response is patently not Philistine indifference, but hypersensitivity: Venice stirs the deep roots of personal feeling in a way that prohibits any easily manageable aesthetic 'appreciation'. As Mrs General reports her as saying, her reaction is one of 'wondering exceedingly'.[45] As her sense of her own reality has been built on servitude to her family, so, the implication clearly goes, its removal and the consequent freedom for her is too fearful to be borne. Her work is not something that she does from pure asceticism, for it is only *through* that that she derives any secure sense of self at all. Similarly, when Arthur first tells her of her family's change of fortune, her realisation that soon 'all the familiar experiences would have vanished away' makes her look not sad but 'frightened'.[46] Nor has her fear got anything to do with a premonition of family *vanitas*. Also, the depression she reports in her letters to Clennam has less to do with moral concern than with her father's acquisition of servants leaving her 'quite lost by her task being done';[47] thus her 'quiet, scared, lost manner' in going about Venice. In this eerily Romantic world in which things seem quite literally to have melted into air, such an unmodern girl can only be expected to conservatively react, clinging anxiously to the only firm ground she knows.

All this, I think, suggests that in the course of the novel Dickens has somehow developed the assurance to look at Amy from a consciously psychological perspective, rather than a simply moralising one. We are still shown her loving concern for her father, but there is a new candour about admitting her own gratification in doing so:

> If Little Dorrit found herself left a little lonely and a little low that night, nothing would have done so much against her feeling of depression as the being able to sit at work by her father, as in the old time, and help him to his supper and his rest.[48]

Even though the coy understatement of the first clause slightly smudges it. Only D. W. Jefferson, I think, has remarked upon this change of tone,[49] but it is not, as he says, inexplicable, but rather, I think, a newly assured detachment, a newly clear recognition that the kind of unproblematic fidelity that Amy embodies need not necessarily be seen as a moral ideal, comparing intimidatingly with the more divided spirit of others. Dickens now seems free to see it as the product of a special kind of temperament, in which, for no intrinsically moral reason, the need for security predominates over the need for self-assertion (the quiescence of the latter being reinforced by the self-protective blindness discussed above).

In this context it is useful to compare the passages cited previously about Amy's attachment to the Marshalsea with one in the Venice chapters where we are shown the actual working of her memory. It is one of the novel's most masterly renderings of consciousness from within:

> Such people were not realities to the little figure of the English girl; such people were all unknown to her. She would watch the sunset, in its long low lines of purple and red, and its burning flush high up into the sky: so glowing on the buildings, and so lightening their structure, that it made them look as if their strong walls were transparent, and they shone from within. She would watch those glories expire; and then, after looking at the black gondolas underneath, taking guests to music and dancing, would raise her eyes to the shining stars. Was there no party of her own, in other times, on which the stars had shone? To think of that old gate now!
>
> She would think of that old gate, and of herself sitting at it in the dead of the night, pillowing Maggy's head; and of other places and of other scenes associated with those different

times. And then she would lean upon her balcony, and look over at the water, as though they all lay underneath it. When she got to that, she would musingly watch it running, as if, in the general vision, it might run dry, and show her the prison again, and herself, and the old room, and the old inmates, and the old visitors: all lasting realities that had never changed.[50]

The *cost* of her integrity is enforced here with a new severity. 'Continuity . . . in self-consciousness' is exemplified in the instinctive play of her thought and imagination, and this instinctiveness suggests that the Past is not just the core of her present being, which the self is free to reject, though at a price, but an almost inflexible prison of it (an emphasis closer to De Quincey's modified version of Romantic psychology than to the Wordsworthian original). She reacts to the memories with a sense of relief, regaining by them her natural sense of gravity, her 'real' self, we are tempted to say. She needs them. Yet inseparable with this is interfused an uncompromising sense of the comparative bleakness of that self: we feel the harsh force of that 'run dry', placed as it is against the dream-like vagueness of the townscape, and the suggestion of those repeated 'old(s)' brings together both reassuring familiarity *and* monotony – a monotony that the poise at this point could not at all see as 'sweet'. Indeed, the pathos here seems to me to be directed not, as we might expect, at her as the virtuous victim of others, but at that, implanted in her by others, by which she is virtuous; the very firmness with which the theory of continuity is shown to guarantee goodness as a psychological necessity, deriving from 'deep immovable roots', too use Eliot's phrase, becomes here a pressure to interpret that goodness as something else, something less unambiguously desirable.

Neither is it something always to be taken quite solemnly. For from at least one point I think we can detect something of the amusement that informs James's view of Miss Birdseye. This occurs in Amy's letters to Clennam from Italy, with their muddlement over how to tell the bad news about the Gowans:

> It will not make you uneasy on Mrs. Gowan's account, I hope – for I remember that you said you had the interest of a true friend in her – if I tell you that I wish she could have married some one better suited to her.[51]

Some hope! One might take this as feeble disingenuousness, or Dickens's own ineptness at conveying harsh news through such a timid vessel. It would be truer to Amy and to her author, however, to see it as a glimpse of the compulsive wish not to upset driving her into ridiculousness – a glimpse that is touching, edged with critical import, and also quietly comic.

I hope it is now clear what I mean by saying that through Amy Dorrit Dickens is not so much echoing the tenets of Wordsworthian psychology as entering into an exploratory dialogue with them. Closely related to this, too, is a further interest in an element in her which actually contradicts the submissiveness and backward-looking fidelity that I have so far been accepting as her defining traits, whatever the understanding and valuation of them may be. On the surface the tale of her love for Clennam and its eventual fulfillment may only seem a matter of the final just discovery of the more than half-hidden violet. In fact, as with Clennam, it is also seen to involve a liberation of the self from the perverse side of self-denial, and even, in the proposal scene, a touch of demure self-assertion:

> He might have released the light little hand after fervently kissing it again; but that, with a very gentle lingering where it was, it seemed to court being retained. He took it in both of his, and it lay softly on his breast.[52]

It is a much too exquisite gesture to be called 'a pass', but it does disclose a quiet sexuality – a womanliness – that finally triumphs over the mutually reinforcing self-doubt and reticence in which their undeclared love has been poignantly imprisoned. For her to be able to make such a gesture is an achievement, the culminating point in a struggle for self-transcendence that has been carefully traced throughout. This dimension of Amy's portrayal has gone unnoticed by critics; but she too, such is the subtlety of Dickens's conception of her, is to some extent immersed – in her own quiet way – in the dialectical conflict between growth and continuity.

This can be further illustrated by recollecting the passage I just quoted about Venice's 'unreality', and adding that it is not quite true to say that Amy is beset by no impulses opposed to those 'lasting realities' of the Marshalsea. For her Turneresque vision here of the de-realising radiance of the city, which so suggestively conveys her isolation from social life, also hints at another and more valuable kind of expansive liberation, the remoteness and impalpability of the visual scene matching the remote and vaguely indeterminate quality of the desire. In a way which deepens our reserve about the unequivocal value of her 'realness', her dream of Venice itself (as of Italy in general), is a positive unreality, beyond her, but not even dreamt of by Mrs General's world. It also associates with a whole series of scenes to do with her pensive brooding over water, looking out of her window, and the illusory play of sunlight upon prison-bars, which has been woven into the narrative since her earlier visits to the Iron Bridge.[53] These all represent a contrary movement of feeling *away* from the terms in which her character has been chiefly established, a tender shoot of fresh growth towards a fuller self. Arthur Clennam is the (at this stage) distant focus of these hopes, and one of the purposes in introducing the comic infatuation of John Chivery is to reassure us of her sexual eligibility. It is in fact in her reaction to his courtship that we are first shown a centre of feeling in her that cannot be accounted for by the purely selfless image we have been given:

> Little Dorrit's lover very soon laid down his penny on the toll-plate of the Iron Bridge, and came upon it looking for the well-known and well-beloved figure ... as he walked on towards the Middlesex side, he saw her standing still, looking at the water. She was absorbed in thought, and he wondered what she might be thinking about.... He walked on, and she did not appear to hear his steps until he was close upon her. When he said 'Miss Dorrit!' she started and fell back from him, with an expression in her face of fright and something like dislike that caused him unutterable dismay.... It was but a momentary look, inasmuch as she checked it, and said in her soft little voice, 'Oh, Mr. John! Is it you?' But she felt what it had been, as he felt what it had been; and they stood looking at one another equally confused.[54]

No wonder he is dismayed! – we are too – for this quite startling lapse from her normal self seems to come from nowhere – her father's stratagem for leading Chivery on has not yet been broached to her. In the context of her enigmatic reflections (the retreat to opaque externality of view being appropriate here) it signals a will to defend herself from the claims of others that qualifies the idea of her as someone who always gives. The well-intentioned harmlessness of Chivery's intrusion sharpens the point. And the suggestion is sustained as the pathos of her secret love gathers and she uncharacteristically seeks out the solitude of her room:

> Howbeit, for this poor place she showed an increasing love; and to sit in it alone became her favourite rest.
>
> Insomuch, that on a certain afternoon during the Pancks mysteries, when she was seated at her window, and heard Maggy's well-known step coming up the stairs, she was very much disturbed by the apprehension of being summoned away.[55]

There is, we realise, a subjectivity beyond the Little Mother persona, a role which even she can at times feel as an imposition.

Surprisingly, then, the received notion of Amy as a static character is a mistaken one: as well as the earlier-discussed complexity of authorical valuation of the overtly given personality there is the further complexity of the developing interaction between this and an impulse towards a more inclusive self. Amy is obviously no Jane Eyre, and the interaction is consequently a matter of quiet struggle, easily missed beneath her surface calm. But it does yield several very perceptive moments. Thus, in a way which echoes *Bleak House's* highly insightful handling of Esther's relationship with Jarndyce, we are invited to see how in such a situation as Amy's even the most solicitous of friends can be subtly unhelpful:

> 'If you were in prison, could I bring such comfort to you?'
> 'Yes, Little Dorrit, I am sure of it!'
> He gathered from a tremor on her lip, and a passing shadow of great agitation on her face, that her mind was with her father.[56]

Clennam is wrong, of course: she is thinking of him. Mixed with this immediate irony against his self-depreciation, though, is the subtler awareness of just how difficult Amy's situation is, even apart from his inhibitions. For his error is a very plausible one, as it interprets her in terms of the filial devotion that is a true and central fact of her being. Anyone else might have been similarly mistaken. Not only by crude stereotyping, so we see, can we obstruct emergent possibilities in others; but also, the passage discerningly suggests, the most seemingly natural and just recognitions can distort things as well.

I may seem to be straining the point, but there is confirmation for this reading in the use made of Amy's imputed likeness to a child. For here we seem to have the same awareness that is shown with Esther and her nicknames,[57] of how naming at once discloses and confines identity. In Amy's case the child-like ascription explicitly arises from her fragile physique and timid manner, though one is also tempted to associate it with the apparent absence in her of the self-assertive will to pull away from childhood dependencies. Thus, given Victorian conventions about femininity, it is only natural that Clennam should slip into calling her 'my child', initially from an affectionate recognition of her, though soon his role of chivalrous and fatherly protector comes to be a means of hiding from himself his true feelings. Amy, in turn, generally accepts the name, it being a congenial description of what she mainly is. Before long, though, she shows unease about it: 'A slight shade of distress fell upon, at his so often calling her a child'.[58] In this discomfort with the non-sexual role into which Clennam has cast her we can sense the emergent self beginning to break through.

This self, however, is as fragile as her physique: it is characteristic that her 'distress' does not articulate itself in words, being left to the sensitive Clennam to notice if not to understand. It is also vulnerable, and she is prone to disavow it under the pressure of embarrassment and anxiety, as when her subsequent letters from Italy show her actually asking Clennam to 'think of (her)' as his 'poor child': it is left to Arthur at the end to come to think of her 'not as the poor child . . . but as a woman'.[59] Her struggle towards growth is as much with herself as with others. In this her meekness is reinforced by the way in which retreat so naturally and plausibly presents itself as loyalty. We see this when, upset by her family's begging-letters to Clennam, she finally justifies her hasty departure home from him in these terms:

> But I had better go home! It was but the other day that my sister told me that I had become so used to the prison that I

had its tone and character. It must be so. I am sure it must be when I see these things. My place is there. I am better there. It is unfeeling in me to be here, when I can do the least thing there. Good-bye. I had far better stay at home![60]

The cruel irony of this is that her best feelings are engaged in it: it looks like a declaration of fidelity and is felt by her as such. In one sense it is, of course, in that it is an abiding by those 'lasting realities' in which her self is founded. Yet while these are indeed at the core of her being, they are not her complete self; the kind of simple true self/false self antithesis that her words imply is a simplification, as the possibilities represented by the Iron Bridge and Clennam that are here renounced are not unreal in the pejorative sense that her father's world is, but only in that, tender growths as they are, they have not been solidified, as it were, by custom. As with all people caught in a nostalgia for origins, however (her behaviour here has a wide bearing), she understandably cannot see that what seems to be integrity is in fact a form of self-betrayal. The same, too, goes for the homesickness with which she reacts to Italy: with her source of security gone, her psyche withdraws upon the past at the sacrifice of its tentative yearnings towards the future. Hence, whereas being called a child by Clennam had previously been a bit cramping, finally, she now welcomes it as a needful reassurance that she is still *somebody's* child. The eventual marriage is so felicitous because, by at once echoing and transforming her original situation, it equally acknowledges both the contrary realities of her being, the old and the new.

* * *

As I have already mentioned, consideration of Amy naturally involves Tattycoram, since through her we have a further pondering of the issues I have been discussing in Amy's case. Her situation is a noticeable variant upon the former's, in which all the terms that link them are deliberately altered, as in a formal experiment. Thus, while it contains the same elements of inequality, condescension and kindness, the kindness in her case would seem to be more disinterested, the inequality perhaps more justifiable, and the condescension possibly mere imagined;

though the difficulty of making such discriminations with any confidence is partly the point of the comparison. Tattycoram's nature, too, is a mirror-opposite of Amy's: her 'lustrous dark hair and eyes'[61] signal an energy and passionateness that contrast with Amy, and this connects with her opposite way of reading and reacting to her circumstances – her 'full red lips'[62] are markedly noticeable when she is being defiant. Likewise, in contrast to Amy's heroism of memory, Tatty's flight from her home is in one sense a revolt against her personal past, as Meagles shows when he appeals to her 'remembrance' in his entreaty to her to return home.[63] Related to this is a similar opposition in their attitudes to dependence. In obvious contrast to Amy's reliance on her family, part of Miss Wade's appeal to Tatty is in her appearance of complete autonomy, though her apologia unconsciously discloses how her vigilantly aggressive stance is a defence against the heightened dependence (presumably the product of her orphan background) revealed in her desperately possessive attachment to her first friend – hence her comment on her spurning the inferred condescension of one of her apparently most kind employers, that it 'made (her) feel independent'.[64] Miss Wade's self-consolatory sense of being singled out, Hamlet-like, in proud isolation, by her ability to see through the falseness of others, is another form of pseudo-independence. (It could be argued, I suppose, that the psychological understanding Dickens reveals here is masked ideology, bourgeois morality dressed up as objective understanding. I, for my part, feel that it is genuinely what it seems to be in this case; though, as Meagles' accounting to himself for Tatty's revolt shows, such psychologising is easily abused.) Explicit comparison of the two women is also invited. They are united for us by their both bearing quaint, identity-conferring names (the differing reactions to which are significant), and they are finally brought together in overt comparison at the end of the novel by Meagle's would-be edifying sermon on Duty.

All this, however, merely deepens our sense of inconclusiveness, for it is equally difficult to decide how we are finally meant to judge Tattycoram. Does she signify a persuasive challenge to Amy's overt status as moral heroine pure and simple, a dramatised proof in her restless vitality that Amy can only be so good because of some deficiency? Does she, that is, represent a revolt of Dickens the whole turbulent being against his sentimental longing to envisage an unproblematic relationship with an embittering past, to imagine someone who *can* forgive his prison? Or does her 'unfortunate temper' simply throw Amy into even more exemplary relief, as Meagles thinks it does? Dickens generally seems to be doing his best to keep this question open. Even simple bodily signs partake of ambiguity: Tatty's 'lustrous dark hair and eyes' and 'full red lips' *can* be taken to express positive vitality, as similar traits do in Sissy Jupe; but they are also close enough to conventional Victorian insignia of the 'dark lady', as seen in their pure form in Miss Wade, to have an air of duplicity about them.

It is not surprising, therefore, that critics have gauged the novel's sympathies on this score so differently, either veering selectively towards extremes – Stanley Tick, for instance, has recently declared Meagles's conduct to be 'without exception exemplary' – or hovering rather vaguely in the middle. Kathleen Woodward, too, who helpfully recognises the thematic importance of the novel's ambivalence towards passion, can nevertheless lapse into such a simplification as 'Miss Wade's analysis of (Meagles's) oppressive paternalism rings true'[65] (another comment in which we can see current radical ideology at once guiding and distorting perception). Some indication of the thoroughness of the novel's double stance towards its chief rebel is needed, therefore, to complete the account of the dialogue with Wordsworth conducted via the novel's ostensible Wordsworthian saint.

To start with, what is the motive of Tattycoram's revolt? Inequality, surely? This would seem to be the point of our being introduced to her at Marseilles, the Revolutionary connotations of which are enforced by Meagles's amiable but obtuse views about the French and about forgiving one's prison. Tattycoram confronts Meagles with a form of 'allonging and marshonging', as it were, within his own family circle. Certainly our first sighting of her suggests someone rattling the bars of a domestic prison, and the political associations are later sustained by Meagles's comments on her flight:

'Left your house?'
'Never to come back,' said Mr. Meagles, shaking his head. 'You don't know that girl's passionate and proud character. A

team of horses couldn't draw her back now; the bolts and bars of the old Bastille couldn't keep her.'[66]

Ideological overtones also mark her relations with Miss Wade, who at the outset is given some of the traits of a revolutionary intellectual. In her opening skirmish with Meagles she identifies herself with the Bastille escapees:

'If I had been shut up in any place to pine and suffer, I should always hate that place and wish to burn it down, or raze it to the ground'.[67]

and her rage soon finds intellectual expression in grand historicist prophecy:

'Your pretty daughter,' she said, 'starts to think of such things. Yet,' looking full upon her, 'you may be sure that there are men and women already on their road, who have their business to do with *you*, and who will do it. Of a certainly they will do it. They may be coming hundreds, thousands of miles over the sea there; they may be close at hand now; they may be coming, for anything you know or anything you can do to prevent it, from the vilest sweepings of this very town.'[68]

This is a slightly amended form of the same notion Dickens himself uses later when he exclaims, 'look to the rats young and old, all ye Barnacles, for before God they are eating away our foundations, and will bring the roofs on our heads!', the difference being that whereas his outcry is prophylactic – it is 'our' foundations that are being eaten away), Miss Wade has a gloating joy in invoking those 'vilest sweepings', and derives an added *frisson* from her conviction of historical determinism ('for anything . . . you can do to prevent it'); this last touch especially being a telling *aperçu* into the psychology of the 'Jacobinical' mind. Naturally enough, then, it is the egalitarian nature of Tatty's resentment that Miss Wade plays upon so skilfully in their opening encounter:

'You must have patience.'
'I *won't* have patience!'

'If they take much care of themselves, and little or none of you, you must not mind it.'
'I *will* mind it.'
'Hush! Be more prudent. You forget your dependent position.'[69]

The allusion to status is the final goad in this clockwork pattern of stimulus and response. Tatty is a nicely observed cameo in the troubled relations between feeling and language, her initial state stemming from the clash of her impulse to rebel and her internalisation of Meagles's dismissal of this as 'temper'.[70] Miss Wade's first role towards her is thus that of the liberating intellectual, performing an act of consciousness-raising by providing the repressed feelings with a legitimating analysis.

Yet there is another explanation of Tatty's conduct than this strictly political one. Meagles persistently explains her to himself in terms of the unhappy temper produced by her orphan background, and this – conveniently for him – dissolves the political question of the inequities of her situation with his family into something which can be indulgently allowed for without cost to his self-esteem. This looks like an intelligent stroke on Dickens's part: the classic self-protective manoeuvre interestingly enhances our sense of Meagles's complacency, and endowing Tatty in fact with a deprived early life makes the needed anti-simplistic point that even the Meagleses need seductive plausibilities to hang their rationalisations upon. Nevertheless, it remains true that we are given no objective evidence that Meagles's account *is* the wrong one – self-interested explanations may be suspect but they are not necessarily false. His report of Tatty's departing accusation, for instance, allows one to infer egalitarian righteousness *or* neurotic jealousy as governing motives, according to one's own ideological fancy:

> ... she was determined to go away. She was younger than her young mistress, and would she remain to see *her* always held up as the only creature who was young and interesting, and to be cherished and loved? No. She wouldn't, she wouldn't, she wouldn't! What did we think she, Tattycoram, might have been if she had been caressed and cared for in her childhood, like her young mistress? As good as her? Ah! Perhaps fifty times as good.[71]

It is only realistic to realise that motives are always mixed; but to leave the question quite so wide open seems to me to be more a matter of hedging bets. To firmly credit Tatty at her revolutionary face-value would have presented a clear choice between either endorsing her at the expense of Amy's status in our eyes, or clearly rejecting the egalitarian values she ostensibly stands for, at least when they conflict with the loyalties of memory and dependence. In leaving open the possibility that her revolt may be unjustified because determined by ulterior motives, Dickens would seem to be side-stepping this decision, which in fact is a further way of maintaining his irresolution about Amy. The question of Dickens's relationship with his readers is also pertinent here, and one thinks again of Mrs Leavis's intriguing hypothesis of a double-text, in which disconcerting suggestions are diplomatically concealed within a bland surface designed for the many Meagleses amongst his readers. In this instance, though, one would need to think of public policy and private vacilations as being both at work together, as the poker-faced presentation provides no authoritative clues for the sophisticated to feel that their deeper reading is indeed the correct one. There is no telling which is the true, and which the false trail.

Uncertainty about the motives behind Tatty's resentment also creates difficulties in assessing Meagles's behaviour towards her. We are certainly not provided with that much objective evidence with which to arbitrate between her grievances against the family and Meagles own bewildered defence – and this is significant. The 'playful' name itself is made the focal index of the failure to take her seriously as a person, together with his recounting having adopted one of 'the little children to be a little maid to Pet',[72] where 'little' may refer simply to her size and age at the time or *perhaps* reveal a generally constrictive attitude. If we are partial to taking Tatty's revolt ideologically we will not need more than these few hints, which we can see as the inevitable product of the master-servant situation, and quite compatible with the Meagles's well-intentioned niceness: we can sympathise with her irritation at her employer-guardians paying so much more attention to Pet than to herself, but given the hierarchic relation one could hardly expect that they would have done otherwise. In fact, this niceness will seem an effective way of making the radical point that it is inequality itself that breeds strain in spirited subordinates, and not the humanity or otherwise of the particular superior involved. Even the odd glimpse of Pet's short temper towards her that we are shown is explained as no more than a young girl in her position is entitled to.[73] (Pet is sentimentalised after the opening chapters, however, into someone too like Arthur Clennam's love-struck idea of her: one cannot see the pampered daughter in the Patient Griselda wife, and her own attraction to Gowan is wilfully exempted from any taint of the family snobbery.[74]) On the other hand, if we subscribe to the deprived-background view the preponderance of niceness in the Meagles mixture will confirm our belief that Tatty's dissatisfaction stems from circumstances purely external to her present situation.

What, then, of Tatty's own explanation of her revolt:

> 'Oh! I have been so wretched,' cried Tattycoram, weeping much more, 'always so unhappy, and so repentant! I was afraid of her from the first time I saw her. I knew she had got a power over me through understanding what was bad in me so well. It was a madness in me, and she could raise it whenever she liked. I used to think, when I got into that state, that people were all against me because of my first beginning; and the kinder they were to me, the worse fault I found in them. I made it out that they triumphed above me, and that they wanted to make me envy them, when I know – when I even knew then – that they never thought of such a thing.'[75]

The perceptiveness at work here first claims our attention. The attribution of a conscious malice has been sheer paranoia, of course – whatever the Meagles's failings we are never shown anything to vindicate this. But Dickens is acute to show Tatty thinking in this way: the angry mind, we realise, just does fantasise a malign intentionality in order to validate its feelings. Earlier on, too, the point has been developed with some nice touches when Meagles first tries to persuade Tatty to leave Miss Wade. Miss Wade counters his appeal by a trenchant restatement of the paranoid case against him, and concludes by sarcastically inviting Tatty to 'have (her) droll name again, playfully pointing (her) out and setting (her) apart.'[76] In protesting his innocence Meagles insists on the old name, however, 'conscious that [he] meant nothing but kindness' by it, and 'conscious that

[she] know(s) it'. Knowing him we agree, but we also sense his obtuseness surfacing again in his naive assumption that his good intentions are equally visible to Tatty, who in her present state is more susceptible to Miss Wade's undeniably intelligent and plausible interpretation of his motives. An intelligent point is being made here about how hard it is to accurately infer the inner feelings of others – Meagles's obliviousness of the difficulty is a nice way of developing our sense of him. Similarly, Miss Wade's much more powerful and incisive mind is barred from seeing the truth by her resentment and, paradoxically, her pride in being incisive: 'I have the misfortune of not being a fool', her apologia begins. We can contrast this with Amy's blank innocence about the inner meaning of many ostensibly benevolent actions.

Nevertheless, here too the text would seem to be cunningly tailored to fit alternative viewpoints. For the phrasing of Tatty's account leaves unresolved whether her paranoia was a *cause* of her anger or a *consequence* of it. The former suits the pro-bourgeois case: Tatty, so one might argue, is driven by the embittering legacy of her early years to blind herself to the Meagleses' goodness, as we can see her doing here. The shift of emphasis once she does leave them, from a seeming resentment of her inequality as such to obviously deluded paranoia, would seem to confirm that her discontent has solely neurotic origins. Yet one could also equally reason that Dickens is recognising that the articulation of hitherto repressed feelings and perceptions is liable to distort as well as to clarify. Having correctly realised the condescending implications of her name, for instance (with, we suspect, Miss Wade's help), it is not surprising that she then takes the slight to be intentional. It is perhaps only true to the confused mixture of truth and falsehood that besets wrathful diagnosis, that the anger caused by her inequitable situation is then displaced *consequently* into the paranoid image of the Meagleses as tormentors, the latter being caused by the former, and not, as the other view would have it, itself its real cause.

These irresolutions all have their bearing, too, upon what we make of the finale of Tatty's story: her repentance. On first inspection the plot-resolving momentum of her return with Mrs Clennam's box seems to carry a matching suggestion of a resolution of her inner tensions. Certainly there is an air of finality about her 'glow and rapture' here. Her contrition embraces

Meagles's definition of her discontent as not a response to her situation but a 'badness' and 'madness'. Now if one is already thinking of this as the true reading of her case, her following admission that she has been deluded about her guardians' malice would then seem to signify a happy ending: cured of her paranoia, in this view the sole objective validation of her resentment, which she now knows clearly for what it is, she is now in a position to commit herself confidently to a future of firmly repressing whatever rebellious tendencies have not yet been excorcised ('I'll count five-and-twenty hundred, five-and-twenty thousand!'[77]). On the other hand, if we have hitherto seen her story as pointing a radical moral, her volte-face need not necessarily be seen as a betrayal of its vision. For if one takes the 'mad and bad' view to be an evasion, her confidence here cannot but strike one as being itself an illusion, her 'glow and rapture' merely one form of an energy that is still liable to revert back into anger. For while the Meagleses' imputed malice has come in the course of her rebellion to seem the main provocation, her enlightenment on this score still leaves her with the real problems of her basically unchanged circumstances. Whether the ensuing tension they give rise to can be satisfactorily dealt with by her newly mystified faith in Meagles's theory about it, plus willpower, would seem doubtful. Will her next break-out, one wonders, be less self-destructive than the last?

I said before that both public policy and a personal wish to avoid commitment appear to be behind all this contrived ambiguity. On one last point, however, Meagles' all-too-predictable sermon on Duty, with Amy Dorrit as exemplum, the novel *is* of one mind. Here one can agree with Mrs Leavis that behind what superficially looks an easily digestible moral, given from a (perhaps admirable) tact as a decoy for the conventionally bourgeois reader, is a disquieting warning that the complexities of Tatty's struggle have been to this moralist very much like those foreign languages of which he is notoriously incapable of learning a word. His sermon, in fact, is the last flourish of that moral stupidity with which his good-heartedness is so compatible; even the enthusiastic amens with which the converted Tatty punctuates his eulogy to Amy cease when he enjoins her to follow in her path. It is as if even in her present state she senses something inappropriate in being asked to emulate someone so unlike herself, someone, in fact, for whose special kind of moral life the word Duty, with its implications of self-discipline, is hardly applicable. Furthermore, the appeal to Duty itself may well seem to be tellingly placed by the whole burden of Arthur Clennam's story, which is that it is an ambiguous virtue, insufficient by itself as a basis of morality, and capable of damaging as well as enhancing life. The persistent suggestion of how it has crushed Clennam is surely meant to make us wonder about its relevance as a panacea for Tattycoram.

* * *

In this essay I have been attempting to explain a number of perplexingly unresolved things at the heart of *Little Dorrit* in terms of Dickens's wrestling with a Wordsworthian doctrine that we can see to be in some ways highly relevant and in others oppressively alien to his own sense of life. I want to conclude with a note about one character, Clennam, in the conception of whom we can see the understanding of Wordsworth to have been more straightforwardly a matter of influence rather than dialogue.

The main reason for doing this now is that Wordsworth seems to me to have been a creative presence behind the most insightful elements of the portrait, those pertaining to the conditions of psychic health in childhood:

'And now, Mr. Clennam, perhaps I may ask you whether you have yet come to a decision where to go next?'
'Indeed, no. I am such a waif and stray everywhere, that I am liable to be drifted where any current may set.'
'It's extraordinary to me – if you'll excuse my freedom in saying so – that you don't go straight to London,' said Mr. Meagles, in the tone of a confidential adviser.
'Perhaps I shall.'
'Ay! But I mean with a will.'
'I have no will. That is to say,' – he coloured a little, – 'next to none that I can put in action now. Trained by main force; broken, not bent; heavily ironed with an object on which I was never consulted and which was never mine; shipped away to the other end of the world before I was of age, and exiled there until my father's death there, a year ago; always grinding in a mill I always hated; what is to be expected from *me* in middle

life? Will, purpose, hope? All those lights were extinguished before I could sound the words.'
'Light 'em up again!' said Mr. Meagles.
'Ah! Easily said. I am the son, Mr. Meagles, of a hard father and mother. I am the only child of parents who weighed, measured, and priced everything; for whom what could not be weighed, measured, and priced, had no existence. Strict people as the phrase is, professors of a stern religion, their very religion was a gloomy sacrifice of tastes and sympathies that were never their own, offered up as a part of a bargain for the security of their possessions. Austere faces inexorable discipline, penance in this world and terror in the next – nothing graceful or gentle anywhere – this was my childhood, if I may so misuse the word as to apply it to such a beginning of life.'[78]

In a general way this well-known passage is but another example where Dickens's broadly Romantic premises about the life of the affections yield him a telling vantage-point from which to diagnose the 'tenderness taboo' at the heart of the severer manifestations of Nonconformity, and its business and work ethic. His reading of *The Prelude*, however (see Chapter One, n. 28), may well have helped him articulate his understanding of the consequences of such a childhood. Clennam's childhood has been the complete negation of the psychological idea delineated in that 'infant Babe' passage I have been adverting to: he is, *par excellence*, an 'outcast... bewildered and depressed'. The absence of affectionate bonds between himself and his parents, and their discouragement in him of anything like the sense of beauty and instinctive empathy that the Wordsworth passage sees to be derived from such bonds, is shown to have resulted, as Wordsworth would have expected, in a feeling of alienation from life as such, of not being at home in the world: 'I am such a waif and stray everywhere', as Clennam puts it. This point is sharpened by our knowledge that he is anything but a drifter through moral lassitude, unlike the 'civilised gypsies'[79] of the Gowan and Barnacle sets. An earnest and conscientious man, his alienation springs from a depth beyond the control of the moral will: the 'void' in his heart leaves him without the instinctive 'filial bond' to life in which a vital moral feeling, in the Wordsworthian sense, must necessarily be rooted. Consequently, though a good man, dutifully grinding in deference to the 'respect' for his mother that has been in her upbringing the alternative to love, he is without 'will, purpose, hope', the emphatic life of the Wordsworthian norm. And contrary to received critical opinion, the mystery plot in which he and his mother figure is not extraneous, but works to sustain this initial analysis: Clennam experiences his return home as a return to childhood,[80] and his vain attempt to glean information from his mother to answer to his intuition of some misdeed in the family past dramatises their original lack of communication:

> To sit speechless himself in the midst of rigid silence, glancing in dread from the one averted face to the other, had been the peacefullest occupation of his childhood.[81]
>
> 'This concerns us all.'
> 'Us all! Who are us all?'
> 'Yourself, myself, my dead father.'
> She shook her hands from the desk; folded them in her lap; and sat looking towards the fire, with the impenetrability of an old Egyptian sculpture.[82]

Clennam's psychology is not understood completely in Wordsworthian terms: there are also several windy outbursts of Carlylean moral gusto, used to explain why, despite deterministic expectations, he has still remained 'a dreamer, after all.'[83] His eventual union with Amy, though, parallels Wordsworth's own recovery from alienation in the later books of *The Prelude*. For just as he is, as her husband and father-figure, both in keeping with the integrity of her experience and a surpassing of it, so she revives and concentrates in him all those fugitive memories that have hitherto composed a kind of half-created soul of his moral being:

> Yet Clennam, listening to the voice as it read to him, heard in it all that great Nature was doing, heard in it all the soothing songs she sings to man. At no Mother's knee but hers had he ever dwelt in his youth on hopeful promises, on playful fancies, on the harvests of tenderness and humility that lie hidden in the early-fostered seeds of the imagination; on the oaks of retreat from blighting winds, that have the germs of their strong roots in nursery acorns. But, in the tones of the voice

that read to him, there were memories of an old feeling of such things, and echoes of every merciful and loving whisper that had ever stolen to him in his life.[84]

Nature here is unmistakably Wordsworth's, the sanctifying medium of the self's wholeness. The Wordworthian assertion of the relatedness of nurture, the imagination, and the adult self is also central (the passage hints at unconscious but abiding memories of his first mother having had at least some influence). At one point, also, the echo is one of idiom as well as idea, as the phrase, 'the early-fostered seeds of the imagination' would seem a direct appropriation of 'Fair seed-time had my soul, and I grew up/Fostered alike by beauty and by fear' – this section contains the *hardest* evidence, as it were, of Wordsworth's presence. The passage centres, too, upon Dickens's development of the borrowed organic metaphor to give his own version of a number of Wordsworthian propositions. 'Tintern Abbey' seems indirectly present, as 'the harvest of humility and tenderness' suggests itself as shorthand for:

> . . . – feelings too
> Of unremembered pleasure: such, perhaps,
> As have no slight or trivial influence
> On that best portion of a good man's life,
> His little, nameless, unremembered acts
> Of kindness and of love.[85]

and the 'oaks of retreat from blighting winds, that have the germs of their strong roots in nursery acorns', have perhaps the same relationship to the equally typical claims in that poem that Nature:

> . . . can so inform
> The mind that is within us, so impress
> With quietness and beauty, and so feed
> With lofty thoughts, that neither evil tongues,
> Rash judgements, nor the sneers of selfish men,
> Nor greetings where no kindness is, nor all
> The dreary intercourse of daily life,
> Shall e'er prevail against us . . .[86]

– except that where Dickens uses the metaphor in a paradoxical sense, 'roots . . . in nursery acorns', he expresses Wordsworth's own epigrammatic summary of his basic premiss, 'The Child is Father of the Man', in 'My Heart Leapt Up'. Amy is shown as the agent of a Nature with which Clennam has always had a hesitant and surreptitious relationship. Now she anchors within him all those intimations of that 'gravitation' and 'filial bond' which have survived the Calvinist ethos. Dickens may in the novel as a whole be unresolved about what Amy actually *is*, but he certainly is at one with Clennam here in the wholeheartedness of his yearning for what she signifies, the serene and restoring tenderness of Wordsworth's saving Mystery, evoked not so much in her speeches as in the poetic creation of that 'healthy autumn day'[87] with which she is here associated. In its subtle fusion of autumnal dignity and quiet with spring-like freshness and animation, it is the best description in this mode that Dickens ever wrote. It is almost proof in itself that for a man, who, as Forster said of him, had 'no 'city of the mind' against outward ills, for inner consolation and shelter',[88] the appeal of such a demure embodiment of the 'oaks of retreat from blighting winds' could not but have been deep indeed, just as her oddly unproblematic relationship with her 'roots' was a fascination; albeit one which, to his credit, Dickens also displays, as I have shown a good deal of intelligence in resisting.

* * *

Consideration of the theme of personal continuity in Amy and Clennam leads inevitably into the novel's examination of the cosmopolitanism to which they are contrasted. Here, however, we find neither the open-ended ambiguity of Amy's portrait nor the unequivocal valuations of Clennam's, but rather an unsteady ambivalence. Dickens's hostility to the expatriate cosmopolitan world Amy finds on her travels has respectable sources in the Romantic anti-cosmopolitanism we find in Wordsworth. This derives logically from the self-continuity idea: the travelling cosmopolitan's sense of Nature must naturally be superficial, so *The Prelude* argues, as his relationship with it lacks that slow interfusing of self and place, begun in childhood and maintained by memory, that is Wordsworth's ideal.[89] Similarly in *Little*

Dorrit there is the useful if not arrestingly realised connection made between the dissipating pointlessness pervading the expatriate ethos, and its inhabitants lack of the kind of involvement in the world around them that could sustain real purpose and responsibility.[90] (George Eliot and Tolstoy were to make the case more interestingly with Maggie Tulliver and her feelings for her home, and the comparison between Levin and Vronsky's social relations in *Anna Karenina*.[91]) On the other hand, the presence of Blandois in the novel represents that element in Dickens that places him halfway between early Romantic attitudes and their coarsening into straight-out Philistine chauvinism of the kind that one finds, for instance, in a minor novel like Bulwer Lytton's *Lucretia* (1846), where the case against the 'intellectual All in All',[92] aided by a tendency in Wordsworth to identify this malady with France,[93] issues in a ridiculous tale of a murderess, educated in France by a hard-hearted Philosophe who has ruined her by 'plunging her mind amidst that profound corruption which belongs only to intellect cultivated in scorn of good, and in suppression of heart'.[94] Here we have the perfect fruit of that 'covert alliance between Romantic anti-rationalism and Victorian Philistine anti-intellectualism', that Philip Collins has indicated:[95] we are here already a good distance along that line that leads downwards from Wordsworth and Coleridge (and Burke), to Thomas Hughes and, worse still, Marie Corelli.[96]

More engaging is Dickens's portrait of the specifically English alternative to cosmopolitanism, Mr and Mrs Meagles. This, too, bears a discerning double judgement, compassing a fond yet measured appreciation of their bourgeois Philistinism without itself being of it. Their warm domesticity expresses the nineteenth-century middle-class ideology of Englishness, as did Wordsworth's earlier celebration of his return from exile to an 'English fire'.[97] However, this conjunction is not given the mindless endorsement we find, say, in Bulwer Lytton ('there ... hisses the welcoming tea urn ... and, best of all, there is the glad face of the sweet English wife'; *Lucretia*, p. 204),[98] but is handled with a deft poise:

> Mrs. Meagles was, like Mr. Meagles, comely and healthy, with a pleasant English face which had been looking at homely things for five-and-thirty years or more, and shone with a bright reflection of them.[99]

At first one sees only praise here in the equation of 'English' with 'homely' and 'pleasant'. But as our sense of the Meagles's develops the irony dawns that it is due to the very lack of paying proper attention to *un*-homely things that they are so obtuse. Sneaking kindness for a lord apart, their virtues and faults spring from the same source: a singularity with which they are themselves that blinds them to the differentness of others. Hence to them prisoners are basically amiable, and orphans quite capable of resisting their sense of injustice.

It is this fact that makes Meagles on tour such splendid material for comedy. The joke, of course, is that for all his gadding about he does not move an inch spiritually:

> we go trotting about the world. This is how you found us staring at the Nile, and the Pyramids, and the Sphinxes, and the Desert, and all the rest of it;[100]

'staring' and 'all the rest of it' reveal the essential incomprehension. Dickens's position of being at once of his bourgeois audience and yet beyond it, facilitates an interesting judiciousness here that can see both the strengths and limitations of such an insulated state.

Nevertheless, this poise (or, as in Tatty's case, equivocation) is not really to be found in Dickens's use of Meagles in his development of the cosmopolitanism theme in its relation to culture and taste. The Romantic critique of an objective and universal model of culture is comically present in Clennam's viewing of Meagles's magpie-like collection:

> Of articles collected on his various expeditions, there was such a vast miscellany that it was like the dwelling of an amiable Corsair. There were antiquities from Central Italy, made by the best modern houses in that department of industry; bits of mummy from Egypt (and perhaps Birmingham); model gondolas from Venice; model villages from Switzerland; morsels of tesselated pavement from Herculaneum and Pompeii, like petrified minced veal; ashes out of tombs, and lava out of Vesuvius; Spanish fans, Spezzian straw hats, Moorish slippers, Tuscan hairpins, Carrara sculpture, Trasteverini scarves, Genoese velvets and filigree, Neopolitan coral, Roman cameos, Geneva jewellery, Arab lanterns, rosaries blest all round by the

Pope himself, and an infinite variety of lumber. There were views, like and unlike, of a multitude of places; and there was one little picture-room devoted to a few of the regular sticky old Saints, with sinews like whipcord, hair like Neptune's, wrinkles like tattoing, and such coats of varnish that every holy personage served for fly-trap, and became what is now called in the vulgar tongue a Catch-em-alive O. Of these pictorial acquisitions Mr. Meagles spoke in the usual manner. He was no judge, he said, except of what pleased himself; he had picked them up, dirt-cheap, and people *had* considered them rather fine. One man, who at any rate ought to know something of the subject, had declared that 'Sage, Reading' (a specially oily old gentleman in a blanket (with a swan's-down tippet for a beard, and a web of cracks all over him like rich pie-crust), to be a fine Guercino. As for Sebastian del Piombo there, you would judge for yourself; if it were not his late manner, the question was, Who was it? Titian, that might or might not be – perhaps he had only touched it. Daniel Doyce said perhaps he hadn't touched it, but Mr. Meagles rather declined to overhear the remark.

When he had shown all his spoils, Mr. Meagles took them into his own snug room . . .

. . .

Clennam's eyes had strayed to a natural picture on the wall, of two pretty little girls with their arms entwined. 'Yes, Clennam', said Mr. Meagles, in a lower voice. 'There they both are. It was taken some seventeen years ago. As I often say to Mother, they were babies then.'[101]

Meagles is the *nouveau riche* gulled both by the fraudulent souvenir-merchant and by Mrs General's system of culture as polite received taste. One can respect the Wordsworthian point about cultural discontinuity, the protest against a centreless eclecticism which uproots things from the life from which they come and which they express, and transplants them into a soil that lacks genuine receptiveness. Less admirable, though, is the way in which the rhetoric of the humour denies any distinction between the meaninglessness of the articles in Meagles's keeping and what they might be in themselves. Rather, the jokes present the legitimate classically inspired stylisation of Renaissance religious art ('sinews like whipcord, hair like Neptune's') as intrinsically ridiculous, an attitude which is reinforced by the contrast drawn between these and the 'natural' portrait in Victorian genre style in the later paragraph.

Yet we should still hesitate before taking this as a sign of that Philistinism with which Dickens has traditionally been charged, most recently by John Carey, as part of his case for Dickens as imaginative genius but intellectual nonentity. For roughly at the same time as he was writing *Little Dorrit*, Dickens himself attacked the prevalence of the kind of art the above passage upholds, finding in its own very conventional bourgeois realism 'a horrid respectability . . . a little, finite, systematic routine',[102] and comparing it with the 'fearlessness . . . bold . . . dashing . . . passion and action' that had marked a contemporaneous Paris exhibition (which had included a large number of works by Ingres and Delacroix). The terms of this enthusiasm for the non-English interestingly accord with Dickens's sympathy for Tattycoram, just as the ambivalence between the public and private view of English painting matches the double attitude in the novel towards Pet Meagles, one of the painted figures in the 'natural' genre portrait. Might one explain the fact that the complexity of outlook on this score does not surface within the novel itself, by suggesting that Dickens's strategy towards the Meagleses of his audience, and their taste, may have ruled it out? The over-riding aim of his satire in this part of the novel is clearly to protect this class, culturally insecure and anxious for 'civilisation', from the Mrs Generals and what they stand for, and to do this by nurturing in them a confidence in their own uninformed but genuine instinctive judgement. It seems highly possible that Dickens felt that the introduction of his own views on Art, in their greater fullness, would only have confused this purpose.

Nevertheless, *Little Dorrit* is not the sort of novel with which we should end on a note like this, for it is the habit of this work to be continually upsetting, qualifying and generally whittling away at our idea of it – its restlessness just will not let our formulations alone. Hence, just when one is settling down into a sense of Meagles as being, for better *and* worse, a late descendant in the Pickwickian line of constitutionally happy men, one's attention is caught by the following conversation that takes place amidst the stasis of the Twickenham retreat:

'Here we are, you see,' said Mr. Meagles, 'boxed-up, Mr. Clennam, within our home-limits, as if we were never going to expand – that is, travel – again. Not like Marseilles, eh? No allonging or marshonging here!'
'A different kind of beauty, indeed!' said Clennam, looking about him.[103]

... 'Ah!' returned Mr. Meagles. 'Something like a look-out, that was, wasn't it? I don't want a military government, but I shouldn't mind a little allonging and marshonging – just a dash of it – in this neighbourhood sometimes. It's Develish still.'[104]

The note of wistfulness is delicately sounded, not insisted upon more than Meagles's nature permits of. He is actually too closely bound up in his radiant social persona, too impervious to alternative suggestions of what he might be (as in his invulnerability to foreign languages and customs), to be other than what he already is. Thus restlessness in him can only register as an enigmatic undertone. Incapable of a fuller and more various being he remains a basically happy man, yet also, for the same reason, unable to satisfy what restlessness he does feel. Still, like Amy Dorrit, that other figure of *apparent* stasis, he is finally *something* of a genuine traveller after all. For all his *Biedermeier*-bourgeois spiritual rotundity, he is still not totally divorced from the revolutionary-bourgeois dynamic restlessness to which the novel as a whole, in its own circling and recircling irresolution, is such an eloquent monument.

4 *Great Expectations*: 'Working Things Through'

In an absolute sense the dialectic of modernity can never be resolved. The relative failure of hippie-style neo-communalism is simply the most recent modern proof that to realise the individual self and to submit to an allegiance beyond the self are polarities that can never be collapsed into each other. Nevertheless, given that it is an inevitable modern condition to live within contradiction and tension, there still remains the possibility of negotiating new equilibriums and new balances, both on the individual and the collective level. Even in *Little Dorrit* Amy's degree of genuine growth stands for the possibility of manoeuvre within the general impasse. It is this 'room' that is in one sense the guiding preoccupation of *Great Expectations*. This novel shares *Little Dorrit*'s dialectical engagement with the Wordsworthian psychology of self-continuity. Like *Little Dorrit*, too, it is susceptible to a simplifying reading which sees it as acquiescing to the conservative nostalgia it explores. Hence the interpretation of Amy as unqualifiedly admirable is matched by the common view of Pip's story as a moral tale about a 'snob's progress', which implies a viably pre-lapsarian hero who would have been better off living in organic harmony with Joe at the forge – whereas Dickens is actually arguing, in accord with Marx on the middle-class revolution, that Pip's 'fall' into bourgeois individualism is a necessary preliminary to further development. In contrast to the earlier work, though, *Great Expectations* foregrounds the possibility of growth within contradiction, and to a real extent therapeutically 'works through' material that *Little Dorrit* for the most part can do no more than adduce. Pip's own name, after all, invites us to see him in terms of growth rather than simply recovery, which makes it a pity that criticism has insisted upon seeing him as such a stunted plant.

* * *

Great Expectations is perhaps Dickens's most subtly concentrated work. The novels from *Dombey* to *Little Dorrit* have a thematic unity organised largely around the interrelations of characters and prominent symbols. By contrast, the dense patterning of detail, and the tautly significant structuring of the narrative as a whole, which recent criticism has thoroughly documented in Pip's story, relates this work to modernist mosaics like *Death in Venice* like nothing else in the *oeuvre*. The reason for this, I think, lies in the novel's quasi-autobiographical nature, or rather in the quality of attention Dickens was now able to bring to his personal history, ten years on from *Copperfield* and having been through the most psychologically testing decade of his adult life. Consequently Pip is the most complex and contradictory of Dickens's characters, and we can see how traits and authorial perceptions that had elsewhere been dispersed into a variety of persons are now gathered up into the one self: William Dorrit's fragility; Clennam's guilt-ridden diffidence and Esther Summerson's guilty self-depreciation; something of David Copperfield's and Amy Dorrit's nostalgia and tenderness; and, co-existent with this, a strong if muffled vein of that energetic force of will that the earlier Dickens had typically displaced into a demonic Quilp, a coldly-powerful Dombey, or a rebellious Tattycoram. Only in Pip does Dickens face up to, as co-existent elements of the one fictional character, the crucial contradictions of his own being.

And being so much a man of his own age this consequently entails a reflection of crucial historical and social contradictions; like Charlotte Brontë with Jane Eyre or George Eliot with Maggie Tulliver, he had only to look into his own divided heart to find, deeply inscribed in his own ambiguous impulses and allegiances, the tensions of the age locked in dialectical play. The restless authorial equivocation of *Little Dorrit* is now the restlessness of Pip the character, and the state in both cases is the unease of Berman's 'experience of modernity'.[1] With Pip, though, the objectification of the authorial condition into the character enables *conscious* recognition of the problematically unresolved identity that pertains to such an experience:

'I was a blacksmith's boy but yesterday; I am – what shall I say I am – today?'

'Say, a good fellow, if you want a phrase,' returned Herbert, smiling, and clapping his hand on the back of mine, 'a good fellow, with impetuosity and hesitation, boldness and diffidence, action and dreaming, curiously mixed in him.'[2]

Herbert's typically prompt tact masks what his ensuing characterisation implies, which is that in Pip's socially mobile limbo traditionally definite identities have melted into airy uncertainty. It is a condition that is both Pip's and arguably Dickens's, as we know him through Forster. But it can also be seen, as Geoffrey Thurley has recently argued,[3] as an increasingly representative one in a dynamic nineteenth-century capitalist world, the world of Berman's 'modernity'.

None of this is massively at odds with the general drift of recent commentaries on *Great Expectations*. Such is the novel's richness, however, that important omissions and simplifications still remain to be redressed, and this can best be done, I want to argue, in terms of the themes I have been pursuing throughout this book. Hence, for instance, A. L. French's suggestive essay, 'Beating and Cringing: *Great Expectations*',[4] whilst having much of interest to say about the novel's Wordsworth-related preoccupation with the ways in which 'the child is father of the man', is flawed by a much too one-sided stress on Pip as a submissive person. Significantly, French organises his account around the oft-cited explicit characterisation Pip gives of himself in Chapter Eight, as being 'morally timid and very sensitive',[5] rather than upon Herbert's more paradoxical view. Actually, one very interesting thing about these quotations *is* the discrepancy between them. If one adhered to the 'blind unconscious genius' school of Dickens criticism, as French tends to do, one might put this down to mere confusion, the analytic head nodding whilst the erratically vital imagination plays on. This line of thinking just will not do, though, for such a wakefully self-conscious work as this one. One should rather see the difference between the formulations as a sign of the development of Pip's self as the tale proceeds – not the moral growth conventionally recognised, though that is important and relevant – but a psychic growth towards the recovery of at least some of that force of will (Herbert's 'boldness' and 'impetuosity') that critics find consistently lacking in him.

A similar incompleteness, too, mars the readings of Robert

Garis and Julian Moynahan, two of the 'classic' modern essays on the novel.[6] These helpfully stress the *alter ego* functions of Orlick, Magwitch and (much less plausibly) Drummle, as embodiments of impulses that Pip, for good and/or bad reasons, has necessarily had to repress in himself. True though this case largely is, it nevertheless presents a too static image of Pip, as someone permanently alienated from his own more self-assertive instincts. This is so even in Peter Brook's recent excellent article,[7] which sees the story's patterning as analogous to the psychological phenomenon of the recurrent return of repressed material – Pip's underlying criminal self-identification – building to the *peripeteia* of Magwitch's literal return. This is illuminating both for our own understanding of Pip and for our appreciation of the novel's intricately interwoven design. What strikes me as misleading, however, is Brooks's related conclusion that after the collapse of his expectations we are to understand Pip as simply drifting in the normalised bourgeois calm of a 'life . . . bereft of movement and desire'.[8] Though this is true of the chastened sobriety of tone of the last chapters, the spirit of the narrative as a whole seems to me in no way the depressed and muted thing it is often taken to be. And if we assume, as I will be arguing that we can, that this tone is not just a superimposition of Dickens's voice upon Pip's character, but an important implied fact about that character, as fictively outliving the narrat*ed* years of his life *as* the narrator, the shared voice being the sign of the psychic continuum between author and character, related to the analogous facts of real and fictive biography[9] – if this is the case, then we can assume that the achievement of a more robust aliveness is, more than has yet been recognised, an important meaning suggested by the conclusion of Pip's psychological journey. Or at least a meaning that is implicitly proferred by the text, if not one unambiguously resolved upon and explicitly affirmed. It is only by realising this, I want to argue, that we can properly understand Dickens's most mature dialogue with Wordsworthian psychology, and his most mature exploration of the dialectic of the post-Romantic 'experience of modernity'.

It is appropriate that it is in the novel's humour that we can most immediately sense the narrative tone I am speaking of. It is a kind of humour that is characteristic of much of Dickens, of course, though it appears in a new light here, as its meaning and function are more clearly revealed through its association with

Pip's character. It is the humour of a vigorously self-assertive spirit, as we can see whenever Pip speaks of his arch-persecutor, the fatuous Pumblechook:

> The worst of it was that that bullying old Pumblechook, preyed upon by a devouring curiosity to be informed of all I had seen and heard, came gaping over in his chaise-cart at tea-time, to have the details divulged to him. And the mere sight of the torment, with his fishy eyes and mouth open, his sandy hair inquisitively on end, and his waistcoat heaving with windy arithmetic, made me vicious in my reticence.[10]

The comic life of this – the superb compression of 'came gaping across', the humoristic fancy of the hair, the general vivid grotesquerie – gives voice to a much more rawly vigorous feeling than, say, George Eliot's consciously humane decorum ever permits of her wit. It associates with the refrain of fantasised threats with which Pip salts his reflections, which are more suggestive of 'boldness' and 'impetuosity' than 'moral timidity':

> Anyhow, Mr. Wopsle's Roman nose so aggravated me, during the recital of my misdemeanours, that I should have liked to pull it until he howled.[11]

> That ass, Pumblechook, used often to come over of a night for the purpose of discussing my prospects with my sister; and I really do believe (to this hour with less penitence than I ought to feel), that if these hands could have taken a lynch-pin out of his chaise-cart, they would have done it.[12]

> I used to want – quite painfully – to burst into spiteful tears, fly at Pumblechook, and pummel him all over.

The slouchingly anomic Orlick, of course, can quell harridans with hammer-blows, whilst Pip, on both good and bad, humane and neurotic grounds, must seethe inwardly, consciously, as above, or unconsciously, as Moynahan has argued, in the case of women like Miss Havisham and Mrs Joe. But in either form such seething bespeaks a vigorous if frustrated fighting spirit buried not too deeply somewhere in his soul, and the especial bounce and exhilaration of the humour comes from the transforming of that tensed force of anger at the prison of fate and circumstance into a more joyfully flowing energy through the fantastical play of imagination that expresses it. If the violence of retaliation cannot be uninhibitedly acted upon, in the interests of social living, it can at least be accepted without guilt as a valid feeling, be creatively channelled into the energy-presence of the personality, and be productively sublimated into socially acceptable behaviour, important amongst this being the civilised art of making good jokes. We can strongly sense the issuance of the submerged fighting spirit of the young Pip, who is the object of the narrative, in the older Pip who is the narrator: Herbert's paradoxes about 'boldness' and 'diffidence' point to a halfway stage. To delineate, or rather fictively enact this development is an important a part of the novel's project, as is the related but distinct matter of becoming free from snobbery. In fact, to see Pip's growth purely in terms of the latter is simply to leave him nowhere, is no growth at all, but a lapsing into the kind of semi-lobotomised tranquillity that invites Brooks's talk of Freudian death-wishes and the end of plot, or the characterisation of the work as a whole as 'muted and depressed'. Which, for all the pain and neurosis it records, it simply is not.

Such a growth in Pip can also be taken, I think, as a step towards wholeness in Dickens. The energetic narrative voice of *Great Expectations* is not in essence different from that of *Little Dorrit*, or the author-narrated half of *Bleak House*. But the identifying of this voice with an objectified and favoured protagonist who is recognisably a partial self-portrait involves a new kind of legitimation of the feelings that the voice expresses, a more conscious acceptance of these as an essential part of the author's self. It is thus also an undismissible factor in whatever resolution might be imaged of the representative social tensions in which that self was enmeshed.

This may all sound more convincing if we glance back at Dickens's earlier self-portrait in *David Copperfield*. That David is in both intention and effect only partially a mirror of Dickens himself, has long been recognised: Forster explains the point very well. But it is helpful to my present argument to look at one possible explanation for the difference between protagonist and author in this case. I have in mind that leading paragraph from the autobiographical fragment that Forster was shown, and which he included in the part of the *Life* that dealt with childhood.

Great Expectations: 'Working Things Through'

It recalls the parental reactions to Dickens's returning home from the traumatising blacking-house, consequent upon a family quarrel:

> My mother set herself to accommodate the quarrel, and did so next day. She brought home a request for me to return next morning, and a high character of me, which I am very sure I deserved. My father said I should go back no more, and should go back to school. I do not write resentfully or angrily, for I know how all these things have worked together to make me what I am: but I never afterwards forgot, I never shall forget, I never can forget, that my mother was warm for my being sent back.[13]

One cannot miss the blatant contradiction here between the avowed philosophical distancing of the disturbing but totally justified resentment of his mother, and the immediate implied retraction of this in the admission of the persistent presentness of that feeling. This contradiction, I suggest, gives us the key to the gap between the earlier and the later autobiographical fictions. *Copperfield*, that is, is written out of the temporarily successful repression of Dickens's resentment: ways in which it both is and is not a full expression of Dickens's complex nature are the measure of this. By contrast, all that I have been saying about *Great Expectations* suggests at least a movement towards the abandonment of this denial.

This contrast holds for David himself, who is passively, boyishly charming, a much more diluted version of Dickens himself than Pip is. It also explains a general difference in the humour, the tone of which in *Copperfield* is closely allied to David and his emotional range. The wry comicality with which David recreates his past is shot through with tenderness, and this intimates the importance of fidelity to the personal sources of emotional power permanently invested in the memories that are now looked back on with comic distance. As with his recall of his child-love for Emily, for instance:

> What happiness (I thought) if we were married, and were going away anywhere to live among the trees and in the fields, never growing older, never growing wiser, children ever, rambling hand in hand through sunshine and among flowery meadows, laying down our heads on moss at night, in a sweet

sleep of purity and peace, and buried by the birds when we were dead!'[14]

The fine accord of lyricism and irony here strikes the novel's distinctive note, with the distancing touches delicately framing but not disturbing the serene nostalgia. We know David most truly in such a mood, which is a comic variant of Wordsworthian continuity, as mediated perhaps by Leigh Hunt's comic essays and critical writings on comedy, which Dickens was familiar with.[15] And if culpable *naïveté* as well as Romantic wonder is involved in the Daisy-like freshness with which David enacts his bonds with his past, the comic charm of the work continually beguiles us into not taking too much notice of it. The novel's argument continues that questioning, begun in *Dombey*, of the Wordsworthian assumption that the claims of self-continuity and of practical morality are compatible. But the comedy genially downplays the importance of this, in the same manner as it converts Micawber's fecklessness into a comic virtue.

By contrast with this, *Great Expectations* articulates rather than suppresses such ambivalence: it is the summation of Dickens's developing debate with himself about the contrary needs to at once acknowledge and transcend his childhood self. Critics have now come to recognise the tautness with which this novel, even more than *Copperfield*, is shaped to suggest the ways in which 'the child is father of the man'. Almost every detail attests to how things have worked together to make Pip what he is, to adopt Dickens's own words in the quotation above. And recently U. C. Knoepflmacher has written several interesting pages on the specific relation the novel has to *The Prelude*,[16] though he only barely hints at the dialectical nature of this. It is this, as a focus of both Dickens's and in a sense the age's tensions, that I want to explore now.

* * *

Probably the most obviously Wordsworthian feature of *Great Expectations* is Joe, and Pip's relationship with him. As with George Eliot in *Silas Marner*, Dickens here seems indebted to Wordsworth's 'Michael', though unlike her he partly treats the hero of pastoral simplicity with comedy, without wanting to forfeit our essential respect for him. Joe's rare combination of rude strength and 'feminine' gentleness recalls Wordsworth's shepherd, and his nursing of Pip after his breakdown echoes the unconventional part played by Michael in his own son's upbringing, when he:

> Had done him female service, not done
> For pastime and delight, as is the use
> Of fathers, but with patient mind enforced
> To acts of tenderness,
>
> (ll. 154–7)

and so 'had rocked/ His cradle, as with a woman's gentle hand'. (ll. 157–8). Similarly, one of the most effective details by which we are given Joe's quietly reassuring presence is distinctively Wordsworthian in flavour. I am thinking here of the moment when, troubled by the news of Pip's expectations but wisely reticent in showing it, Joe smokes his pipe late into the night:

Looking towards the open window, I saw light wreaths from Joe's pipe floating there, and I fancied it was like a blessing from Joe – not obtruded on me or paraded before me, but pervading the air we shared together.[17]

This little metonymic touch (which rounds off the chapter's presentation of Joe), strikes me as a whimsical variant upon the atmospheric detail near the end of the first verse-paragraph of 'Tintern Abbey': 'wreaths of smoke/Sent up, in silence, from among the trees'. This may seem far-fetched, but the effect is, I think, exactly the same (and we know of Dickens's familiarity with the poem from his more extended echoing of it elsewhere[18]). As such it poignantly gauges the depth of Pip's Wordsworthian alienation at this moment, ashamed of home and poised to betray it:

I put my light out, and crept into bed; and it was an uneasy bed, and I never slept the old sound sleep in it anymore.[19]

Joe, then, is the creator and representative of Pip's beneficent Wordsworthian past, and Pip's betrayal of him in quest of the troubled pleasures of gentility, and his subsequent return, enact a path of estrangement and restoration that stands as a qualified version of the spiritual-cum-psychological autobiography Wordsworth had traced in *The Prelude* (which poem had been in publication for a decade by the time *Great Expectations* came to be written). In contrast to Wordsworth's self-interpretation, though, Pip also has a 'bad' past to contend with: the efforts of Mrs Joe, Pumblechook, and others, which have created his guilty, insecure, 'morally timid' self. His path towards psychic health is thus necessarily more tortuous than the Wordsworthian schema provides for, for he needs at once to free himself from the hold of this negative past, whilst retaining fidelity to the positive one. The novel's argumentation is hence more complex than Wordsworth's, dialectically confronting it at every turn.

This is nowhere more apparent than in the treatment of Joe in his by now recognised double agency as both the nurturer and inhibitor of Pip's positive selfhood, the living proof both of the inevitability of Pip's break with his childhood world, and of the spiritual cost this entails. It is there, for instance, in Joe's account of his own upbringing, early in the novel. Before this his merely partial protection of Pip from his domestic persecutors has seemed to be arguably the only realistic strategy available, un-ideal though it might be. Now, however, his tale of his own childhood innocently reveals a highly problematic and unresolved personality. Significantly for our general argument, too, the appealingly Wordsworthian side of his nature is shown to contribute to this impasse. Not only has his failure to achieve a poised distance from his mother's suffering robbed him of the capacity to assert himself against his wife's domination. Also, his will has been doubly sapped – or rather dammed up – by an inability to acknowledge a clean and simple hatred for his simply brutal father:

> My father, Pip, he were given to drink, and when he were overtook with drink, he hammered away at my mother, most unmerciful. It were a'most the only hammering he did, indeed, 'xepting at myself. . . . . . . Consequence, my mother and me we ran away from my father, several times; and then my mother she'd go out to work, and she'd say, 'Joe', she'd say, 'now, please God, you shall have some schooling, child,' and she'd put me to school. But my father were that good in his hart that he couldn't abear to be without us. So, he'd come with a most tremenjous crowd and make such a row at the

doors of the houses where we was, that they used to be obligated to have no more to do with us and to give us up to him. And then he took us home and hammered us. Which, you see, Pip,' said Joe, pausing in his meditative raking of the fire, and looking at me, 'were a drawback on my learning.'

'Certainly, poor Joe!'

'Though mind you, Pip,' said Joe, with a judicial touch or two of the poker on the top bar, "rendering unto all their doo, and maintaining equal justice betwixt man and man, my father were that good in his hart, don't you see?"

I didn't see; but I didn't say so.

'Well!', Joe pursued, 'somebody must keep the pot a biling, Pip, or the pot won't bile, don't you know?'

I saw that, and said so.

'Consequence, my father didn't make objections to my going to work; so I went to work at my present calling, which were his too, if he would have followed it, and I worked tolerable hard, I assure *you*, Pip. In time I were able to keep him, and I kep him till he went off in a purple leptic fit. And it were my intentions to have had put upon his tombstone that Whatsume'er the failings on his part, Remember reader he were that good in his hart.'[20]

One might sense a touch of suppressed glee, perhaps, in that image of the elder Gargery going 'off in a purple leptic fit', which suggests a festive version of Krook's 'spontaneous combustion'. However, as Dickens enforces with comic repetition, a totally natural filial resentment in Joe is sharply blocked off by a perverse loyalty. This may seem endearing in him in the ludicrous parody it offers of Christian forbearance and sentimental ways of talking about 'the real self'; but it is also judged by the implication that it has contributed to Joe's later conjugal passivity. This particular kind of repression parallels Amy Dorrit's mystified sense of *her* father, subtler though his kind of tyranny is, of course. And it also echoes Dickens's own denial of his feelings in the passage cited above from the *Autobiographical Fragment*, just as certain details of Joe's story – his interrupted education, his being sent to work early in his life – recall the key facts of Dickens's childhood trauma. One might say of both Joe and Amy, in fact, that they are ironically placed embodiments of something that one side of Dickens yearned towards but could not be, in that he himself was (fortunately) incapable of the repressions he fictionally located in them. For better and/or worse, he was too much of a self-assertive individualist for their Tory quiescence to have more than a nostalgic appeal.

All this points towards the interesting complication of suggestion we find in Joe's relations with Pip. This is wonderfully apparent in the episode that follows soon after Joe's autobiography, to do with Pip's 'lies' about his first visit to Miss Havisham's. It is surely one of the most exhilarating moments in the novel. As Mrs Joe and Pumblechook hound Pip to disclose the mysteries of the genteel inner *sanctum*, we realise that for the first moment in his tale Pip has the chance to turn the tables. We have just heard Joe explain that Mrs Joe 'would not be over partial to my being a scholar, for fear as I might rise'.[21] Now Pip has a splendid chance to realise that Knowledge can indeed be Power, and one cannot but delightedly approve as he proceeds to seize it. Hence, moving swiftly from defensive obstinacy to an assault which ridicules his oppressors' momentary ignorance (and the more general *petit bourgeois* narrowness that we can associate with it), he gloriously indulges himself in a free flow of fantasy:

> 'Now, boy! Wha was she a doing of, when you went in today?' asked Mr. Pumblechook.
> 'She was sitting,' I answered, 'in a black velvet coach.'
> Mr Pumblechook and Mrs. Joe stared at one another – as they well might – and both repeated, 'In a black velvet coach?'
> 'Yes,' said I. 'And Miss Estella – that's her niece, I think – handed her in cake and wine at the coach-window, on a gold plate. And we all had cake and wine on gold plates. And I got up behind the coach to eat mine, because she told me to.'[22]

This best and most timely of practical jokes takes its especial appeal from the domestically political context in which it occurs: it is the first moment in Pip's early life where we can see his normally cowed spirit springing free in delighted self-assertion. Consequently, when Pip confesses the truth to Joe, Joe's condemnation is obviously to be judged as exemplifying the serious limitations of his stolid strengths, and the way in which his Wordsworthian influence is not an unmixed blessing. His blunt dictum, 'Lies is lies', does not comprehend the meaning the incident has had for Pip; which is inevitable, as it has unleashed a retaliatory aggressiveness that it is the very business of Joe's personality to keep suppressed. Pip as narrator does not himself explicitly extract this meaning from the episode, possibly because its subversion of conventional morality is of the kind that Dickens characteristically chooses not to make explicit; or – more unlikely I think – because Dickens himself is not fully conscious of where his imagination is leading him. But the implied suggestion of Joe's only partial adequacy as moral mentor would seem to be clearly there, given the joyfulness of the lie-telling. And both this and the likelihood of Dickens's awareness of what he is doing are reinforced by a scene several chapters afterwards where Joe himself is shown to relish the role of having had privileged access to Satis House, in his 'subtle and deep design'[23] of keeping his wife and her relative on tenterhooks as to the amount of money Miss Havisham has given for Pip's services.

Another reason, though, why Pip the narrator does not overtly disclaim Joe's advice is that, as Pip the child himself admits to Joe, the lies had 'come . . . somehow' of the disturbing wish to be other than 'common', disturbing in that it has catalysed a radical self-dissatisfaction about class that exacerbates the already existent tendency to think of himself as a criminal. An already low self-esteem takes a further battering when Estella causes Pip to regard his plebianness – coarse hands and non-U diction – as further proof of his inferiority. Nevertheless, the un-Wordsworthian paradox at the heart of Dickens's argument *is*, I think, that the wish for 'un-commonness' also expresses a profound need of Pip's being, so that we associate the joy of discovering a temporary distance from and power over his oppressive relations with the pleasure of briefly identifying with the exotic, his invented fantasy of life at Satis House being an idealised version of its real, more sinister exoticism. And surely it is a profundity of need that Dickens has in mind when he stresses the paralysing of any capacity for choice that Pip's first contact with Satis House has upon him, as in the image with which the relevant chapter closes:

> think for a moment of the long chain of iron or gold, of thorns or flowers, that would never have bound you, but for the formation of the first link on one memorable day.[24]

Taken in isolation this image would seem to ascribe all responsibility to the riveting power of the bonds, rather than the eagerness of the victim to be bound. Such a reading would support the conservative nostalgic position on the novel. But it would also run counter to the overall spirit of this stage of Pip's story, which strongly implies the life-seeking inevitability of Pip's individualistic break with his childhood self and surrounds, though at the same time acknowledging all that is lost by such a violation.

Similarly, it does seem to me a mistake to suppose that Pip's passion for Estella, perversely self-destructive though it is, can simply be written off as 'infatuated folly', to quote Angus Calder's comments in the Penguin edition,[25] which represents the consensus of modern opinion. Pip's love *is* radically flawed, a neurotic parody of courtly idolatry in its class-motivated self-abasement. But it is not all just a matter of an 'errant heart' straying from home-wisdom into snobbery, as he himself puts it to Biddy in a moment of contrition that is at once self-recovering and self-betraying. Rather, I think Dickens wants us to recognise an essential value somewhere at the heart of Pip's dream, his 'great expectations', that ought not to be forfeited in the cause of a too narrow notion of integrity. The book is of course strongly critical of what Pip calls his 'wretched hankerings after gentility'.[26] But neither does it want to deny his urge to dream as such. The complexity of the case is revealed in Pip's reflections upon his feelings for Estella in Chapter 29:

> We sat in the dreamy room among the old strange influences which had so wrought upon me, and I learnt that she had but just come home from France, and that she was going to London. Proud and wilful as of old, she had brought those qualities into such subjection to her beauty that it was impossible and out of nature – or I thought so – to separate them from her beauty. Truly it was impossible to dissociate her presence from all those wretched hankerings after gentility that had disturbed my boyhood – from all those ill-regulated aspirations that had first made me ashamed of home and Joe – from all those visions that had raised her face in the glowing fire, struck it out of the iron on the anvil, extracted it from the darkness of night to look in at the wooden window of the forge and flit away. In a word, it was impossible for me to separate her, in the past or in the present, from the innermost life of my life.[27]

Pip is in no position to understand the inner contradictions that emerge here, and as his thoughts swell away from moral self-reproach ('ill-regulated aspirations') to a deeper self-acknowledgement that confutes it ('the innermost life of my life'), he sounds confused. In the Romanticism of his final sentences, however, I think we can sense a deeper idealism, both in Pip *and* in his sense of Estella, than 'hankerings after gentility' quite accounts for, a yearning for beauty and pride which goes beyond that but which has sadly become entangled with it in the process of social living, and thus – by Pip as by many readers – become identified with that. It is a bourgeois, individualistic idealism, of course: the goal that Pip yearns towards is primarily one of *self*-realisation and not collective fulfillment. But the force of the distinction I am suggesting is not thereby diminished by our realising this.

What we have, in fact, is another classic instance of the sort of thing Lukàcs has demonstrated in Balzac and Stendhal. By this I mean that movement of the dialectical historical process by which heroic aspirations of a general kind become displaced into particular social forms that subvert and degrade the spirit of the original aspiration – as Julien Sorel's vaguely Napoleonic longings are displaced into the forms of a professional hypocrite and place-seeker in an anti-Napoleonic regime that he loathes. With Pip, whilst there is at first no particular *name* or *ideal* he can give to the urge to become something more – that urge visible in the joyous energy of the scene I have mentioned, for example – I think we can sense a similar displacement and betrayal of something deeply valuable when, in the scene where Estella first makes Pip ashamed of calling the Knaves Jacks, Pip's longings begin to focus upon (or *cathect* with, perhaps) the specifically socially-real form of 'gentility'. Both Julien and Pip are, in all this, generic nineteenth-century heroes. Thus, when Herbert calls Pip 'romantic',[28] and Estella, with some affection, chides him as 'visionary',[29] their off-hand colloquialisms naturally suggest themselves as historical classifications.

This whole dilemma of displacement is in fact nicely summarised by implication in Pip's early whimsical aside about the seeds in Pumblechook's shop:

> Mr. Pumblechook's premises in the High-street of the market town, were of a peppercorny and farinaceous character, as the premises of a corn-chandler and seedsman should be. It

appeared to me that he must be a very happy man indeed, to have so many little drawers in his shop; and I wondered when I peeped into one or two on the lower tiers, and saw the tied-up brown paper packets inside, whether the flower-seeds and bulbs ever wanted of a fine day to break out of those jails, and bloom.[30]

If they had escaped from this horticultural Bastille, the problems besetting them would have been very much the same as those of liberated humans: that how they fared would depend on what kinds of seeds they were and where they landed. Likewise with Pip, whose name points the analogy: *his* modestly Promethean impulse to get out of the Pumblechookian jail of his life is not itself discredited by the twisted form it is made to take by where Fate conspires to have him land, and how the psychology of class determines that he shall react.

It is perhaps towards the end of the novel, however, that it becomes most clear that Dickens is both bringing to bear and finally transcending the Wordsworthian critique of Romantic expansiveness. Pip's hopes of self-fulfillment are tempered in the pain and self-knowledge enforced by the resurgence of Wordsworthian pieties: his realisation of how he is betraying Joe, and what this means as self-betrayal. But they nevertheless remain intact. Where George Eliot in *The Mill on the Floss* collapses Maggie's similar moral tensions into a nostalgic harmony in death, the expectations of a sentimentally pastoral resolution cultivated for us towards the end of Dickens's novel are pointedly frustrated by Joe's return home as Pip recovers from his Wordsworthian breakdown, and the ensuing revelation of his marriage to Biddy. Like Adam and Eve at the end of *Paradise Lost*, Pip must trudge his way on into a world of separation and loss – of adulthood. Against the regained and reviving symbiosis of his childlike dependence on Joe during fever and convalescence (that standard form of primal therapy in the Victorian novel), and the hint of a similar dependence latent in his feeling for Biddy ('If you can receive me like a forgiven child'), we have the insistence on the necessity of individuality, sustained by a new acceptance of the positive memory of the past, but living apart and pushing away from it. (One might speak of this as a synthesis of the contrasting paradigms of growth exemplified by Blake's 'Infant Sorrow' and Wordsworth's *Prelude*.) It is in this context that the generally ill-received final chapter of the novel makes sense, following up the echoed end of *Paradise Lost* at the end of Chapter 58, with Biddy and Joe's connubually linked arms barring Pip from the path of regression, with a modest and tentative image of a Paradise Regained. Here the scenic symbolism attending the reunion with the now humanised Estella, the resurgent ivy newly greening the site of the burnt-out Satis House – is a way of at least beginning to point towards a recovery of a vital essence in Pip's love, a passion for Estella's un-Biddy-like beauty and charm that is now purged of the snobbery and self-inflicted pain that has previously befouled it. To finally reward Pip's striving in this way may lack verisimilitude: the drawing on the Christian doctrine of spiritual improvement through suffering to come up with an Estella all too conveniently 'bent and broken' into this particular shape is simply sentimental, a choice of doctrinal panacea over probability. But it *is* true, I think, to the novel's abiding perception of where an essential value lies in Pip's feeling for her.

Before going further in my argument I do want to record one important qualification to the distinction I have been accepting between the positively valuable drive that leads Pip to seek gentility, and the generally negative picture the novel presents of gentility itself. For, as Mrs Leavis has valuably emphasised, there is a variousness in the depiction of gentility, and Dickens does stress that the same broad ideal that can be responsible for the neuroticism of the Pip–Estella relationship or the ridiculousness of a Mrs Pocket, can also produce the genuinely delightful Herbert Pocket, whose own version of gentility represents another of the positive gains to be salvaged from the meretricious in Pip's expectations. There is value, for instance, in the way in which delicacy of feeling (which Pip shares with him) is in Herbert effectively translated into social behaviour. It is this that makes him such a suitable teacher for Pip, whom he has to induct into the ways of his new world, beginning with such basics as table manners:

> We had made some progress in the dinner, when I reminded Herbert of his promise to tell me about Miss Havisham.
> 'True,' he replied. 'I'll redeem it at once. Let me introduce the topic, Handel, by mentioning that in London it is not the

custom to put the knife in the mouth – for fear of accidents – and that while the fork is reserved for that use, it is not put further in than necessary. It is scarcely worth mentioning, only it's as well to do as other people do. Also, the spoon is not generally used over-hand, but under. This has two advantages. You get at your mouth better (which after all is the object), and you save a good deal of the attitude of opening oysters, on the part of the right elbow.'

He offered these friendly suggestions in such a lively way, that we both laughed and I scarcely blushed.[31]

Herbert's lightness of touch is endearingly comic, but also makes an important point: the essential art of his gentlemanly style is to be able to pedagogically draw attention to Pip's lack of genteel accomplishments in such a way as to avoid causing embarrassment and a sense of inferiority. Thus Pip's comment that 'we both laughed and I scarcely blushed' – the advice is given without the overall egalitarian nature of their fellowship being disturbed. It seems likely that a deliberate contrast is intended to the young Estella's deployment of her genteel manners to demean Pip: in her 'gentility' aims at and achieves the very effect which it is Herbert's skill to avoid. Here, as elsewhere in the mature novels, Dickens's considerations of the gentility ideal take place in the context of his whole personally motivated exploration of the psychology of social mobility, the specific social context in which the 'experience of modernity' has most typically occurred. The Estella–Herbert contrast here shows an interesting awareness of how gentility, variously interpreted, can in this context be either a highly destructive force or a very useful one, by working either to exacerbate or to minimise inevitable insecurities. In Estella's hands it is a weapon of privilege, a last-ditch tactic of the established genteel against newly powerful but psychologically vulnerable classes. In Herbert's it is a paradigm of the kind of action educated classes can take in acceptance of a social and cultural democracy, whilst resisting the notion that democratisation must entail a levelling-down on all sides.

Despite all this, however, to emphasise what Dickens offers as the positive content of Pip's aspirations to gentility, is only to give a very partial and in itself misleading account of his interest in affirming Pip's capacity for self-assertion. For whilst Pip's desire for the genteel expresses his natural impulse for growth, and at least partially puts it to good effect, the main outcome of his 'romantic', 'visionary' involvement with 'uncommonness' is rather to undermine the self-assertion necessary for growth than to confirm it. To use Jungian terms for a moment, one might argue that whilst Estella, in what she symbolises, is an *anima* figure for Pip, embodying the 'otherness' which is undeveloped in his present, limited self, the neurotic terms on which his relationship to her inevitably establishes itself, given their natures, prevent in him any growth through incorporation of 'otherness'. Through the novel he and she remain frozen into a rigid duality of the common and the uncommon, bound together by his love and her dependence on Miss Havisham, but with no interchange of being: the 'to-be-born' in Pip (the 'great expectations' in the fullest sense of the words) remains locked away in her as (as he sees her) the forever inaccessible object of his desire. We have, one might say, a version of the Beauty and the Beast fable in which the narrative remains fixated midway in its development.

The only way out of this impasse is for Pip to be cured of his self-demeaning tendencies, which spring from that deeply ingrained negative self-image that we have seen the novel tracing in him from its opening chapters. Therapy towards just such a cure is actually what Dickens has in mind, I think, with that culminating strand of the narrative that deals with the greatly unexpected return of Abel Magwitch, the strand which Peter Brooks has recently discussed in terms of the Freudian concept of the 'return of the repressed'. Various critics previous to Brooks have naturally commented on the Magwitch *perepeteia* as the return of something studiously forgotten about, but they have misleadingly singled out only its function as a way of pointing an essentially *moral* meaning, as demolishing Pip's (in their eyes) simply snobbish pretences. Brooks's approach is contrastingly helpful in seeing the 'return' in psychological terms, offering a picture in which the actual reappearance is also the climactic breakthrough (and point of psychic breakdown) of a whole pattern of defensive flight from and persistent returns of the haunting sense of personal criminality that lies at the heart of Pip's sense of himself – a pattern around which the narrative, as Brooks demonstrates, is very tightly structured. This emphasis is closer to Dickens's more interesting aim at this stage of his tale.

However, as I want to argue, Dickens does himself seem to equivocate between psychological and moral meanings in such a way as to muffle his therapeutic case, and to mislead Brooks, in following him, into offering as a cure something which sounds more like an admission of defeat.

One major contribution the idea of the flight-return pattern makes is to disclose quite fully the intricate weave of interrelations throughout the text. We can see the significance of the otherwise not fully explained disquiet in the various scenes where those buried memories of criminal association threaten to return upon Pip. We can appreciate the particular force, for instance, in the off-handedly whimsical analogy used to describe the strange man with the file in Chapter Ten:

> The strange man looked at nobody but me, and looked at me as if he were determined to have a shot at me at last, and bring me down.[32]

Or the 'revival for a few minutes of the terror of childhood' that besets Pip after travelling together with two convicts on the coach he takes to visit Estella.[33] Or Pip's feeling of being personally contaminated by the atmosphere of criminality in the Little Britain office.[34] All these moments are symptomatic premonitions of the psychological inevitability that is literally played out in Magwitch's actual arrival. Pip's anxiety is quite clearly recorded and understood by his adult narrating self for what it is. Even in the last-cited instance, whilst Pip as narrator simply wonders at the strangeness of how the taint of crime keeps on 'starting out like a stain that was faded but not gone . . . [pervading his] fortune and advancement',[35] the implication is quite clear that, whatever the morality involved, the past is something that Pip, or anyone for that matter, cannot run away from. The same point is elsewhere made by a beautiful stroke of parallellism by which the 'two fat sweltering one pound notes'[36] that Magwitch earlier forwards to Pip, with the reek of his unacceptability so metonymically upon them, are later repaid by the genteelly sterilised 'clean and new' pair[37] that the shocked Pip proffers back. Magwitch immediately burns them, and the little episode symbolises in miniature the necessary destruction of Pip's genteel persona in so far as it exists as a defensive apparatus against repressed feelings.

And these are only some of the examples of Dickens's artistic resourcefulness here, as elsewhere, in exploring and dramatising his personally distinctive awareness of the fragility of such a persona. There is also, for example, the masterful coda to the hilarious episode of Wopsle's Hamlet:

> Miserably I went to bed after all, and miserably thought of Estella, and miserably dreamed that my expectations were all cancelled, and that I had to give my hand in marriage to Herbert's Clara, or play Hamlet to Miss Havisham's Ghost, before twenty thousand people, without knowing twenty words of it.[38]

The logic is clear: Wopsle's pathetic failure as Hamlet, comic though it has been to Pip the detached spectator, has unconsciously catalysed a sense of a similar inadequacy in himself in his role as gentleman, which the dream declares. It is a good example of the poise with which the mature Dickens characteristically balances the claims of comic liveliness and those of his abiding themes and insights.

Now where, at this point, does the novel's argument stand in relation to Wordsworthian psychology? Like Wordsworth it is insisting that the personal past cannot be denied: the return of the repressed Magwitch, and of the repressed sense of self as a kind of Magwitch, grimly enforces the idea that the child is indeed the father of the man. Impulses to further growth, however valuable they might be, are finally of no avail if they exist in denial of this fact – or, as with Pip's gentility, come to function as the main mechanism of denial. In contrast to Wordsworth, though, the returning memories are not in any way beneficial in their present form. In Wordsworth 'the shaping power of fear' is typically presented as playing a constructive role in the nurturing of the psyche, sternly but justly tempering overweening egoism. 'Fair seed-time had my soul, and I grew up/Fostered alike by beauty and by fear':[39] the Wordsworthian psyche is obviously cast in idyllically familial terms, with severe paternal and supportive maternal principles working in harmonious alliance. In Dickens, however, family discord reigns: fear and beauty simply compete, which of course reflects the domestic politics of Pip's childhood home. Hence the legacy of fear, rooted in the original incident with Magwitch but also produced by those others responsible for Pip being the sort of person who experiences that occasion as he does, remains in Pip's psyche as something quite divorced from, and set against, the positive legacy stemming from the maternally Wordsworthian Joe. Whereas guilt is consequently depicted in Wordsworth as a creative emotion (however unpleasant an experience it is), a guarantor of the self's integrity, Dickens gives increasing prominence, from Esther Summerson in *Bleak House* onwards,[40] to the psychic damage wrought by irrational, unmotivated guilt. Though Pip's guilt at betraying Joe is obviously of the more creative kind, it is the only one of his many guilt feelings that is.

Given this, then, it is quite clear that it is by no means just snobbery and egotism that Pip needs to be cured from. In fact, given that these things are, as I have suggested, best seen as defences against his underlying problem, the 'moral discovery' interpretation, that even Mrs Leavis takes as a complete account of the novel's aims,[41] stands exposed as analogous to a therapy that destroys a patient's provisional coping mechanisms only to abandon him naked and helpless before his original traumas. One might indeed argue that this is exactly what is happening, that Dickens is too uncomfortably caught between psychological and moral modes of interpretation that are, in this case, quite incompatible. But whilst there are some signs of this being so, it is not wholly the case, I think. For the concluding sections of the novel do attempt very interestingly to imagine and dramatise a cure that does get to the roots of Pip's condition.

To understand what this is we need to go back to the original encounter with Magwitch. This is depicted as a doubly traumatic incident, both for what it is in itself, and for its crystallisation in Pip of the negative idea of himself that has been bred into him, as Dickens carefully shows in his initial social-psychological coverage of the significant influences in Pip's early life. Brought up by hand by Mrs Joe and eternally lectured as a criminal by Pumblechook, it is no wonder that he takes the complicity Magwitch enforces upon him as proof that he is 'clearly on [his] way' to the 'great[ly] convenien[t] . . . hulks'.[42]

'I had begun by asking questions, and I was now going to rob Mrs Joe.'[43] The comic pathetic alignment of these two acts obviously invites us to see the present response in the light of early conditioning. Hence, too, the poignantly comic moment ingeniously contrived at the end of Chapter Four, in which Pip instinctively assumes that the soldiers searching for Magwitch,

Great Expectations: 'Working Things Through' 145

who have called in at the forge to get their handcuffs repaired, have come to arrest him instead.[44]

And what of the 'real criminal'? Though sufficiently frightening in the comic-horror mode of the distancing narrator, he is from the start established along the lines of an inclusive image of what one might call human primality. The ravenous eating, the obsessive vengefulness, the pitiable sense of desolation so perfectly caught in that line about the 'something' that 'clicked in his throat, as if he had works in him like a clock, and was going to strike':[45] all these things compose a very credible portrait of an actual convict, but one clearly recognisable as an archetype of a universal human condition, the 'poor, bare forked animal' of the storm scenes in *Lear*. Pip himself spontaneously recognises this, in the pity that Magwitch awakes in him.

This recognition is important if we are to realise the significance of Pip's guilt and his attempted repression of it. For in construing the bond between Magwitch and himself *as* simply one of criminality – which he cannot but do, as the product of his upbringing – and thus continually striving to flee from this underlying feeling, it is inevitably his own primality, his animality (in the rich Shakespearian sense of the word), that he comes to deny. In this gentility is his natural refuge, especially since its own deprecation of the primal, as communicated initially and traumatically through Estella's comments on his coarseness, positively reinforces the alienating process. Pip grows up a split man, a brittle aspiringly genteel ego guiltily trapped within an unacknowledged, rejected animality that forever threatens to start out – like the stain in the carpet – and incriminate him.

This is perhaps nowhere better brought out than in his fight with the 'pale young gentleman' who will later turn out to be Herbert. Herbert's insistent provocation speaks to the 'coarse' instincts Pip has been trying to forget about, and after temporary mystification by the didactically proffered Rafferty's rules approach, they finally leap out:

> My heart failed when I saw him squaring at me with every demonstration of mechanical nicety, and eyeing my anatomy as if he were minutely choosing his bone. I never have been so surprised in my life, as I was when I let out the first blow, and saw him lying on his back, looking up at me with a bloody nose and with his face exceedingly fore-shortened.

But, he was on his feet directly, and after sponging himself with a great show of dexterity began squaring again. The second greatest surprise I have ever had in my life was seeing him on his back again, looking up at me out of a black eye.

His spirit inspired me with great respect. He seemed to have no strength, and he never once hit me hard, and he was always knocked down; but, he would be up again in a moment, sponging himself or drinking out of the water-bottle, with the greatest satisfaction in seconding himself according to form, and then came at me with an air and a show that made me believe he really was going to do for me at last. He got heavily bruised, for I am sorry to record that the more I hit him, the harder I hit him: but, he came up again and again and again, until at last he got a bad fall with the back of his head against the wall. Even after that crisis in our affairs, he got up and turned round and round confusedly, not knowing where I was; but finally went on his knees to his sponge and threw it up: at the same time panting out, 'That means you have won.'[46]

'The more I hit him, the harder I hit him': if we stop and consider this little clause we can see that there has indeed been a letting go, a resurgence of the primal, on Pip's part. Nevertheless, the reluctant admission is tucked away amidst the comically affectionate tribute to Herbert's gallantry and his endearingly odd attempt to be in the one moment pedagogue and practitioner of the pugilistic art. Pip the adult narrator still seems embarrassed to face up to what took place in him during the fight, and we can associate this with his ensuing report of the guilt he felt consequent upon his victory, a guilt intensified by the fact that he has reverted to the role of plebeian predator upon the very gentility to which he himself aspires. Nevertheless, the contextual facts of his innocent passivity until coerced into fighting clearly indicates the neurotic irrationality of this guilt; and we can associate the naturalness of his small-scale retaliatory violence with the equally understandable naturalness of Magwitch's violent vengefulness towards Compeyson. But this is of course the point about Pip's divided psyche at this stage of the novel: what is 'natural' in him is disowned as 'criminal' and 'coarse'.

It is therefore no mystery that Pip should react as he does upon Magwitch's return and subsequent revelation of his role as

Great Expectations: 'Working Things Through'   147

benefactor, which collapses the Romance plot of being chosen from above upon which Pip has founded his sense of himself as gentleman. Mrs Leavis is right in defending Pip against the charge of simple snobbery here: surely no Victorian gentleman in his situation could have been expected to welcome such a discovery. However, her urge to chastise the egalitarian blindness of non-English critics does seem to have led her into missing the peculiarly intense, even hysterical quality of Pip's revulsion:

> He took out of his pocket a great thick pocket-book, bursting with papers, and tossed it on the table.
> 'There's something worth spending in that there book, dear boy. It's yourn. All I've got ain't mine; it's yourn. Don't you be afeered on it. There's more where that comes from . . .'
> 'Stop!' said I, almost in a frenzy of fear and dislike.[47]

That detail about the 'bursting pocket-book' is wonderfully felicitous, not just because (like the 'fat, sweltering one-pound notes') it is vivid with Magwitch's uncompromising criminality, but also because it catches the particularly violent way in which this quality implodes upon Pip's horrified consciousness at this point. A similar intense and disturbed subjectivity characterises the whole presentation of Magwitch in the chapters immediately following his return. Dickens seems to explicitly pinpoint its feel and significance when he has Pip comment on the futility of Magwitch's attempts to use powder to disguise himself as a gentleman:

> so awful was the manner in which everything in him that it was most desirable to repress, started through that thin layer of pretence, and seemed to come blazing out at the crown of his head.[48]

We might recall, as further proof of the subjectivity involved in Pip's reaction here, that he has previously spoken of that incriminating stain as 'starting out', just as Magwitch's vulgarity here 'start(s) through'. The truth of the matter is that Magwitch is a powerful embodiment of everything that Pip has striven to repress in himself, so that Pip's hysteria when his benefactor confronts him is the last desperate attempt of his genteel ego to preserve itself against the feeling that it is itself turning to little more than a 'thin pretence' of powder under the glare of a now irrepressible animality. Again we see how, in this novel, the seemingly incidental detail can work as precise and deep-probing metaphor! Similarly suggestive, too, in its sense of Magwitch as a psychic threat, is the way in which the very details of his uncouthness that most horrify Pip are those that have to do with things that we know Pip himself to be still somewhat edgy about. Magwitch's primitive table-manners, for instance, which Pip records with fascinated horror, minutely and at length, remind us that Pip's own first lesson in gentility at Herbert's hands was in not putting one's knife in one's mouth,[49] and that he has been preoccupied by 'keeping a bashful watch upon [his] company-manners' whilst dining with the parental Pockets.[50] He too has been 'a heavy grubber' in his day, to cite Magwitch's happy phrase, and is presumably even now not a confidently exquisite one.[51] Likewise, his startled account of the strangely demotic card game Magwitch plays with himself ('a complicated kind of Patience with a ragged pack of cards of his own – a game that I never saw before or since, and in which he recorded his winnings by sticking his jack-knife into the table') reminds us that Pip's first humiliation at the hands of gentility occurred through his calling the 'knaves' 'jacks', even though now, as he has mentioned in an aside several chapters previously (another instance of the text's taut patterning) he and Estella are 'skilful' players, and play 'French games'.[52]

It is not surprising, then, that the returned Magwitch is a 'dreadful mystery', as Pip tells us, even in his horribleness. I do not think this phrase is meant to be a casual one: given Pip's revulsion it is too curiously paradoxical for that. Rather, it is perhaps a significant clue to how we can best see Magwitch; that is, as something akin to a Jungian *alter ego* in the same way that Estella is, though in an opposite psychic direction, albeit one which must be taken *before* the attraction to Estella can be fruitfully pursued.

This is, I think, what Dickens is at least groping towards in his depiction of the final stages of the Pip–Magwitch relationship. For it seems to me that only such an interpretation can really explain the movingly impressive figure which Magwitch becomes as he unfolds his story and generally makes his presence felt in chapters forty to forty-two. It is an impressiveness not in spite of but in its coarseness, in the elemental boldness with which certain primal human emotions figure themselves forth. There is the need for love and acceptance, irrepressibly demonstrated, as when his eyes fill with tears at Pip's initial rejection of him (and to which, in a beautiful stroke, Dickens has Pip respond in the chilly tones of genteel 'concern': 'How are you living? ... I hope you have done well.')[53] And there is the monomaniac determination of his rise to wealth, and the fierce pride in this achievement and in thus being able to scorn his genteel taunters in what he has done for Pip, the virility of which feeling surely redeems its vulgarity. And finally there is the impassioned resentment against the society that has forced him to become a criminal in order to survive, and his passionate wish for revenge against Compeyson, all together with a firm conviction in himself as essentially innocent – as indeed an Abel and not a Cain. All these emotions may be problematic in their unalloyed form, but set against Pip in his alienation they do present a picture of a basic psychic health that contrasts strongly with Pip's own thwarted and self-thwarting vitality. This impression is supported by the way in which certain details of Magwitch's autobiography echo, albeit with variation, against our memory of Pip's early years. His first moment of self-awareness parallels Pip's in its cold and lonely desolation,[54] for example. Similarly, his being 'took up, took up, took up'[55] recalls Pip's being 'brought up by hand'. However his childhood of pragmatic thieving for survival, unfortunate in its consequences though it has been, has about it a comparatively robust guiltlessness that contrasts in context with Pip's neurotic guilt about *his* theft. In fact what Dickens has in mind by the comparison, I feel, is not just the possibility for Pip to Christianly humanise himself in relinquishing false values and accepting fellowship with Magwitch, but also to deeply *revitalise* himself through coming to accept, in his acceptance of Magwitch in *his* essential innocence, the innocence of his *own* animality, which he has up till now repressed as criminal. Which is to effect a cure for his basic sickness, in converting the threatening confrontation with the experiential source of his negative self-image into a positive triumph by reliving that experience *as* innocent.

Such an interpretation may well sound wilfully speculative, but let me emphasise that I am merely giving an account of where, in the way he aligns Magwitch against Pip in these chapters, Dickens seems to be wanting to go. For it does seem to me to be equally true that this kind of regenerative identification just is not clearly delineated in the chapters that follow this. Pip's reactions to Magwitch largely recede into the background as the narrative turns to the logistics of the escape plan, and when any change is explicitly mentioned it is merely towards 'pity'.[56] Pip's last gestures of friendship – holding Magwitch's hand in the dock, etc.[57] – pointedly reverse his earlier flight from his initial compassion. But it is a tired and softened Magwitch that Pip opens himself up to, a suitable case for compassion, and this invites us to see Pip's actions more in terms of traditional Christian humility than of the reading I have just canvassed. Nevertheless, whilst consciously seeming to balk at the possibilities earlier so richly prepared for, there is at least one aspect of the curious interlude of the rendezvous with Orlick at the lime-kiln, which takes place at this point,[58] that does in fact seem to carry them through. For it is at this moment, bound and helpless before Orlick's murderous *ressentiment*, that he discovers in himself for the first time the capacity to guiltlessly entertain an aggressive plan of action:

> Above all things, I resolved that I would not entreat him, and that I would die making some last poor resistance to him. Softened as my thoughts of all the rest of men were in that dire extremity; humbly beseeching pardon, as I did, of Heaven; melted at heart, as I was, by the thought that I had taken no farewell, and never never now could take farewell, of those who were dear to me, or could explain myself to them, or ask for their compassion on my miserable errors; still, if I could have killed him, even in dying, I would have done it.[59]

The conventional piety of most of this can easily distract one from noticing how unusual, for Pip, that last clause is. It is indeed, as Pip puts it several pages later in describing his last-ditch attempt to free himself, the discovery of a 'force, until then unknown, that was within (him)'.[60] One could perhaps call it the Magwitch within him: it certainly looks like an incorporation by Pip of his benefactor's ability to unabashedly stand up for himself against persecutors. One could also see the contrast between past and present in this regard as being indicated by the scenic symbolism at the beginning of this chapter:

My back was turned towards the distant hulks as I walked on, and, though I could see the old lights away on the spits of sand, I saw them over my shoulder.[61]

This would not be the first time that we have seen Dickens seem to invite contradictory readings of the one situation (see, for example, my argument in my chapter on *Little Dorrit* about his related ambivalence towards Amy Dorrit and Tattycoram). To me, anyway, the reverberations in the quotations above do suggest that he is at least feeling his way beyond the conventional moral denouement to a psychic relearning, a reclaiming of the bad past as good. And if we accept this we can also take it as forming an explanatory link between past and present Pips, between the mixture of 'boldness and diffidence' who is the narrative's object, and the much more assured and robustly aggressive humorous tone of the *persona* who is the narrative's subject.

And it is pre-eminently this tone that declares a measure of freedom from trauma. For me, it is summed up in that triumphant comic gesture Dickens gives to Orlick near the end of the novel, of stuffing Pumblechook's mouth full of flowering annuals. (It reminds me of Pope's line about laughing Ceres at the conclusion of his Fourth Moral Essay.) Orlick's burglary can hardly be called a *political* act – he is a distinctly pre-political animal, or rather a potential National Front member. Yet his inspired parting touch seems to me the most perfect expression of the deeply serious yet exhilarating comic spirit of this work, and in this stands with Pancks's demolition of Christopher Casby as at least a beautiful piece of revolutionary *imagining*. It is more than Pip can achieve in any of those infuriating encounters with Pumblechook, but it does seem to embody in essence that fighting spirit we sense in Pip's voice, for all his confusions and self-divisions. It is the triumphant sign that his life has not finally been a journey towards a state 'bereft of movement and desire' (to cite Brooks again), but towards a desire liberated by a return to and positive if incomplete working through of the dominating past. In this it is at once an adherence to and partial transcendence of the imperative of Wordsworthian self-continuity, and the conservatism of that. It is a Wordsworthian return to the past in order to reclaim an un-Wordsworthian energy of self-assertion by which a release from that past's negative aspects can be achieved. The spirit we are thus left with may not be capable of successfully resolving the paradoxes of 'the experience of modernity', of reconciling nostalgia with adventure, the longing for community with the drive to individual fulfillment. Who can, after all? But it is one that we can trust to live energetically within these contradictions, beginning with a fresh approach to Estella, on healthier terms.

* * *

I want to conclude with a brief discussion of Jaggers, especially since the uncertainties we have just seen in how the Pip–Magwitch reconciliation is to be understood, do seem to be interestingly echoed in Dickens's treatment of him. One can begin with his disclosure to Pip, in Chapter Fifty-one, of the secret of Estella's background, which also entails an explanation of his role towards Molly, her mother, now Jaggers's housekeeper:

> Put the case, Pip, that passion and the terror of death had a little shaken the woman's intellects, and that when she was set at liberty, she was scared out of the ways of the world and went to him to be sheltered. Put the case that he took her in, and that he kept down the old violent nature whenever he saw an inkling of its breaking out, by asserting his power over her in the old way.[62]

This sounds benevolent enough, and indeed Jaggers's whole explanation provides very usable evidence for those, like Alan Dilnot,[63] who see him as a Law and Order hero, whose lack of feeling is just the toughness necessary to function effectively in life's battle, in which human nature is essentially criminal. Yet Molly, as a caged Medea, 'a wild beast tamed', as Wemmick puts it,[64] is so akin in outline to the violent Magwitch as to suggest that the simple repression Jaggers practices on her might not have Dickens's unqualified endorsement. Certainly the incident at Jaggers's dinner-party, where he forces Molly to show her wrists to the guests, reveals less admirable emotions at work in his control over her than his later rationale admits to. '"There's power here", said Mr Jaggers, coolly tracing out the sinews with his forefinger'[65] – his manipulation of her vulnerability and his appallingly detached air of connoisseurship here clearly instances the essential truth that is variously conveyed about him: that he is in fact *drawn* to crime by the opportunity it affords him of exerting power. As Pip continually reports, this is an egotistic habit that pervades even his private relations, right down to sacrilegiously cross-examining the wine.[66] His baffling partiality for Bentley Drummle is of the same kind, as we can see where he follows up his dinner-party 'triumph' over Molly by encouraging Drummle to show his parts and assert himself. The predictable fight at table that ensues seems deliberately provoked in order that Jaggers can give another virtuoso exhibition of his power by stepping in and 'dexterously seizing' the glass Drummle is about to throw at Pip, then announcing magisterially that the party is at an end.[67]

To a writer so committed to the festive and the genial as Dickens, such a violation of sociability is a violation of life. And in this the novel's purpose in Jaggers can be seen to partly involve an exploration of a converse possibility to the relations with life, and especially 'primality', to that which it traces through Pip. For whereas Pip is restored to fuller life through vital contact with the primal in Magwitch, as also through Joe's primal tenderness, so Jaggers's power, a power of Will in the negative sense Lawrence uses of Gerald Crich, is based upon a repressive denial of primality through obsessional mastery of it. This power may be socially useful (as Gerald Crich's is, too), but if this is to some extent presented in the novel so as to partially legitimise it, it is also there to judge the civilisation of which it is the mainstay. One could in fact see Jaggers as a further study, along the lines of Dombey, of a neurotic form of masculinity. For as with Dombey the prime index of the malady is the rupture of psychic continuity which the particular form of male 'strength' entails. Jaggers's maleness is more harshly energetic and more worldly; compare, for instance, the 'high-backed chair ... of deadly black horse-hair, with rows of brass nails round it',[68] with the similar metonymic décor surrounding Dombey.[69] But there is a basic similarity of suggestion, nevertheless, between Dombey's placing encounter with Toodles in Chapter Two of that novel, and the juxtaposition of Jaggers, in his first full-length appearance, against the Toodles-like Joe:

> 'It was understood that you wanted nothing for yourself, remember?'
> 'It were understood,' said Joe. 'And it are understood. And it ever will be similar according.'
> 'But what,' said Mr. Jaggers, swinging his purse, 'What if it was in my instructions to make you a present, as compensation?'
> 'As compensation what for?' Joe demanded.
> 'For the loss of his services.'
> 'Joe laid his hand upon my shoulder with the touch of a woman. I have often thought him since, like the steam-hammer, that can crush a man or pat an egg-shell, in his combination of strength with gentleness. 'Pip is that hearty welcome,' said Joe, 'to go free with his services, to honour and fortun', as no words can tell him. But if you think as Money can make compensation to me . . .'[70]

'With the touch of a woman'; 'his combination of strength with gentleness' – such phrases declare that a questioning of notions of the masculine and the feminine informs this novel's concerns just as it did the earlier one's. Though with a crucial difference. *Dombey*'s modification of Wordsworthian doctrine lies, as I have argued in Chapter 2, in its positing an implacable dichotomy between psychic integrity and successful social adaptation (implausibly bridged by Walter Gay, who is only half-seriously offered as a solution, anyway). By contrast, Pip's whole self finally unites a vital communion with psychic sources and a personality, seen emergent through his story and felt vividly in the narrative voice, which we can confidently believe to be equipped both for the world's work and the world's play.

Nevertheless, having made out this case about Jaggers, what do we make of the way in which Chapter Fifty-one, from which my first passage about him and Molly comes, works so thoroughly to retract the critically diagnostic account of him that has been so carefully built up? It is of course Jaggers himself who tells the tale of which the justification of his treatment of Molly is a part; but there is no immediately adjacent narrative rejoinder to expose the cover-up one feels is involved. Why this sudden volte-face? Perhaps we can associate it with Dickens's equivocation in interpreting Magwitch's reconciliation with Pip. In both cases what is revealed is a final ambivalence about the place of primal (retaliatory, self-protective) aggression in the self; in both cases, that is, a partially argued insight into its necessary role is blocked off by a muffling reinterpretation or, in Jaggers's case, a sudden championing of what has already been diagnostically disposed of. This is understandable, given Dickens himself and his socio-cultural context: it is a sign of the 'modern' bourgeois age's characteristic ambivalence about the self-assertive individualism that such aggression supports and is justified by, and the alternating allure and peril of the freedom it seeks. More particularly, too, it explains the discrepancy between the authoritarianism in Dickens's publicly expressed views on crime and punishment, which Philip Collins drew attention to some years ago in his *Dickens and Crime*, and the intelligent liberalism about these matters that for the most part informs *Great Expectations*. It also enforces again the truth that whilst Dickens in many ways has a piercing intuition of things, he does not share Blake's single-minded confidence in his radicalism and the need to express it: as my emphasis upon his dialectical *engagement* with Wordsworthian conservatism has made clear, his creative thinking takes place within the ideological contradictions of the age in a continual effort of self-disentanglement and self-clarification. Dickens is in fact unsure as to whether there is such a thing as psychic growth quite separate from moral considerations. His equivocations as to what Pip's reconciliation with Magwitch really means, or as to how we are to judge Jaggers, reveals a reluctance to consciously acknowledge a radicalism of insight towards which his imagination is drawing him. But it hardly impairs one's sense of the marvellous suggestiveness of his work.

Notes and References

PREFACE

1. Robin Gilmour, 'Memory in *David Copperfield*', *Dickensian*, LXXI (Jan. 1975) pp. 30–42.
2. Alex Zwerdling, 'Esther Summerson Rehabilitated', *PMLA*, LXXXVIII (May 1973), pp. 429–39; William F. Axton, 'The Trouble with Esther', *Modern Languages Quarterly*, XXVI (December 1965), pp. 545–57; William F. Axton, 'Esther's Nicknames: A Study in Relevance', *Dickensian*, LXII (September 1966), pp. 158–63.

1 INTRODUCTORY: DICKENS, ROMANTIC PSYCHOLOGY AND 'THE EXPERIENCE OF MODERNITY'

1. Marshall Berman, *All that is Solid Melts into Air: the Experience of Modernity* (New York: Simon and Schuster 1982).
2. See the recent account of Romanticism and its influence on the Victorian novel, in terms of similar paradoxical oppositions, in Donald D. Stone, *The Romantic Impulse in Victorian Fiction* (Cambridge and London: Harvard University Press, 1980).
3. Judith Armstrong, *The Novel of Adultery* (London: Macmillan, 1976); Tony Tanner, *Adultery in the Novel* (Baltimore and London, 1979).
4. *The Novel of Adultery*, chs 4 and 5.
5. Michael Black, *The Literature of Fidelity* (London: Chatto and Windus, 1975); ch. 8.
6. F. R. Leavis, *Anna Karenina and other Essays* (London: Chatto and Windus, 1967); ch. 1.
7. *Anna Karenin* (Penguin), p. 570.
8. Ibid., pp. 578–9.
9. Ibid., p. 320.
10. Cf.

Notes and References 157

> I love the bold, uncompromising mind,
> Whose principles are fixed, whose views defined:
> Who scouts and scorns, in canting CANDOUR'S spite,
> All *taste in morals*, innate sense of right,
> And Nature's impulse, all uncheck'd by art,
> And feelings fine, that float about the heart:
> Content, for good men's guidance, bad men's awe,
> On moral truth to rest, and gospel law.

'The New Morality', ll. 223–30 (these lines by W. Canning); in L. Rice-Oxley (ed.), *Poetry of the Anti-Jacobins* (1924) pp. 172–90 (p. 180).
11. Thomas de Quincey, *Collected Writings*, ed. D. Masson, 14 vols (Edinburgh, 1889–90); xi. 244.
12. *The Prelude*, II, 233–52.
13. 'My Heart Leaps up when I Behold', ll. 8–9.
14. 'Lines composed of a Few Miles Above Tintern Abbey', ll. 109–111.
15. Ibid., ll. 32–5.
16. Cf. the passage from which my quotation comes:

> if men laugh at the falsehoods that were imposed upon themselves during their childhood, it is because they are not good and wise enough to contemplate the Past in the Present, and so produce by a virtuous and thoughtful sensibility that continuity in self-consciousness which Nature has made the law of their animal life. [Ingratitude, sensuality, and hardness of heart, all flow from this source. Men are ungrateful to others only when they have ceased to look back on their former selves with joy and tenderness. They exist in fragments. Annihilated as to the Past, they are dead to the Future, or seek for the proofs of it everywhere, only not (where alone they can be found) in themselves. A contemporary poet has exprest and illustrated this sentiment with equal fineness of thought and tenderness of feeling.] ("My heart leaps up" is then cited)

This, and other essays from *The Friend* are reprinted in *The Complete Works of Samuel Taylor Coleridge*, ed., Barbara E. Rooke, vol. IV, (1969); from 'Ingratitude' to end of quote is note to main text.

A concern with the continuity of the self is as central to Coleridge as it is to Wordsworth (and also was to their mutual friend and disciple, Thomas de Quincey, whom I argue elsewhere in this book to have been an important mediating influence between the first generation Romantics and Dickens – see Chapter 2, Appendix A). Hence, see also Coleridge's distinction between 'genius' and 'talent':

> To carry on the feelings of childhood into the powers of manhood, to combine the child's sense of wonder and novelty with the appearances which every day for perhaps forty years has rendered familiar,
> With sun and moon and stars throughout the year,
> And man and woman –
> this is the character and privilege of genius, and one of the marks which distinguish genius from talent.

(*The Friend*, quoted from Kathleen Coburn (ed.), *Inquiring Spirit* (London: 1951) pp. 42–3.)

As critics such as Peter Coveney and William Walsh have commented, Coleridge's regard for the powers of childhood is at the heart of his concern for the creative Imagination ((Peter Coveney, *The Image of Childhood* (Penguin, 1967) pp. 84–90; William Walsh, *The Use of Imagination* (Chatto and Windus, 1959) pp. 11–14).) The unconventionality of such a notion can be seen by comparing it with the following from the 1814 review of Wordsworth's *The Excursion* by the still Augustan-oriented critic Francis Jeffrey:

> An habitual and general knowledge of the few settled and permanent maxims, which form the canon of general taste in all large and polished societies – a certain tact, which informs us at once that many things, which we still love and are moved by in secret, must necessarily be despised as childish, or derided as absurd, in all such societies, – though it will not stand in the place of genius, seems necessary to the success of its exertions.

(*Edinburgh Review* 1814); quoted from John Wain (ed.), *Contemporary Reviews of Romantic Poetry* (London, 1953) p. 74.

17. For a fine reading of 'Nutting' along these lines, see R. L. P. Jackson, *Leavis, Tragedy and the Novel*', *The Critical Review*, no. 24 (1982), pp. 94–107.
18. *The Prelude*, XIII, 24, 34.
19. Ibid., XIII, 62.
20. Ibid., XIII, 9; XII, 158.
21. George Eliot, *The Mill on the Floss* (first published 1860; OUP 1931) pp. 151–2.
22. S. L. Goldberg, 'Morality and Literature', *The Critical Review*, no. 22 (1980) pp. 3–20.
23. *The Romantic Impulse in Victorian Fiction*, ch. 6.
24. John Forster, *The Life of Charles Dickens*, ed. J. W. T. Ley (London: 1928; first published 1872–74) book 8, ch. 2, 'What Happened at this Time'.

25. Edmund Wilson, 'Dickens: the Two Scrooges' in his *The Wound and the Bow* (London: Methuen, 1960, essay first published 1940; book in 1941).
26. John Carey, *The Violent Effigy* (London: Faber, 1973).
27. Forster, book 6, ch. 7.
28. See J. H. Stonehouse, *Reprints of the Catalogues of the Libraries of Charles Dickens and W. M. Thackeray* (London: 1935) p. 119. A few years ago Philip Collins advised me that evidence had come to light showing that Dickens had bought a copy of *The Prelude* upon its publication. As far as I know this has not yet been published.
29. 'William Wordsworth (25 May 1850) pp. 210–13. The article has been attributed to William Weir – see Ann Lohrli, *Household Words* (1973) p. 455.
30. *The Household Narrative* (July 1850) p. 167. The *Narrative* was a supplement to *Household Words*. *The Prelude* was also reviewed in *The Examiner*, which was under Forster's editorship at the time (see H. Lindenberger, 'The Reception of *The Prelude*', *Bulletin of the New York Public Library*, LXI (1960) pp. 196–208).
31. For a list of such allusions see the comprehensive discussion of the evidence (pre-1955) of Dickens's reading of Wordsworth, in Harry Stone, *Dickens's Reading* (unpublished PhD dissertation, University of California, Los Angeles, 1955) pp. 416–19.
32. Forster, book 5, ch. 5.
33. David Wilkie to Mrs Ricketts, 14 October 1839; quoted from A. de Suzannet, 'Dickens' Love for Wordsworth', *Dickensian*, XXIX (June 1933) pp. 197–8.
34. To Burdett-Coutts, 15 November 1848: in *Letters from Charles Dickens to Angela Burdett-Coutts* ed., Edgar Johnson (London, 1955) p. 133.
35. Philip Collins, *Dickens and Education* (London: Macmillan, 1965) pp. 194–6. In pondering the Dickens–Wordsworth connection I have been greatly helped by Professor Collins's suggestion in this work that an important role was possibly played in transmitting Wordsworth's influence to Dickens by the Romantic essayists, De Quincey, Lamb and Leigh Hunt. I pay some attention to this idea in the present book – see Chapter 2, Appendix A regarding De Quincey, and comments on Leigh Hunt in Chapter 4 – but unfortunately not as much as I would have liked to.
36. Angus Wilson, 'Dickens on Children and Childhood', in Michael Slater (ed.), *Dickens 1970* (London: 1970) pp. 195–227.
37. *Pickwick Papers*, Penguin, p. 489.
38. *Nicholas Nickleby*, New Oxford Illustrated, Dickens (1950), pp. 57–66 (p. 65).
39. *Oliver Twist*, Oxford Clarendon edition, p. 191.

40. Edgar Johnson, *Charles Dickens: his Tragedy and Triumph*, 2 vols (London, 1953; first published 1952).
41. John Carey, *The Violent Effigy* (London: Faber, 1973); Garett Stewart, *Dickens and the Trials of Imagination* (Harvard Uni. Press, 1974); S. J. Newman, *Dickens at Play* (St Martin's, 1981).
42. Forster, back 1, ch. 3.
43.   My mother groan'd. my father wept.
            Into the dangerous world I leapt:
            Helpless, naked, piping loud:
            Like a fiend hid in a cloud.

            Struggling in my father's hands,
            Striving against my swadling bands,
            Bound and weary I thought best
            To sulk against my mother's breast.
            (from *Songs of Experience*)
44. For example: Q. D. Leavis in F. R. and Q. D. Leavis, *Dickens the Novelist*, (London: Chatto & Windus, 1970); and especially Robin Gilmour, 'Memory in *David Copperfield*', *Dickensian*, LXXI (January 1975) pp. 30–42, and Michael Black, *The Literature of Fidelity*, ch. 7.
45. Forster, book 6, ch. 7.
46. See Chapter 4 of this book, note 15.

2 THE IDEAL OF VICTORIAN MANLINESS IN *DOMBEY AND SON*: RADICALISING WORDSWORTHIAN PSYCHOLOGY.

1. Dickens to Forster, 5 September 1857; quoted in Forster, book 8, ch. 2.
2. 'Politics and Sexuality in *The Princess* and *In Memoriam*', in Barker and Coombs (eds), *1848: The Sociology of Literature* (University of Essex Press, 1978).
3. John Carey, *The Violent Effigy* (1973).
4. See, for instance, William Axton, '*Dombey and Son*: from Stereotype to Archetype', *ELH*, XXXI (September 1964), pp. 301–17, for the novel's debt to Douglas Jerrold's stage comedy, *Black-Eyed Susan*.
5. Nina Auerbach, 'Dickens and Dombey: a Daughter after all', *Dickens Studies Annual*, V (1976), pp. 95–114.
6. Ibid., p. 99.
7. Wilhelm Reich, *Character Analysis*, tr. Theodore Wolfe (Vision Press, 1948).

8. Mrs Gaskell is also trying to do somewhat the same thing in *North and South*, of course, with the industrialist Thornton, though she brings a very different outlook and point-of-view to bear: Thornton's Northernness is determined not just by the facts of the social-historical situation, but also by her identification (albeit qualified in the course of the novel) with a rather idealised picture of the traditional squirearchy.
9. Speech at the dinner of the General Theatrical Fund, 14 April 1851; cited from Norman and Jeanne Mackenzie, *Dickens: A Life* (Oxford Uni. Press, 1979).
10. Legitimation of bourgeois pursuit by associating it with the imagery and *dramatis personae* of the military and naval past was, of course, a pervasive rhetorical habit of Victorian culture.
11. Forster, book 1, ch. 3.
12. Michael Cooke, *Acts of Inclusion* (Yale Uni. Press, 1979); ch. 3: 'The Feminine as Crux of Value'.
13. Thomas De Quincey, *Collected Writings*, xi, p. 294.
14. In his *The Origins of Love and Hate* (1935); reprinted in Penguin, 1960.
15. *Personality Structure and Human Interaction* (Hogarth Press, 1968) p. 175.
16. *Dickens the Novelist*, p. 14.
17. I am assuming here, in contrast to the claims of structuralist-inspired scepticism, that to identify an interpretative and evaluative schema 'behind' or 'within' a novel's presentation of things is not *necessarily* to explode the novel's pretensions to truth *per se*, but simply to alert one to the probable selectiveness of that truth.
18. 'Dealings with the Firm of Dombey and Son: Firmness versus Wetness', in John Gross and Gabriel Pearson (eds), *Dickens and the Twentieth Century* (Routledge & Kegan Paul, 1962) pp. 121–32.
19. Ibid., p. 125.
20. 'Reward, Punishment and the Conclusion of *Dombey and Son*', *Dickens Studies Annual*, VII (1978) pp. 103–28.
21. Kathleen Tillotson, *Novels of the 1840's* (Oxford University Press, 1954) pp. 165–71.
22. See, for instance, 'Metapsychological and Clinical Aspects of Regression, within the Psychoanalytical Set-Up' (1954) in his *Collected Papers* (1958), republished as *Through Paediatrics to Psychoanalysis* (1975) pp. 278–94; also Guntrip, op. cit., 'Winnicott and thereapeutic regression'.
23. Mark Roberts, *The Tradition of Romantic Morality* (Macmillan, 1973).
24. *The Idler*, LXXXII, September 1759, in *The Works of Samuel Johnson*, The Yale Edition, ii, 224–7.

25. V. Skultans, *Madness and Morals: Ideas on Insanity in the 19th Century* (Routledge & Kegan Paul, 1975).
26. *Dickens the Novelist*, p. 14.
27. *The Violent Effigy*, p. 106.
28. A. E. Dyson, 'The Case for Dombey Senior', *Novel*, II (Winter, 1969) pp. 123–34.
29. A. L. French, 'Beating and Cringing: *Great Expectations*', *Essays in Criticism*, XXIV (April 1974) pp. 147–68.
30. Although Louise Yellin has recently argued that the novel does actually reveal a bitterness towards her father at work in Florence which it will not consciously admit to (('Strategies for Survival: Florence and Edith in *Dombey and Son*', *Victorian Studies* (Spring 1979) pp. 297–319).)
31. Note the following statement by a patient of R. D. Laing's quoted in his *The Divided Self*:

    If you had actually screwed me it would have wrecked everything. It would have convinced me that you were only interested in pleasure with my animal body and that you didn't really care about the part that was a person. It would have meant that you were using me like a woman when I really wasn't one and needed a lot of help to grow into one. It would have meant you could only see my body and couldn't see the real me which was still a little girl. The real me would have been up on the ceiling watching you do things with my body. You would have seemed content to let the real me die. When you feed a girl, you make her feel that both her body and her self are wanted. ((*The Divided Self* (Penguin, 1965; first published 1959) p. 166))

    The hard-boiled idiom of this obviously suggests a world remote from Florence's, but the emotional situation is essentially the same, I feel.
32. *The Prelude*, V, 411.
33. Ibid., V, 294–425. Cf. also, of course, the Smallweeds in *Bleak House*, the Gradgrinds in *Hard Times*, etc. See also Coveney, *The Image of Childhood* (Penguin, 1967) and William Walsh, *The Use of Imagination*, (London, 1959), for Dickens parallels with other Romantic writers, such as Charles Lamb, on this score.
34. Dickens to Forster, 25 July 1846; M. House and G. Stanley (eds), *The Letters of Charles Dickens*, The Pilgrim Edition (ONP, 1965–) I, p. 771.
35. 'Essay on his Own Times'; quoted from Coburn (ed.), *Inquiring Spirit*, p. 82.
36. 'A Prophecy', *Westminster Review*, VI and XXVIII (1838); quoted

from K. J. Fielding, 'Mill and Gradgrind', *Nineteenth-Century Fiction*, XI (June 1956) pp. 148–51 (p. 150).
37. As in, for instance, '*The Chimes*', in *The Christmas Books* New Oxford Illustrates Dickens (1947–59), i, 245.
38. I myself am indebted to Philip Collins's hint that Dickens's connections to the English Romantics can perhaps be better approached through the essayists than through the poets (Philip Collins, *Dickens and Education*, p. 213). See also my ch. 1, n. 35.
39. See James T. Fields, 'Charles Dickens', in his *Yesterdays with Authors* (1899; first published 1872) p. 238.
40. *Catalogues of the Library of Charles Dickens and W. M. Thackeray* p. 27.
41. Reprinted as part of the '*Autobiographic Sketches*', *Writings*, i, 28–54.
42. See, for instance, letters to James White, 23 Sept. 1849; and to W. H. Wills, 5 Sept. 1855, in Wolte Dexter (ed.), *The Letters of Charles Dickens*, 3 vols 'The Nonesuch Dickens' ii, 173 and iii, 687. Dickens first read George Eliot's 'Scenes of Clerical Life' in *Blackwood's* in 1843 (see Forster, p. 292).
43. *Writings*, i. 28–9.
44. 'On Wordsworth's Poetry', *Tait's Magazine* (September 1845); in *Writings*, xi, 294–325.
45. Ibid., p. 294.
46. Ibid., i, 43.
47. See, for example, his reference to 'the superior manliness, generosity and self-control' of those who benefit by the disciplines of public-school life. Ibid., i, 59.
48. Ibid., xiii, 359.
49. Ibid., xiii, 348–49. Cf. also the climactic return of the past in Tom and Maggie's death by drowning at the conclusion of *The Mill on the Floss*.
50. Ibid., i, 46.
51. The specific tension between Romantic and Evangelical ideologies of childhood and child-rearing in nineteenth-century England has recently been documented by David Grylls, in his *Guardians and Angels* (London: Faber, 1978).
52. Reprinted in various forms; I have used it as it appears in *Christmas Stories*, New Oxford Illustrated; pp. 315–55.
53. Ibid., p. 337.
54. Ibid., pp. 340–41.
55. Ibid., p. 346.
56. Charles Dickens, *Miscellaneous Papers*, ed. B. W. Matz (1914) p. 569.
57. Ibid., p. 658.
58. Charles Dickens, *Pictures from Italy* (1973; first published 1846) pp. 168–76.

59. Charles Dickens, *The Uncommercial Traveller and Reprinted Pieces* (1958; *The Uncommercial Traveller* first published 1860) pp. 269–79. *Miscellaneous Papers*, pp. 566–72.
60. Dickens to Forster, 5 September 1847; Nonesuch *Letters*, ii, 52.
61. George Orwell, 'Charles Dickens', in *The Collected Essays, Journalism and Letters of George Orwell*, ed. Sonia Orwell and Ian Angus, 4 vols (1968), i, pp. 413–60 (p. 43).
62. *Miscellaneous Papers*, p. 569.
63. R. H. Hutton, 'Mr. Dickens's Moral Services to Literature', *Spectator*, XIII (17 April 1869) pp. 474–75; reprinted in Philip Collins (ed.), *Dickens: the Critical Heritage* (Routledge & Kegan Paul, 1961) pp. 489–91 (p. 490).
64. *Christmas Stories*, p. 337.

3 WORDSWORTHIAN PSYCHOLOGY AND *LITTLE DORRIT*: THE UNRESOLVED DIALOGUE

1. See Forster, book 4, ch. two.
2. ll. 34–5.
3. Walter Bagehot, *The English Constitution* (1867), esp. ch. 7.
4. Dickens to Forster, 30 September 1855; *Letters*, ii, 693.
5. Charles Dickens, *Little Dorrit* (1857; all my quotations are from the Penguin edition, 1967) pp. 269–70.
6. Ibid., p. 678.
7. Lionel Trilling, '*Little Dorrit*,' in his *The Opposing Self* (Harcourt, Brace & Johannovich, 1979; first published 1955). See also William Myers, 'The Radicalism of *Little Dorrit*,' in J. Lucas (ed.), *Literature and Politics in the Nineteenth Century* (Methuen, 1971) pp. 77–104; Marie Peel, '*Little Dorrit* – Prison or Cage', *Books and Bookmen*, XVII (September 1972) pp. 38–42; Kathleen Woodward, 'Passivity and Passion in *Little Dorrit*', *Dickensian*, LXXI (September 1975) pp. 140–48.
8. Walter Bagehot, 'Charles Dickens', in his *Literary Studies*, ed. Richard Holt Hutton, 3 vols, 1895; ii, 161.
9. *Little Dorrit*, p. 742.
10. Ibid., p. 839.
11. Lionel Trilling, *The Liberal Imagination* (Scribner, 1976; first published 1950).
12. Terence Hawkes, *Structuralism and Semiotics* (Methuen, 1977) pp. 153–6.
13. *Little Dorrit*, p. 419.
14. *The Prelude*, XII, 158–61.

15. (Composed? – published 1807); in Wordsworth's *Miscellaneous Sonnets*.
16. *Little Dorrit*, p. 895.
17. Ibid., p. 216.
18. Ibid., p. 109.
19. See, for instance, *Daniel Deronda* (Penguin, 1967; first published 1867) pp. 50–1.
20. *The Prelude*, I, 269–81.
21. *Dickens the Novelist*, p. 226.
22. *The Mill on the Floss*, book one, ch. five.
23. Percy Fitzgerald (ed.), *Life, Letters and Writings of Charles Lamb*, 6 vols, 1875; Lamb to Wordsworth, ii, 69–71; 'The Londoner', iv, 322–4.
24. Cf. *The Prelude*, II, 233–54.
25. *Little Dorrit*, p. 275.
26. Ibid., p. 703.
27. Ibid., p. 666.
28. Raymond Williams, *The English Novel from Dickens to Lawrence* (Chatto & Windus, 1970) p. 53.
29. Woodward, ibid.; P. J. M. Scott, *Reality and Comic Confidence in Charles Dickens* (Macmillan, 1979) ch. 3.
30. *Dickens the Novelist*, pp. 119–23.
31. *Little Dorrit*, p. 111.
32. Ibid., pp. 111–12.
33. Ibid., p. 122.
34. Ibid., p. 137.
35. Ibid., p. 139.
36. Ibid., p. 138.
37. Ibid., p. 139.
38. Ibid., p. 138.
39. Ibid., p. 61.
40. Ibid., p. 420.
41. Ibid., p. 558.
42. Ibid., p. 557.
43. Ibid., p. 646.
44. Ibid., p. 519.
45. Ibid., p. 527.
46. Ibid., p. 467.
47. Ibid., p. 519.
48. Ibid., p. 668.
49. D. W. Jefferson, 'The Moral Centre of *Little Dorrit*', *Essays in Criticism*, XXVI (No. 4, 1976) pp. 300–17.
50. *Little Dorrit*, p. 520.
51. Ibid., p. 521.

52. Ibid., p. 884.
53. Ibid., pp. 337–8; p. 343.
54. Ibid., p. 260.
55. Ibid., p. 338.
56. Ibid., p. 306.
57. See W. Axton, 'Esther's Nicknames: A Study in Relevance', *Dickensian*, LXII (September 1966) pp. 158–63.
58. *Little Dorrit*, p. 209.
59. Ibid., p. 829.
60. Ibid., p. 308.
61. Ibid., p. 55.
62. Ibid., p. 240.
63. Ibid., p. 378. The more articulate Arthur, in replying to Miss Wade earlier in the interview on the dumbfounded Meagles's behalf, refers to Tatty's 'passionate sense' occasionally getting 'the better of better remembrances' – p. 376.
64. Ibid., p. 728.
65. Stanley Tick, 'The Sad End of Mr. Meagles', *Dickens Studies Annual*, III (1974) pp. 87–99 (p. 88); Woodward, ibid., p. 145.
66. *Little Dorrit*, p. 369.
67. Ibid., p. 61.
68. Ibid., p. 64.
69. Ibid., p. 65.
70. Cf. ibid., p. 56 and pp. 65–7.
71. Ibid., p. 371.
72. Ibid., p. 56.
73. Ibid., p. 240.
74. Even at the outset Dickens alternates between seeing her from the viewpoint of a contrasting sympathy for Tattycoram, and a more conventional male chivalry. Compare the following:

> There was something in the manner of these words that jarred upon Pet's ear. It implied that what was to be done was necessarily evil, and it caused her to say in a whisper, "O Father!" and to shrink childishly, in her spoilt way, a little closer to him. (p. 64)

> She was round and fresh and dimpled and spoilt, and there was in Pet an air of timidity and dependence which was the best weakness in the world, and gave her the only charming crown a girl so pretty and pleasant could have been without. (pp. 54–5)

75. *Little Dorrit*, p. 880.
76. Ibid., p. 377.

77. Ibid., p. 880.
78. Ibid., pp. 58–9.
79. *Little Dorrit*, p. 359.
80. In spontaneous feeling as well as conscious reminiscent preoccupation, as the novel sensitively observes: 'The old influence of [his mother's] presence and her stern strong voice, so gathered about her son, that he felt conscious of a renewal of the timid chill and reserve of his childhood.' (p. 73) This sense of the ever-possible vertiginous collapse of the self in time further exemplifies what I have called the negative version of the Wordsworthian continuity-doctrine, as developed in William Dorrit's psychology.
81. *Little Dorrit*, p. 73.
82. Ibid., p. 87.
83. Ibid., p. 80.
84. Ibid., pp. 883–4.
85. 'Tintern Abbey', ll. pp. 30–35.
86. Ibid., ll. 125–34.
87. *Little Dorrit*, p. 883.
88. Forster, ibid., book 8, ch. 2.
89. *The Prelude*, XII, 110–30. The explicit attact on picturesque travel here spells out the implications of Wordsworth's conception of Nature elsewhere, as in the repeated celebration in *The Excursion* of retirement into the reassuring bounds of locality:

> ... Thus I breathed
> A parting tribute to a spot that seemed
> Like the fixed centre of a troubled world.
> . . .
> How vain, thought I, is it by change of place
> To seek that comfort which the mind denies;
> (*The Excursion*, V, 15–17; 21–22)

Cf. the Wordsworthian exit of Amy and Clennam: 'They went quietly down into the roaring streets, inseparable and blessed;' (p. 895)
90. *Little Dorrit*, p. 565.
91. As in the detailed comparison between Levin and Vronsky as landlords, which connects the egoism and role-playing of Vronsky's performance with his cosmopolitan modernising.
92. William Wordsworth, 'A Poet's Epitaph', l. 32.
93. See, for instance, the Wanderer's attack on Voltaire, 'the laughing Sage of France', a nation of 'most frivolous people' in *The Excursion*, IV, 996, 1009.
94. *Lucretia* (1853; first published 1846) p. 60.

95. *Dickens and Education*, p. 193.
96. For an account of this, see Peter Coveney, *The Image of Childhood* pp. 184–93.
97. 'I travelled among unknown men', l. 12.
98. For an earlier, more 'high-cultural' appropriation of feminine sweetness as a peculiarly English characteristic, see Hazlitt's 'On a Portrait of an English Lady, by Vandyke', *Plain Speaker*, in *The Complete Works of William Hazlitt*, ed. P. P. Howe, 21 vols (London and Toronto, 1930–34), XII, 280–94.
99. *Little Dorrit*, p. 54.
100. Ibid., p. 58.
101. Ibid., pp. 236–38.
102. Forster, book 7, ch. 5.
103. *Little Dorrit*, pp. 235–6.
104. Ibid., p. 236.

4 *GREAT EXPECTATIONS*: 'WORKING THINGS THROUGH'

1. *All That Is Solid Melts Into Air*; see discussion in the first chapter of this book.
2. *Great Expectations*, p. 269.
3. Geoffrey Thurley, *The Dickens Myth* (Routledge & Kegan Paul, 1976).
4. A. L. French, 'Beating and Cringing: *Great Expectations*', *Essays in Criticism*, XXIV (April 1974) pp. 147–68.
5. *Great Expectations*, p. 92.
6. Robert Garis, *The Dickens Theatre* (Oxford University Press, 1965); Julian Moynahan, 'The Hero's Guilt in *Great Expectations*', *Essays in Criticism* 10 (1960) pp. 60–79.
7. Peter Brooks, 'Repetition, Repression, and Return: *Great Expectations* and the Study of Plot', *New Literary History*, 2 (Spring 1980) pp. 503–36.
8. Ibid., p. 522.
9. See Forster, book 1, ch. two.
10. *Great Expectations*, p. 95.
11. Ibid., p. 59.
12. Ibid., p. 124.
13. Forster, p. 32.
14. *David Copperfield*, p. 202; and we do know by this stage that Emily is not quite what David takes her to be:

> "You would like to be a lady?" I said.
> Emily looked at me, and laughed and nodded 'yes'. (p. 202)

15. Hunt's critical writings, for instance, draw on the Wordsworthian-Romantic 'self-continuity' idea in formulating a theory of comedy. This contribution lies within and significantly extends the tradition of 'genial' comic theory which develops throughout the eighteenth century but reaches its apogee in Romantic critical writings. It is Hunt specifically whom Forster seems to echo in accurately declaring *Copperfield* to be 'the perfection of English mirth' (Forster, book 6, ch. 7). Indeed, Forster's preferences within the variousness of Dickens's comedy are largely governed by the outlook of this tradition, and his perceptive and seemingly blindly unresponsive moments relate to its general strengths and limitations: the patriotic equation Forster makes here between 'mirth', in the special Huntean meaning of the word he probably has in mind, and Englishness, gives a clue to where the balance between these lies. Hunt's non-critical essays generally exemplify his own comic theory, and his exercises in nostalgia look forward to the particular blend of tenderness and amusement in recalling the personal past that we find in *Copperfield*.

    Stuart Tave's *The Amiable Humorist* (University of Chicago Press, 1960) provides an excellent introduction to the rise and development of the idea of 'genial' comedy.
16. U. C. Knoepflmacher, 'Mutations of the Wordsworthian Child of Nature', in U. C. Knoepflmacher and G. B. Tennyson (eds), *Nature and the Victorian Imagination*, (Uni. of Cal. Press 1977) pp. 391–425 (422–5).
17. *Great Expectations*, p. 172.
18. See, for instance, the distinct echoes of the poems in *Hard Times*, p. 223 ('the dreams of childhood . . . so good to be remembered when outgrown, for then the least among them rises to the stature of a great Charity in the heart'); and *Little Dorrit*, pp. 883–4 ('the harvests of humility and tenderness'). Both of these read like glosses on the well-known lines about the 'feelings . . . of unremembered pleasure . . . as have no slight or trivial influence /On that best portion of a good man's life' (ll. 30–35) in 'Tintern Abbey'. Also, in the same passage of *Little Dorrit*, the reference to 'the oaks of retreat from blighting winds, that have the germs of their strong roots in nursery acorns', would seem to be a figurative variant of ll. 125–34. This would seem to be an especially important example, as it further suggests that Dickens's interest in Wordsworth was a curiosity in someone who seemed to live and write from deeply-rooted sources of psychic stability that were more and more obviously lacking in himself.
19. *Great Expectations*, p. 172.
20. Ibid., pp. 76–7.

21. Ibid., p. 79.
22. Ibid., pp. 96–7.
23. Ibid., p. 130.
24. Ibid., p. 101.
25. Ibid., p. 495.
26. Ibid., p. 257.
27. Ibid., p. 257.
28. Ibid., p. 271.
29. Ibid., p. 377.
30. Ibid., p. 83.
31. Ibid., p. 203.
32. Ibid., p. 106.
33. Ibid., p. 252.
34. Ibid., p. 284.
35. Ibid., p. 284.
36. Ibid., p. 107.
37. Ibid., p. 336.
38. Ibid., pp. 278–9.
39. *The Prelude*, I, ll. 301–2.
40. On Esther as a complex study in an irrationally guilt-ridden childhood, and the persistent legacy of this adult life, see Q. D. Leavis in F. R. and Q. D. Leavis, *Dickens the Novelist*, pp. 154–60; W. Axton, 'The Trouble with Esther', and 'Esther's Nicknames: A Study in Relevance', ibid. and Alex Zwerdling, 'Esther Summerson Rehabilitated', ibid.
41. *Dickens the Novelist*, ch. 6.
42. *Great Expectations*, p. 46.
43. Ibid., p. 46.
44. Ibid., pp. 61–62.
45. Ibid., p. 50.
46. Ibid., p. 120.
47. Ibid., p. 347.
48. Ibid., p. 353.
49. Ibid., p. 203.
50. Ibid., p. 214.
51. Ibid., p. 346.
52. Ibid., p. 325.
53. Ibid., p. 335.
54. Ibid., p. 36; p. 360.
55. Ibid., p. 361.
56. Ibid., p. 366.
57. Ibid., p. 466.
58. Ibid., ch. 53.
59. Ibid., p. 437.

60. Ibid., p. 440.
61. Ibid., p. 433.
62. Ibid., p. 425.
63. Alan Dilnot, 'The Case of Mr. Jaggers', *Essays in Criticism*, 25 (1975) pp. 437–43.
64. *Great Expectations*, p. 224.
65. Ibid., p. 237.
66. Ibid., p. 263.
67. Ibid., p. 238.
68. Ibid., p. 188.
69. *Dombey and Son*, p. 25.
70. *Great Expectations*, pp. 168–9.

Index

Armstrong, Judith, *The Novel of Adultery*, 8, 156
Arnold, Matthew, 7, 21, 59, 86
Auerbach, Nina, on *Dombey and Son*, 38–9, 160
Austen, Jane, 3, 9
Axton, William, on *Dombey and Son* and *Bleak House*, 10, 156, 160, 165, 170

Bagehot, Walter, 164; on deference in *The English Constitution*, 81, 84, 86
Black, Michael, author of *The Literature of Fidelity*, 10, 156
Blake, William, 155; 'Infant Sorrow', 31–2, 138
Balzac, Honoré, 137
Barnaby Rudge (character in *Barnaby Rudge*), 26
Berman, Marshall, author of *All that is Solid Melts into Air*, ix, 3, 5, 6, 83, 84, 156
Bleak House (novel by Charles Dickens). *Characters*: Jarndyce, 102; Krook, 133; Esther Summerson, 28, 67–8, 77, 91, 102–3, 124, 144
Brooks, Peter (on *Great Expectations*), 126, 141, 151, 168
Brontë, Charlotte, 35; and 'dialectic of modernity', 23; *Jane Eyre*, 102
Brontë, Emily, 22
Burdett-Coutts, Angela, 25

Canning, William, 157
Carey, John, author of *Dickens: the violent effigy*, ix, 24, 35, 48, 57, 58, 121, 159, 160

Carlyle, Thomas, 14, 34, 71
Christmas Carol, A (story by Charles Dickens), 41
Coleridge, Samuel Taylor, 69, 118, 157; 'Kubla Khan', 44; on Wordsworth, 18
Collins, Philip (author of *Dickens and Education*, *Dickens and Crime* and much else on Dickens), xi, 25, 26, 118, 155, 159
Cooke, Michael, author of *Acts of Inclusion*, 41, 161
Conrad, Joseph, *The Secret Agent*, 7
Corelli, Marie, 118
Coveney, Peter, 167

De Quincey, Thomas, 157, 161; *Confessions of an English Opium Eater*, 73; influence on Dickens, 73–6; mediation between Wordsworth and Dickens, 75ff; 'return of the repressed' in, 75–6; *Suspiria de Profundis*, 73; on Wordsworth, 16, 25, 42; writings as model for Paul Dombey's 'creative regression', 76
David Copperfield (novel by Charles Dickens), 'dialectic of modernity' in, 32–3, 72; Dickens's partial self-portrait in, 128–30; ; 'perfect English mirth' of, 32, 129–30; psychology versus morality in, 130; 'social vertigo' in, 82; *Characters*: David Copperfield, 32–3, 72, 77, 124, 128–9; Romantic naïveté of, 130; Little Emily, 23, 129; Mr Micawber, 94, 130; Mr and Mrs Murdstone, 64

Index

Dickens, Charles (*see also individual novel entries*); 'Autobiographical Fragment', in relation to novels, 128–9; coexistence of hardness and feminine susceptibility in, 30, 40; 'dialectic of modernity' personified in, 24, 124; conflict of moral and psychological understanding in, *see* psychology and morality; on English versus French Art, 121; fascination with passive heroines, significance of, in, 33; personal past explored through characters unlike self in, 105–6, 128–9, 133; alleged Philistinism of, 121–2; prose of, balance of the playful and the referential in, 36–7, 48–50; restlessness of as seen by Forster (*see also* Forster), 23–4, 117; self-portrait (in part or in whole) in novels in, 26–8; 32, 72, 124, 128; influence of Wordsworth in early novels of, 25–8; reading of Wordsworth, 24–5

Dilnot, Alan (on *Great Expectations*), 152, 170

Dombey and Son (novel by Charles Dickens). *Characters*: Major Bagstock ('taboo on tenderness in'), 47–8; Cornelia Blimber, 37, 62; Dr Blimber, 38, 69; Mrs Brown, 66; Carker ('taboo on tenderness' in), 48; Mrs Chick (and the ideology of effort), 55, 58, 64; Mr Chick, 50, 64–5; Captain Cuttle, 37, 65; Paul Dombey, 28, 29, 36; 'taboo on tenderness' in upbringing, 42–5; imagination and withdrawal, 56–63; speech and Victorian poetry, 58–60; Mr Dombey, 30–39, pseudo-masculinity in, 46–7; 'taboo on tenderness' in, 51–2; breakdown, and regression as restored continuity, 52–4, 68; Mrs Dombey, 36; Florence Dombey, 37, 44–6, 65; Walter Gay, 30–1, 37, 67–8, 69–72, 154; Solomon Gills, 70; Edith Granger, 47; Mrs Pipchin, 55, 64; Sir Barnet Skettles, 37; Mrs Skewton, 71; Mr Toodles, 153; Toots, 37, 57, 60; Miss Tox, 40; suppressed femininity in, 63; Mrs Wickham, 62. *Themes*: breakdown and therapeutic regression in, 52–4; denial of feminine in, 42, 63–4; ideas of manliness and the Wordsworthian self-continuity idea in, 35–71; psychological insight and religious language in, 61–3; psychological versus moral understanding in, 55ff; sibling romance pattern and the self-continuity idea in, 67–8; concept of the 'taboo on tenderness' in, 42–3, 44, 46,

Dostoevsky, Fyodor, 5

Dyson, A. (on *Dombey and Son*), 65, 162

Eagleton, Terence, on Victorian poetry, 35

Eliot, George; 5, 6, 14; anti-cosmopolitanism in, 118; 'dialectic of modernity' in, 22; humour in as compared with Dickens, 127; *Middlemarch*, 6, 8, 14–15; *Silas Marner*, 130; Wordsworth's 'self-continuity' idea in, 15; in *Daniel Deronda*, 20; in *The Mill on the Floss*, 20–21, 88–9, 138, 158

'dialectic of modernity', the; and novel as social criticism, 80; in *David Copperfield*, 32; in early Dickens novels, 28–9; George Eliot and, 22; in *Little Dorrit*, 33; worked through in *Great Expectations*, 33, 155

'experience of modernity', the; Marshall Berman's concept of, 3–5

Index

Fields, James T., 73
Fitzgerald, Percy, 165
Flaubert, Gustave, 6; Manichean dualism in *Madame Bovary*, 9–10
Forster, John, 158, 160; on Dickens's determination, 34, 40, 53; on Dickens's 'feminine susceptibility', 30; on Dickens's restlessness, 23–4, 117; 'perfect English mirth' in *David Copperfield*, 24, 32
Freud, Sigmund, 2, 17, 44

Garis, Robert (on *Great Expectations*), 126, 168
Gaskell, Elisabeth, 161
Gilmour, Robin (on *David Copperfield*), x, 156
Goldberg, S. L., xi, 22, 158
Great Expectations (novel by Charles Dickens); complex treatment of gentility in, 136–9; dialectical engagement with Wordsworthian–Romantic psychology in, 123, 126, 130, 151; 'dialectic of modernity' in, 33, 41, 123, 152; guilt in as compared with Wordsworth, 143–4; patterning of motifs in, 142–3; Prometheanism in *re* Pip, 136–9; psychological versus moral understanding in, 152–5; thematic significance of humour in, 126–7, 134, 151–2. *Characters*: Biddy, 138–9; Estella, 136–9; Joe Gargery, childhood of, 132–3; compared with Amy Dorrit, 133; as Wordsworthian, 131–4, 139, 144, 153; Miss Havisham, 127, 134–5; Jaggers, psychology versus morality in Dickens's understanding of, 152–4; Mrs Joe, 127, 132; Abel Magwitch, as *alter ego* of Pip, 145–8; 'primality' of, 145–6, 148–9; Molly, 152, 154; Orlick, 126–7, 150–1; Pip, 66, 67; and authorial voice, 126, 128; aggression suppressed in, 145–6; aggression reclaimed in, 150–1; as authorial self-portrait, 124, 133–4; 'dialectic of modernity' in, 124–5; and Estella, 136, 139, 141; gentility, uneasy in, 140–3; growth in, 123, 125, 128, 135, 141, 145–8; guilt in, 135, 143–4; humour and aggression in, 127–8; and Joe, 134–5; bourgeois idealist Prometheanism in, 137; psychology versus morality in authorial understanding of, 141–4; 'return of the repressed' in, 141–3, 146–8; 'social vertigo' in, 82; Herbert Pocket, 125, 137, 139, 146; Mrs Pocket, 139; Pumblechook, 127, 134, 137; Wemmick, 152; Wopsle, 143
Grylls, David, 163
Guntrip, Harry, 42, 161

Hard Times (novel by Charles Dickens). *Characters*: Louisa Harthouse, 23; Sissy Jupe, 106
Haunted Man, The (story by Charles Dickens), 31, 41; Redlaw, character in, 32
Hawkes, Terence, 86, 164
Hogarth, Mary, 25
Household Words (publication of Dickens), 25
Hutton, R. H., on Dickens as un-English, 78
Hazlitt, William, 167
Hughes, Thomas, 118
Hunt, Leigh, 25, 130, 168; humour and the 'self-continuity' idea, 32–3

illness as therapeutic regression in the Victorian novel, 52, 138

Jackson, Arlene (on *Dombey and Son*), 52
Jackson, R. L. P., 158
James, Henry, Miss Birdseye in *The Bostonians*, 96, 99
Jefferson, D. W. (on *Little Dorrit*), 98, 165

Index

Jeffrey, Francis, 158
Johnson, Edgar (author of *Charles Dickens: his Tragedy and Triumph*), 28, 160
Johnson, Samuel, 7, 55; 'The Vanity of Human Wishes', 8, 10–11

Knoeplmacher, U. C., 130, 169

Lacan, Jacques, 17
Laing, R. D., 162
Lamb, Charles, 25; 'The Londoner', 90
Lawrence, D. H., 14; *Women in Love*, 49, 153
Leavis, F. R., x, 7, 10, 36, 44, 56, 89, 156, 160
Leavis, Q. D., x, 36, 91, 112, 144, 147, 160, 170
Little Dorrit (novel by Charles Dickens), 'dialectic of modernity' in, 80–5; French Revolution in, 106–8; gentility in, 81–2; liberal spirit of, 85–6; moral status of discontent in, 83–6 (*see also* Amy Dorrit *and* Tattycoram *listed below in this entry*); non-conformity, Dickens's ambivalence about in, 84–5; Philistinism in, 118–22; Romantic anti-cosmopolitanism in, 117–21; Romantic anti-intellectualism in, 118–22; 'self-continuity' idea (Wordsworthian–Romantic psychology) in, 80–122.
Characters: Affery, 85; Barnacles, 114; Christopher Casby, 151; Cavalletto 78, 84; Chief Butler (Merdle's), 83; John Chivery, 84–5, 101–2; Arthur Clennam, 66, 77, 84–5, 90–3, 97, 99–104; 110, 113, 124; significance *re* Wordsworthian–Romantic psychology, 113–17; Mrs Clennam, 85; Amy Dorrit, 28, 33; as Dickensian *alter ego*, 72, 81–4; attachment to Marshalsea, 87–8, 98–9; and family dynamics, 90–5; growth of in relationship with Clennam, 100–4; 'self-continuity' idea (Wordsworthian–Romantic psychology) in, 86–104, 123; psychology versus morality in Dickens's understanding of, 91–104; as converse of Tattycoram, 104–5; reaction to Venice, 96–9; and Wordsworthian feminine ideal, 86–8; Fanny Dorrit, 90, 95; William Dorrit, 81, 83; Flora Finching, 82; Mrs General, 95, 97; Henry Gowan, 110, 114; Mr Meagles, 56, 84, 94, 118–22; Dickens's ambivalence towards, 104–13; Pet Meagles, 109–10, 166; Nandy, 82, 95; Pancks, 151; Plornish, 84; Rigaud/Blandois, 85, 118; Tattycoram, 33, 81, 94; Dickens's ambivalent understanding of (*re* moral status of discontent, *see above this entry*), 104–13; Miss Wade, 94–5, 105–7, 110–11
Lohrli, Ann, 159
Lucas, John, 57
Lukàcs, Georg, 10, 137

McKenzie, Jeanne and Norman, authors of *Dickens: a Life*, 161
Mill, J. S., on the need for imagination and idealism in education, 69–70
Milton, John, *Paradise Lost*, 138, 139
Moynahan, Julian (on *Dombey and Son* and *Great Expectations*), 51, 52, 126–27
Myers, William (on *Little Dorrit*), 9, 164

Newman, S. J., author of *Dickens at Play*, 10, 160
Nicholas Nickleby, novel by Charles Dickens, 26; Smike (character in), 26
'novel of adultery', the, 8–9; in Dickens, 23

Old Curiosity Shop, The, novel by
  Charles Dickens, 27, 28; Little
  Nell (character in), 26, 27, 28;
  Quilp (character in), 28, 124
Oliver Twist (novel by Charles
  Dickens), 27; Maylies
  (characters in), 27; Oliver
  Twist (character in), 27, 28
Orwell, George, 164; on Dickens
  and nationalism, 78

Pecksniff (character in *Martin
  Chuzzlewit*), 82
Peel, Marie (on *Little Dorrit*), 164
Pickwick Papers (novel by Charles
  Dickens), 26; Gabriel Grub
  (character in), 26
Pope, Alexander, 9, 83, 151
Prometheanism, 4–6, in *Great
  Expectations*, 139
'psychology and morality' (*see also*
  'self-continuity'), in *David
  Copperfield*, 130; in *Dombey and
  Son*, 59ff; Dickens's
  equivocation between
  psychological and moral
  interpretation, in *Little Dorrit*,
  90–113; and in *Great
  Expectations*, 135, 140ff, 152–4;
  in Tolstoy, 14

Reich, Wilhelm, 160; his concept of
  the 'phallic-narcissistic' type of
  pseudo-masculinity as
  applicable to Mr Dombey, 39,
  47
Roberts, Mark, author of *The
  Tradition of Romantic Morality*,
  161
'Romantic psychology,' *see*
  Wordsworth, 'self-continuity'
Romanticism, Romantic anti-
  cosmopolitanism in *Little Dorrit*,
  as related to 'self-continuity',
  117–22; Romantic anti-
  intellectualism in *Little Dorrit*,
  118–22; Romantic 'myth of the
  artist', ix, 6; Romanticism and
  'the incorporation of the
  feminine', 41; Romanticism as
  adversary sub-culture within
  Victorian culture, 34–5
Rousseau, Jean-Jacques, 22;
  Confessions, 2

Salveson, Christopher, author of *The
  Landscape of Memory*, 18
Scott, P. J. M., author of *Reality and
  Comic Confidence in Charles
  Dickens*, 91, 93, 94, 165
'self-continuity', idea of in
  Wordsworth, Dickens, *et al.* (*see
  also* 'taboo on tenderness',
  psychology and morality); 1–2,
  8, 15–19, and 'the feminine',
  41ff; in Dickens compared with
  Wordsworth, 23–33, 41–72, 88–
  121, 130–55; in Emily Brontë,
  22; in George Eliot, 15, 20–2,
  88–90; restoration of 'self-
  continuity' and nervous
  breakdown, 52–4, 147–52;
  restoration of 'self-continuity'
  and Imagination (in Paul
  Dombey), 58–63; in
  Wordsworth (*see also*
  Wordsworth), 16–20, 41–2
sentimentalism, 2
Shakespeare, William, 1, 39
Shelley, Percy Bysshe,
  Prometheanism in, 6–7; Nature
  in, 18
Skultans, V., 162
'Somebody's Luggage' (story by
  Charles Dickens), 77–9; Bebelle
  (character in), 77
Stendhal (Henri Beyle), 137
Stewart, Garret, author of *Dickens
  and the Trials of Imagination*, ix,
  160
Stone, Donald H., author of *The
  Romantic Impulse in Victorian
  Fiction*, 22, 28, 156
Stone, Harry, on Dickens's reading,
  159
Stonehouse, J. H., 159
Suttie, Ian (*see also* 'taboo on
  tenderness'), 42, 47, 50–1, 161

Index 177

symbiosis (and individuation), in Blake and Wordsworth in relation to Dickens, 31; in *Great Expectations*, 138; in Wordsworth, 17

'taboo on tenderness' (*see also Dombey and Son*), and Dickens on Englishness in 'Somebody's Luggage', 77–9
Tanner, Tony, author of *Adultery in the Novel*, 8
Tave, Stuart, author of *The Amiable Humourist*, 169
Tennyson, Alfred, 35, 59
Thackeray, William Makepeace, 7
Thurley, Geoffrey, author of *The Dickens Myth*, 168
Tick, Stanley, on *Little Dorrit*, 106, 166
Tillotson, Kathleen, on *Dombey and Son*, 52
Tolstoy, Leo, 5, 6; the ambiguous nature of vitality in, 11–13, the authority of psychological law in, 14; *Anna Karenina*, 10–14
Tomlinson, T. B., x
Trilling, Lionel, 83, 84, 85, 91, 164

Walsh, William, 158
Wilkie, David (painter), 25

Williams, Raymond, 35, 91, 165
Wilson, Angus, 159
Wilson, Edmund, 24, 33, 159
Woodward, Kathleen, on *Little Dorrit*, 9, 93, 106, 164
Wordsworth, William (*see also* 'self-continuity'), ix, 2, 3; ideal of the feminine in, 20, 87; ideological implications of the 'self-continuity' idea in, 19, 81; psychology and morality in the 'self-continuity' idea, 15–16, 19, 44–5; Romantic anti-cosmopolitanism in, 117; Romantic anti-intellectualism in, 118; poems: 'The Immortality Ode', 61–2; 'The Idiot Boy', 26; 'Michael', 130–1; 'My Heart Leaps Up', 17, 117; 'Nuns fret not at their convents' narrow room', 87; *The Prelude* (*see also* 'self-continuity'), 15–17, 44–5, 61, 69, 81, 88–9; 90, 114, 117; 'Tintern Abbey', 18, 116, 131, 138; 'We Are Seven', 25, 26

Yellin, Louise (on *Dombey and Son*), 162

Zwerdling, Alex (on *Bleak House*), x, 156, 170

GPSR Compliance

The European Union's (EU) General Product Safety Regulation (GPSR) is a set of rules that requires consumer products to be safe and our obligations to ensure this.

If you have any concerns about our products, you can contact us on

ProductSafety@springernature.com

In case Publisher is established outside the EU, the EU authorized representative is:

Springer Nature Customer Service Center GmbH
Europaplatz 3
69115 Heidelberg, Germany

www.ingramcontent.com/pod-product-compliance
Lightning Source LLC
Chambersburg PA
CBHW031541230426
43749CB00025B/440